Women's Studies

Women of the F

_____

Women of the Praia

WORK AND LIVES IN A
PORTUGUESE COASTAL COMMUNITY

Sally Cole

PRINCETON UNIVERSITY PRESS

PRINCETON, NEW JERSEY

Library of Congress Cataloging-in-Publication Data

Cole, Sally Cooper, 1951–
    Women of the praia : work and lives in a Portuguese coastal
community / Sally Cole.
        p. cm.
    Includes bibliographical references and index.
    ISBN 0-691-09464-0 -- ISBN 0-691-02862-1 (pbk.)
    1. Women fishers--Portugal--Vila Chã (Porto)--Case studies.
2. Women fish trade workers--Portugal--Vila Chã (Porto)--Case
studies. 3. Women--Portugal--Vila Chã (Porto)--Social conditions.
4. Women--Portugal--Vila Chã (Porto)--Economic conditions.
I. Title.
HD6073.F652P83   1991   91-2359
331.4′8392′0946915--dc20   CIP

For Michael,
Samuel,
and Isabella

CONTENTS

ILLUSTRATIONS

TABLES AND MAPS

PREFACE

IN THE SPRING of 1984 I went to Vila Chã, a village on the north coast of Portugal, to study women, work, and social change. I was interested in women in fishing economies, and there had been little written on the subject at that time. I was also interested in Portugal. I knew that, since the Revolution of April 25, 1974, Portuguese society had been undergoing rapid social, economic, and political changes but that, until the decade leading up to 1974, the country had, under the Salazarean New State, experienced the slowest rate of growth in Western Europe. And I knew that, despite rapid and radical change, it remains the most underdeveloped country in Western Europe. In a Portuguese rural community, I thought, changes in women's work might be documented through an analysis of the changes in the work of three generations of women—the earliest being the generation born before the First World War and married before the Second World War, during the Salazarean regime. I chose to focus on the coastal zone north of Porto where fishing was an important part of the traditional economy, an area that has been among those of most intensive industrialization in the contemporary period.

As a graduate student at the time, I was also concerned with theoretical and methodological problems I had identified in two bodies of literature, the ethnography of Southern or "Mediterranean" Europe and the writing on women and economic development. I was concerned that despite the avowed interest in Mediterranean women and the assertion that Mediterranean societies are societies "preoccupied with gender" (Ortner and Whitehead 1981), we knew very little about the women. Through the anthropologists' concept of "honor and shame" we knew that women were daughters of fathers, wives of men, and mothers of sons, but we knew little about women's work, their property relations, their relations with other women, their values and aspirations, or their own perceptions of themselves and of the role of women in society. We knew about women only in their relationships with men. Men were the subjects of Mediterranean ethnography; women were the "other." And the result of this framework was that women were understood primarily as "victims of their sexuality" (Schneider 1971).

Although I recognized the validity of the then-current feminist socialist women-and-development theoretical framework, the resulting literature was also problematic for me, and for reasons similar to those that rendered the traditional ethnography problematic: the values, agendas, and strategies of the women themselves were not heard. In the ethnography, the analysis of external and global processes of change took precedence over the subjective experiences of individuals and groups. In this literature women were being portrayed as "victims of development." The women-and-development framework apparently had not been applied to a Mediterranean case—and this was one of my tasks—but I was interested in integrating the voice and experience of actual women into a discussion of women and socioeconomic change in Portugal. It was for these reasons that I chose to record women's life stories.

Finally, I was interested in the relationship between women's work and the social construction of gender. I believed there was a strong relationship between the two: that the work which women do is related to the gender images that are operative in societies, and that as women's work changes, so do gender ideologies. But the burgeoning literature on the anthropology of women in the late 1970s and early 1980s treated these as two separate spheres of analysis. There were abundant studies of women and work where ideology was neglected (Beneria and Sen 1981; Etienne and Leacock 1980; Fernández-Kelly 1983; Luxton 1980; Young, Wolkowitz, and McCullagh 1981; Zavella 1987), and there were abundant symbolic analyses of gender that ignored the analytical importance of material conditions and social change (Ardener 1975; McCormack and Strathern 1980; Ortner and Whitehead 1981). Rarely were the two integrated. The anthropology of women was mirroring the split between materialist and symbolic anthropologists but was not reflecting the actual experience of women for whom the symbolic and the material worlds are both real. Again, I hoped to present an integrated view that would more accurately represent the lived experience of real women rather than create an artificial separation between the different spheres of women's lives.

The extent to which I have realized my agenda is for the reader to judge. I certainly had the full cooperation and assistance of the women of Vila Chã, who know better than I how their lives are integrated. I am extremely thankful to them and to them I hope I have been true. My concern in this regard was significantly allayed by one of these very women: having sent a copy of the dissertation on which this study is based to Vila Chã, where it circulated among numerous households, I received a letter of reply. Laura's student daughter (Laura's story appears in the text) wrote to tell me that her mother "recognized herself and was pleased." I would like to thank Laura and the women of Vila Chã for the warmth, openness, and hospitality they showed me during the time I was a resident of their community. Especially, I would like to thank Clara and her family, Alice and her family, Carmelina and her family, and Beatriz (now deceased), Gracinda, Constância, Angelina, Teresa, Maria, Inês, Maria Inês, and Ana Maria.

I lived in Vila Chã for thirteen months from May 1984 to June 1985 and returned during the summer of 1988. I went to Vila Chã after three months' residence in Lisbon, where I had been studying the Portuguese language and exploring Portuguese secondary and primary source material. After the traffic, pollution, and crowded apartment living of the city, Vila Chã in the spring and summer offered a welcome opportunity for outdoor life and physical work. My first view of the community was on a rainy May morning when women were at work on the beach, wading waist-deep in the water, collecting seaweed in huge circular hand nets and spreading it to dry on the sand. The women welcomed an extra pair of hands, and I felt that the characteristics of this community, where women are engaged in such physical work and where they work in public view rather than isolated in their homes, would make easier the anthropologist's initial task of finding a place in the community. When one of the women mentioned a small house that was usually rented to Portuguese vacationers during the summer but that could be rented to me for the entire year, Vila Chã seemed the obvious place to unpack my bags. This three-room house—a renovated shed once used to store fishing gear and dried seaweed—stood on the main street that runs across the head of the beach in the heart of the fishing community, and it became my home during my year in Vila Chã. My neighbors on both sides were the owners of small grocery shops that also served as taverns for the fishermen. The fishing boats and fish auction were only a few meters away.

I spent the summer months working with women on the seaweed harvest, baiting lines and traps, sorting the catch, and selling the fish. And, with the assistance of a high school student, Teresa Maria Ramos Moreira, I mapped the parish (map 2 in the text) and conducted a household survey. The parish is large, comprising almost three thousand residents, an estimated seven hundred households, and thirteen hamlets, and occupying an area of 10.5 square kilometers. I needed the household survey in order to develop a preliminary understanding of the economic bases of, and the relationships among, the different hamlets, and in order to understand the composition and economic structure of households in the community. It was during this task that I became aware of the history and basis of the antagonism between agricultural and maritime households in Vila Chã that I describe in the book.

As the rainy weather of fall and winter settled in, I began to divide my time between research in the fisheries offices and archives in Vila do Conde and in neighboring Póvoa de Varzim, hand copying the parish registers of births, marriages, and deaths in the parish priest's office in Vila Chã, and working with individual women in their homes recording their life stories. I continued as well to attend the daily arrival of the fishing boats on the beach, to assist with the unloading, to watch the auctioning of the fish, to wash my laundry in the river and hang it out on the beach to dry alongside the other women's—theirs sparkling white, mine a dull yellow that was much commented upon—and to attend Saturday evening mass and participate in the ritual life of marriage, baptism, and mourning. The women and men of Vila Chã opened their homes and shared their lives with me. In doing so, they enriched my life immeasurably. To them I owe the greatest thanks.

Funding for field research was provided through a Social Sciences and Humanities Research Council of Canada (SSHRCC) doctoral fellowship, an Ontario Graduate Scholarship, and a University of Toronto Fellowship. While writing this book I have been supported by an SSHRCC postdoctoral fellowship and the Department of Anthropology of Memorial University of Newfoundland.

To my teachers—Raoul Andersen, Janice Boddy, Gordon Inglis, Richard Lee, Robert Paine, and especially my thesis supervisor, Michael Levin—I express thanks for teaching me about peasantries and fisheries, about gender and social change. And, to the feminist caucus of the Department of Anthropology at the University of Toronto, thank you for intellectual challenges.

For teaching me about Portuguese anthropology and culture, I would especially like to thank Caroline Brettell, Alice Duarte Geraldes, Manuela Marujo, João de Pina-Cabral, and my colleagues in the Noroeste Group. In Portugal, I would also like to thank Sr. Manuel Lopes, Director of the Museu Municipal de Etnografia e História da Póvoa de Varzim, Sr. Antonio Monteiro dos Santos of the Biblioteca Municipal de Vila do Conde, and Sr. Antero Coutinho, retired officer of the Capitania do Porto in Vila do Conde for their assistance with archival and fisheries sources. And in Vila Chã I would like to thank Sr. Armando da Costa e Silva for his interest in history and anthropology, and for his friendship and continuing support of my work.

I would like to thank Brian O'Neill and Ruth Behar for their critical reading of the manuscript, and Gail Ullman, editor at Princeton University Press, for her initial interest in my work and her encouragement throughout the writing. Also at Princeton, I would like to thank Lauren Lepow for her careful editing of the manuscript.

At home, I thank Ellen Bielawski, Marlene Kadar, and Lynne Phillips for their faith and friendship. I thank my parents, Alfred and Jean Cole, for nurturing my interest in history and culture. Finally, I thank Michael Huberman for his perennial encouragement and good humor, and our children, Samuel and Isabella, whose births during the writing were not only a joy to us but—because *um casal sem filhos é como uma árvore sem ramos*—a relief to our friends in Vila Chã.

Women of the Praia

Chapter 1

VILA CHÃ

ARRIVING

VILA CHÃ is located on the north coast of Portugal, twenty-three kilometers north of the district capital Porto, Portugal's second largest city, and eight kilometers south of the town of Vila do Conde (map 1). Two clusters of rocks define a harbor of sorts on an otherwise exposed and inhospitable stretch of sandy coastline. This small natural harbor permits the launching and landing of small open wooden boats on the beach. The rock outcrops catch several varieties of seaweeds that, since at least the sixteenth century, have been harvested and dried for use as fertilizers to grow corn, wheat, and rye, and later potatoes, carrots, onions, and cabbages. From the sea, Vila Chã appears as a continuous row of small masonry houses strung out just above the high tide mark of the beach. Colorful fishing boats are pulled up the beach and clustered together above the harbor entrance. Women wearing fluttering aprons and kerchiefs and bareheaded children are seen climbing on the rocks at low tide, collecting seaweeds or perhaps mussels and other mollusks. Paper and plastic garbage litters the beach. Rows and rows of laundry wave in strong sea breezes from the clotheslines strung out between poles planted in the beach sand. Flat expanses of green fields of hay and corn extend back behind the row of houses to the interior of the parish. In the distance, due east through the harbor entrance past the beached fishing boats, one can see the white steeple of the parish church that serves as a navigation point for fishermen.

But the present-day visitor to Vila Chã enters the parish by road and sees a different picture. Leaving the national highway, we traverse a forest of tall, thin, cool and fragrant eucalyptus trees. Gradually, houses begin to line the road—small detached stuccoed houses and some newer bungalows and duplexes. We pass a sawmill, a gas station, and a clothing shop, The Boutique. Then the road forks and we turn left, west toward the coast rather than inland again, although we see many more homes along the fork that goes to our right. We pass an old café where numerous bicycles and small motorbikes are parked outside. Then the road narrows and winds, lined on both sides by high stone walls and the walls of extremely large old homes. It is quiet here. We cannot see into the houses or their yards, but we can see grapevines above the walls. We realize that the owners must be farmers and are away at work in their fields. But we seem to be lost. Where is the

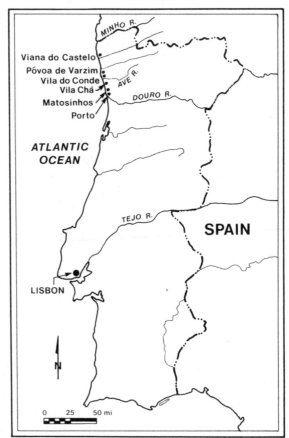

Map 1. Map of Portugal showing location of Vila Chã

beach? Where are the fishing boats? The road forks and we head right. We see the church and the cemetery and think we must have found the center of the parish, but all is quiet here too. There are small old stone houses but no shops and no people. We pass a blacksmith working alone at his forge and stop to ask the way to the beach. He tells us to retrace our steps and take the left-hand fork, which we now do. The road here is also lined by high walls and houses, and we have no sense of our direction. Then the narrow road opens out onto an expanse of fields across which we can see in the distance, perhaps a kilometer away, the sea and a string of houses following the coastline. This must be the fishing community—so separated from the rest of the parish. And Vila Chã is larger and more dispersed than we had expected it would be. What are the relations among these different neighborhoods? Where is the center of the community?

We follow the road down through the green fields toward the sparkling blue expanse of the Atlantic Ocean. The road turns right when it reaches the beach and immediately narrows. From here it goes north following the coastline. On both sides the road is lined by rows of small attached houses whose fronts are painted stucco—green, blue, white, and orange—or tiled in bright colors. These are the houses we saw earlier in our view of the village from the sea.

Not only does the road narrow, but women shouting in conversation in the middle of the street and motorbikes parked outside cafés make navigation difficult. Slowly we pass, amid the houses, a pharmacy, a butcher shop, a hairdresser's, two cafés, and two small grocery shops. The road opens onto a small square. To our right we see women washing clothes in a trickle of a river. To our left is the fish auction, the *lota*. It is now almost noon. Two refrigerated trucks, and women vendors on foot pulling loaded handcarts, are leaving with their purchases of the morning's catch to begin their rounds selling fish in the interior. Behind the lota are the gaily painted fishing boats pulled up the beach and at rest. We have arrived.

VILA CHÃ

In 1985 the parish of Vila Chã had a population of three thousand residents living in approximately seven hundred households.[1] Parish residents worked in agriculture, fishing, factories, and construction.

The parish comprises 10.5 square kilometers of cultivated lands and pine and eucalyptus forest that slope up gently to the east away from the coast. Within this area, the population is divided into thirteen hamlets (*lugares*) of residence. The thirteen hamlets, with their different histories, have the character of neighborhoods.

The fisherwomen and men (*os pescadores*) live in two large contiguous hamlets, Lugar da Praia and Lugar do Facho, on the coast. The landowning agriculturalists (*os lavradores*) live about one kilometer inland in nine small hamlets clustered together in the center of the parish and surrounded by their small cultivated plots.[2] Factory and construction workers live either in the coastal hamlets as members or neighbors of maritime households, or they live in the hamlets of Rio da Gândara and Rio da Igreja farther inland from where the lavradores live (map 2).

The houses of the pescadores are strung out along 1.5 kilometers of coastline. At about the center point, the coastline is interrupted by the two rocky outcrops that form the natural harbor, a cove encompassing a 200-meter stretch of sand known locally as "the beach" (*a praia*). Here the pescadores launch their small open boats each morning and afternoon, and here, at the end of each day, they haul the colorfully painted boats up to rest.

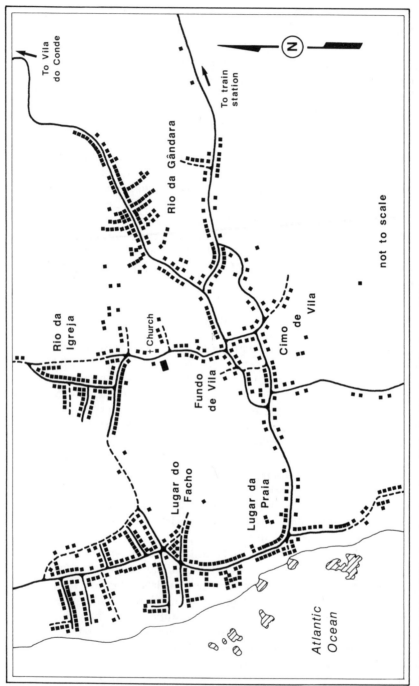

Map 2. Vila Chã, 1985, showing hamlets of Rio da Gândara, Facho, and Praia

The beach is the center of activity of the maritime households. Men, women, and children spend many hours each day on the beach, baiting lines and traps, mending nets, sorting the catch, working on the boats, or enjoying conversation with one another. During the summer, women also spend hours wading in the shallows collecting seaweed and spreading it to dry on the beach.

At the head of the beach where the boats are hauled up, the pescadores have small stone huts where they store their gear. To one side of these huts is a new building, the state-run fish auction, the lota, built in 1971. A cobblestone street parallels the coastline at the head of the beach behind the lota, winding through Lugar da Praia and Lugar do Facho. On this street near the lota are two small shops that sell groceries to women, and wine and beer to men; this is where the men spend their time when not fishing and where women and children come and go in the course of a day's errands. Also lining both sides of the street are the homes of the pescadores: small, painted stucco houses attached to one another. This is the heart of the fishing community in Lugar da Praia, and it was between the two shops on this street that I lived, in one of these small attached houses, from May 1984 to June 1985. Immediately to the north in Lugar do Facho are the newer detached homes of some pescadores and their wage-earning sons and daughters. This study focuses on the 171 households of these two hamlets, Lugar da Praia and Lugar do Facho.

The street is busy and noisy at all hours of the day. Televisions blast from the cafés. Felt-capped fishermen stand talking at the doors of the shops. Women, wearing head scarves, dark-colored woolen shawls, skirts, and aprons, bustle up and down the street on their way to sell fish, to wash laundry at the river, or to buy groceries at the shop. They stop to talk along the way. From 5:00 to 7:00 A.M. and from 5:00 to 7:00 P.M. is "rush hour" on the street as factory hands and construction workers riding motorcycles or transport trucks travel to and from work. In the evenings the workers go to the cafés to have coffee and to watch television. The street is quiet only after 11:00 P.M. when the cafés close.

In the interior of the parish, about one kilometer from the coast, are the homes of the lavradores. A visitor to Vila Chā is struck by the quiet here, by the contrast to the noise and bustle of life on the street and on the beach in Lugar da Praia and Lugar do Facho. The large old houses of the lavradores are separated from one another and surrounded by large walled yards. The lavradores leave their houses to go to their fields, and when work there is done they return home to work behind the walls in their dairies. Vila Chā lavradores own on average less than four hectares (9.88 acres) of land divided into a number of separate small plots (Moreira da Silva 1983:93). They work in commercial dairy farming and cultivate potatoes as a cash crop.

Factory workers and construction workers live on the coast among the maritime households, or they live in small houses strung out along one of the three roads that lead out of town, one to the east toward the train station, one to the south, and one to the north toward the town of Vila do Conde eight kilometers away at the mouth of the Ave River.

The dispersed pattern of residence and work in the parish means that there is no "downtown." The church and cemetery are located in the geographical center of the parish near the homes of the lavradores; the pescadores and other parish residents walk the kilometer or so to the church for mass on Saturday evenings and Sunday mornings. Most hamlets have their own shop and café, but other services are spread throughout the parish. In 1985, these included ten grocery shops (most of which also sold glasses of beer and wine over the counter), seven cafés, two fruit stores, two butchers, two clothing boutiques, two shoe repair shops, two bicycle shops, one gas station, one pharmacy, one hairdresser, and one furniture shop. Parish residents tend either to patronize the shops and use the services in the hamlet where they live or to fulfill their needs in the town of Vila do Conde.

The visitor to Vila Chã is struck by a confusion of contrasting images of new and old: elaborately tiled new homes abut old, plain, stucco homes; small motorcycles whiz past cattle-drawn carts; a gas pump and garage sit next to the blacksmith's workshop; and a clothing boutique and furniture store are new neighbors to the old shoemaker's shop. The visitor is also struck by the different life-styles of the lavradores, pescadores, and wage workers.

Parish Institutions

Vila Chã is one of thirty-two parishes in the *concelho* (municipality) of Vila do Conde.[3] The parish itself has relatively few institutions. The major institutions and services are located in the town of Vila do Conde (pop. 20,226), the seat of the concelho.[4] Vila do Conde is the location of the *câmara municipal* (town council) and the weekly market, as well as the hospital, high school, banks, tribunal, jail, post office, public library, convent, cinema, and major shops. The offices of the fisheries authorities, the Capitania do Porto, are also located in Vila do Conde, and the pescadores of Vila Chã come here to renew their licenses. Vila Chã residents can reach the town by taking one of five daily buses or one of several daily trains departing from the parish station located three kilometers inland from the beach.

1. Vila Chã beach. Houses. Laundry. Seaweed spread to dry.

2. Vila Chã from the water. Boats pulled up on beach.

3. The street and houses of pescadores in Lugar da Praia.

4. The beach on a winter morning.

The parish has an elected council (*a junta de freguesia*) that represents its interests to the câmara municipal in Vila do Conde. The parish council is the smallest elected body in the Portuguese administrative structure. The only other elected bodies are the câmaras and the National Assembly in Lisbon.

The office of the parish council is located in the church hall and is open two nights a week for parish residents to meet with the councillors. The council consists of four men, all of whom live in the center of the parish and all of whom grew up in lavrador households, although they are now employed as public servants or bank clerks in either Vila do Conde or Porto. Until the 1960s, under the authoritarian New State (the *Estado Novo*), the parish council was appointed by the state, and the parish priest often was also the president of the council.[5]

The parish council concerns itself mainly with public improvements in the parish. In 1985, one of its projects was to build a large public wash tank in Lugar da Praia so that the women would no longer wash clothes kneeling at the edge of the small river that flows through the parish to the beach. Council members apparently considered the washerwomen to be an eyesore. The women, however, did not request the wash tank, and most continue to prefer doing their laundry in the river. The pescadores, men and women, generally do not consider that the parish council represents their interests. For more than twenty years they have been requesting that a flashing beacon be built on the beach to assist them in navigation, but the beacon has never been a priority with the council.

Two elementary schools (one inland and one on the coast) offer grades 1 to 6; grades 5 and 6 are taught by television. Students who continue their schooling past grade 6 go by bus to the high school in Vila do Conde. Three local doctors operate part-time clinics from their homes, and the nearest hospital is in Vila do Conde. There is one Roman Catholic church in the parish, and the majority of residents are, at least nominally, Roman Catholic. There is also an evangelical Protestant church, the *Assembleia de Deus*, in Vila Chã; most of its congregation comes from outside the parish and no pescadores are members.

POPULATION, HISTORICAL SETTLEMENT, AND SOCIOECONOMIC DIFFERENTIATION IN THE PARISH

In 1864, according to the first national census of Portugal, Vila Chã had a population of 549 living in 125 households. By 1890, the population had increased to 740, and the number of households had increased to 167; by 1911 there were 1,030 individuals living in 190 households (table 1.1).

TABLE 1.1
Population Growth, Vila Chã, 1527–1985

	Number of Residents	Number of Households	Average Number of Persons/ Household
1527		30	
1706		46	
1758	275	53	5.2
1789	279	58	4.8
1857	406	103	3.9
1864	549	125	4.4
1874	606	144	4.2
1890	740	167	4.4
1900	837		
1911	1,030	190	5.4
1920	1,112		
1930	926	276	3.4
1940	1,315	270	4.9
1950	1,645	374	4.4
1960	1,933	456	4.2
1970	2,156	469	4.6
1981	2,781	665	4.2
1985[a]	3,000	700	4.3

Sources: Anonymous (1937, 1938); Memórias paroquiais (1758); Instituto Nacional de Estatística.

[a] The secretary of the parish council estimated the figures for 1985; he also maintains that the official 1981 figures are too low.

Steady population growth stimulated new areas of settlement within the parish. Until the mid-nineteenth century, settlement had been concentrated in nine hamlets in the center of the parish. These hamlets were settled by the lavradores who owned and worked all the surrounding lands within the parish boundaries. Only the beach lands were not privately owned; beach lands were state property.

New settlement spread first into the interior of the parish in the mid-nineteenth century, and then down onto the coast by the turn of the century (map 3). New patterns of settlement were precipitated by local inheritance practices. Legally, each child of a household was entitled to an equal inheritance, but local practice in the late nineteenth century increasingly favored consolidation of household property and inheritance by a single heir. The gap between rich and poor widened as one heir received most of a household's property and other children

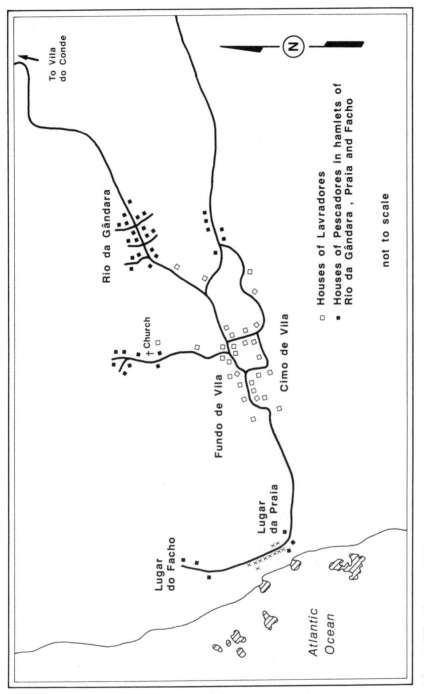

Map 3. Vila Chã, ca. 1900

became landless and land-poor members of the parish. The first maritime households in Vila Chã were established by sons and daughters of lavradores who either had received as their inheritance, or *dote*,[6] a small plot of land on which to build a house or who had simply squatted on a piece of land and built there.

In the interior the members of the new maritime-based households established the hamlet of Rio da Gândara (map 3). Here they built small (5 × 7 meters) one-story stonemasonry cottages side by side along narrow lanes off the road. By 1863, there were twelve households in Rio da Gândara; ten were fishing households, and two were carpenters' households. Fourteen years later there were at least twenty fishing households in Rio da Gândara. By the turn of the century, settlement had begun on the coast, and in 1905 there were at least seven fishing households established on the beach in the new hamlets of Praia and Facho. Here the fishermen and women squatted illegally on state-owned beach lands. They built stone and thatch huts to live in, and they began to reclaim the dunes for small garden plots. By 1911, there were 308 individuals in sixty-five households in Rio da Gândara, and 133 individuals in twenty-nine households in the coastal hamlets of Praia and Facho. Rio da Gândara had become the most populated hamlet in the parish, and Praia and Facho were the next most populated ones.[7] The majority of these households were engaged in a maritime economy; the remainder were those of agricultural day laborers (*jornaleiros*) and of craftsmen such as stonemasons and carpenters. Rio da Gândara, Praia, and Facho continued to grow rapidly throughout the twentieth century, while the interior hamlets where the lavradores resided remained almost stable in population (map 2).

Population increases and inheritance practices not only stimulated new areas of settlement but also encouraged the diversification of the parish economy and especially the development of a maritime economy. In the early nineteenth century, the parish population consisted of lavradores, a small number of tenant farmers (*seareiros*), and a small number of jornaleiros who worked for the lavradores. The population also included craftsmen: carpenters and stonemasons, and a blacksmith and shoemaker. Electoral censuses for the late nineteenth century document differentiation and increasing stratification in the parish economy as the number of households unable to earn their subsistence through agriculture increased relative to the number of landowning agriculturalists (lavradores). The landless and land-poor turned to fishing, or they worked as jornaleiros for the lavradores, or they took up a craft such as carpentry or boat building. They were concentrated in the recently settled outlying hamlets. The lavradores

TABLE 1.2

Occupations of Male Voters, Vila Chã, 1869–1928 (in percent)

	Agri-culture[a]	Fishing	Skilled Trades[b]	Services[c]	Total
1869	64.7	11.8	15.7	7.8	100.0 (N = 49)
1877	60.7	29.8	2.4	7.1	100.0 (N = 84)
1905	51.7	28.5	12.1	7.7	100.0 (N = 116)
1911	45.7	28.7	12.8	12.8	100.0 (N = 164)
1918	56.6	25.9	10.4	7.1	100.0 (N = 182)
1928	54.6	28.9	7.2	9.3	100.0 (N = 152)

Source: Electoral Censuses, Vila Chã. Available for 1862; 1865–1877; 1905–1928; 1966–1973. Pescadores first appear in the 1869 census.

Note: Only males over the age of 25 who paid taxes of 1,000 reis or more were eligible to vote. After 1905, males over 25 who could read and write were also eligible to vote. Both criteria excluded women and the poorest households of the parish.

[a] Those employed in agriculture include lavradores (landowning farmers), seareiros (tenant farmers), and jornaleiros (day laborers).

[b] Skilled trades include the blacksmith, tailor, and shoemaker, and several carpenters.

[c] The "Services" category includes shopkeepers, priests, military personnel, and, after 1911, teachers.

remained concentrated in the old hamlets in the center of the parish. Over time, these two groups (the lavradores and the land-poor, especially those who were now fishing) became defined locally as two antagonistic social groups, and their opposition dominated parish life.

Table 1.2, summarizing the available census data for Vila Chã for the years 1869 to 1928, reveals the occupations of voters (taxpaying males over the age of twenty-five). By 1877, approximately 30 percent of male taxpayers (and therefore more than 30 percent of parish households) were engaged in fishing. The fishery continued to employ more than one-third of parish households until the mid-1960s.

HISTORY OF THE FISHERY

Situated in the extreme southwest of Europe, on the western shores of the Iberian Peninsula, Portugal is bordered by a single country, Spain, and a single sea, the Atlantic. Her territory of 89,626 square kilometers has the approximate shape of a rectangle, and the Atlantic coastline, 845 kilometers long, comprises the western and southern sides of the rectangle. Despite its small size, Portugal exhibits the same geographical contrasts that characterize the rich variety of Iberian landscapes, a variety that is attributed to the interaction of maritime, Mediterranean, and semiarid climates with a complex geological structure of which the main feature is the deeply eroded western slope of the Iberian Meseta.

The historical importance of fishing in Portugal results from a particular set of environmental conditions: the shortest continental shelf in Atlantic waters, the sandy and/or rocky nature of the ocean floor, the water temperature and salinity, and the sea currents. Portugal is also crossed by a considerable number of rivers that flood annually, link sea and hinterland, and provide spawning grounds for a variety of migratory fish, including salmon, sturgeon, lamprey, shad, and eels. The combination of environmental conditions is highly favorable for breeding and nurturing more than three hundred species of marine life; as early as 1599, the fisheries of Portugal were described as the greatest in Europe. In addition to its national fisheries, offshore fishing has also played an important part in the history of Portugal. A fourteenth-century treaty authorized Portuguese fishing rights in English coastal waters. Henry the Navigator established the Morocco and Cape Verde fisheries in the fifteenth century, and cod fishing on the Newfoundland Grand Banks off the coast of Canada was under way as early as the sixteenth century (Ribeiro 1986).

Salt extraction and the gathering of sea plants and animals for fertilizer are also centuries-old maritime activities. In the north, *pilado* (the small crab *Portunus puber*) and small sardines and seaweed (*sargaço*) were gathered, the latter now in great demand by the pharmaceutical industry, especially for cosmetics. In the central region waterweed (*moliço*) from the lagoons was the most sought-after fertilizer, while in the south only the pilado was used. The practice of exploiting marine algae for use as fertilizer developed primarily on the north coast, north of the Douro River, where land is held in small family farms (*minifundia*). The northern shoreline is broken by rocky outcrops that trap a variety of seaweeds (principally *Chondrus crispus*, *Gelidium sesquipedale*, and *Laminaria succharina*, known locally as *botelho*, *francelha*, and *taborrão* respectively). Heavy winds blow the trapped seaweeds up onto the beaches where they can be harvested easily and spread to dry. These seaweed varieties contain valuable nitrogen, phosphoric acid, potassium, and calcium, which become three times more concentrated in the drying process and make seaweed a valuable local source of fertilizer (Veiga de Oliveira, Galhano, and Pereira 1975:181). The richness of these natural fertilizers promoted the reclaiming of large coastal sandy areas that had remained bare and uninhabited until the last century.

Regional diversification of the small coastal fisheries—the *pesca artesanal*—prevents any generalization. Filgueiras (1984) identifies three regions: the north, central, and south; within each of these regions he describes much local variation. Vila Chã exhibits the general characteristics of the north coast fisheries: seasonal fishing from small, open, keeled, and double-prowed boats for a variety of fish, but especially for sardines, with a surface drift net; seaweed gathering using a large conical hand net with a long wooden handle and the *graveta*, a big wooden rake; octopus hunting with the *bicheiro*, a wrought-iron hook with a wooden handle; fishing close to the rocks using the *ganha-pão* (literally, "breadwinner"), a small hand net with a wooden handle attached to a supporting iron hoop; and shellfish catching, either by hand or with the ganha-pão.

The pescadores of Vila Chã, as in other northern Portuguese coastal fishing communities, typically built houses in continuous rows along streets parallel to the shoreline. The basic model was a simple wooden hut, covered with a double-pitched roof (thatched, later tiled), with a single all-purpose room. Originally built of wood, the walls were later built of white-washed, roughly rendered granite masonry. Inside there was a single partition, parallel to the street, dividing the front main room from the back kitchen. The kitchen was used only for cooking (over an open hearth), bread making, and dyeing nets with a willow bark infusion. The front room was used for family life, including sleeping, for all other activities such as net and cloth making, and also to store fishing gear and dried seaweed. The main room had a wooden floor; the floor in the kitchen was compacted earth. The pescadores who lived inland in Rio da Gândara also built small thatched huts on the beach to store their boats and gear.

The development of a small-boat fishery in Vila Chã was part of a general process of social stratification that occurred on the north coast of Portugal during the second half of the nineteenth century and was similar to the development of small fisheries in other parts of Western Europe (Veiga de Oliveira, Galhano, and Pereira 1975:17–18). In Vila Chã, where the lavradores had owned small boats and gone to sea to harvest seaweed for use as fertilizer on their fields, some exploitation of marine resources had been important since at least the eighteenth century. But it was not until the mid-nineteenth century that a fishery began to develop in Vila Chã. As we have seen, inheritance practices at this time began to favor consolidation of property, and this created increasing numbers of landless and land-poor. In Vila Chã many of the land-poor turned to fishing. At the same time, increased demands on agricultural productivity during the nineteenth century required more intensive cultivation of the land and greater quantities of fertilizer than the lavradores could produce themselves, either from livestock manure or from seaweed harvested by members of their own households. And, after 1880, when people who had no land began to settle the dunes

along the north coast, additional quantities of fertilizer were needed to
reclaim these lands for gardens. More intensive cultivation encouraged the development of a commercial market for seaweed fertilizer in
Vila Chã and at other centers along the coast to the north. Many of the
landless and land-poor households in Vila Chã and elsewhere began to
organize their economy around the production of seaweed fertilizer for
sale or exchange to lavradores, and for use in their own gardens.

In Vila Chã, these households developed a seasonal round of maritime economic activities centered on the production of seaweed fertilizer. They harvested and dried seaweed during the summer months
from June to September and they supplemented their earnings from
the sale of seaweed with a variety of other seasonal activities. They
worked as day laborers for the lavradores on the land during either the
busy spring planting season or the autumn harvest, or they worked on
the sea. They line fished for their own household consumption and
sold any surplus. Ideally each household also kept a pig and a small
vegetable garden. From the woodlots surrounding the parish they collected kindling and pine cones, which they also sold or exchanged.
They produced a meager subsistence from this seasonal round, and
there were frequent periods of hunger and hardship, particularly during the stormy winter months when they could not go to sea and had no
fish to sell. At these times the pescadores often were forced to beg for
food from the lavradores.

The first report on the fishery in Vila Chã is found in the *Inquérito
industrial e comercial: a pesca* (Anonymous 1890), a government report on the state of the fishery in each of the more than thirty ports and
beaches along the north coast between the Douro River and the Minho
River. By this time, maritime activities in Vila Chã included the harvest
of seaweed and pilado for fertilizer, and net and hand-line fishing for a
variety of fish, especially sardines, *faneca* (whiting-pout), and *congro*
(conger). In total, the fishery in Vila Chã employed 166 people, including 24 women, and including both lavradores and pescadores. The
lavradores exploited marine resources in order to produce fertilizer for
their own fields; the pescadores were entirely dependent on the seasonal round of activities and especially on the commercial seaweed
harvest that began in early June and lasted until late September.

The 1890 *Inquérito* also reported that the pilado fishery was important between August and October. The pilado is a small crab that trav-
els in schools and is therefore easily caught in nets. When dried, it
produces a fertilizer three to six times richer in mineral content than
seaweed. The development of the pilado fishery, like the development
of the commercial seaweed harvest, is generally associated with the
intensification of agriculture in the late nineteenth century, and with

the recovery of the sand dunes for cultivation along the northern coast of Portugal (Veiga de Oliveira, Galhano, and Pereira 1975:182). Certainly, by 1886, pilado fishing was important in Vila Chã (Baldaque da Silva 1891); as early as 1876, two women drowned when a boat loaded with pilado overturned. Although superior in composition to seaweed, the pilado was more difficult to harvest, required systematic organization of labor, and was harvested only in small volume. Pilado was also an unreliable resource, better in some years than in others.[8] Thus, despite its superior properties as a fertilizer, pilado was less widely used than seaweed, which could be harvested annually in larger volume, with little equipment and no special organization of labor. Nonetheless, the pilado harvest remained an important part of the fishery until the 1940s when its numbers were depleted, and when the lavradores turned to chemical sources of fertilizer.

Fresh fish were caught year-round, but especially between October and February. Sardines were caught in nets, and other fish were caught by line. Lobster (*lagosta*) was caught especially between November and January, and mussels (*mexilhão*) were harvested in all seasons from the rocks along the beach and used as bait. Fishing gear, all of which was made in the parish, included sardine nets, pilado nets, lobster pots, lines and hooks, and the hand net, the ganha-pão. Boats also were built in the parish; they were keeled and double-prowed open boats less than six meters in length, each equipped with oars and a mast and sail.[9]

The *Inquérito* further revealed that markets were local. Dried seaweed and pilado were sold to local lavradores. Fish were sold by auction on the beach. And, if more fish were caught than could be consumed within the parish, women and girls would carry the surplus to neighboring parishes to sell. If there was an exceptional catch of sardines, the boats would row to Póvoa de Varzim or Matosinhos to sell the fish. Póvoa de Varzim was the principal center supplying fresh fish to the interior regions of Douro, Minho, and Trás-os-Montes, and Matosinhos was the largest sardine processing center in Europe (Barbosa 1985; Filgueiras 1984; Santos Graça 1982). Lobster was carried by Vila Chã women into Porto and sold door-to-door or on the streets.

Methods of calculating payment to crew members varied. The large pilado boats belonged to lavradores and, if they themselves did not go to sea, they hired a jornaleiro or a pescador, offering a small daily wage and food, to fish for them. The pilado fishery required that two boats fish together and, as few lavradores owned two boats, most fished in partnership with another lavrador, each supplying an equal number of nets and crew members. Each owner of a boat received an equal share (*quinhão*), and from that share he took one-third for his boat and net.

The remaining two-thirds was divided among the three crew members. Payment was in pilado.

The sardine fishery allowed greater flexibility in crew composition. Pescadores and lavradores joined in groups of two to five to crew a boat. Each crew member brought two nets, and the catch was then divided equally. Line fishing was even more flexible, because crew members fished independently and kept the fish they caught as their share. Boats would go out line fishing with crews of two to five, often including women. As the *Inquérito* notes, the inclusion of women as crew members was a special feature of the Vila Chã fishery.

Throughout the first half of the twentieth century, the Vila Chã fishery remained essentially as it was described in the 1890 *Inquérito*. It was a small-scale, inshore fishery based on household production of seaweed and pilado fertilizers and on both net and hand-line fishing from small boats. Little capital outlay was required for the boats, nets, lines, and other gear, all of which were made in the parish and were maintained by household members. The fishery was dependent on the availability of diverse and seasonal marine resources, the exploitation of which required specialized gear and varying patterns of labor organization.[10]

Up until the 1940s, lavradores continued to engage in fishing through their ownership of boats and their management of the pilado fishery. Changes began to take place in the organization of the fishery in Vila Chã only after the Second World War. These included the termination of pilado fishing, increased male emigration, and recruitment of men to the Grand Banks cod fishery.

The pilado had begun to disappear from the northern coast in the 1940s. Their disappearance coincided with an increased use of chemical fertilizers by local agriculturalists, and the result was the collapse of the market for pilado and the end of the pilado fishery by 1950. Low prices for fresh fish and decreased markets after the war forced many of the men to seek employment outside Vila Chã. (At this time it was rare for women to emigrate in search of work, and women did not work in offshore fisheries.) Throughout the decades of the 1950s and 1960s almost every Vila Chã fisherman emigrated and worked abroad for at least a few years. The men emigrated to work in the larger fisheries of Brazil or Angola and Mozambique.

Fishermen who did not want to emigrate from Vila Chã for long or indefinite periods joined the "White Fleet," the Portuguese fleet that fished for cod on the Grand Banks off the coast of Newfoundland. The first Vila Chã man joined the national cod fleet in 1947; between 1960 and 1965, more than sixty men from Vila Chã took out licenses as cod fishermen (*bacalhoeiros*) and were making the annual six- to eight-month voyage to the Grand Banks. The cod fishery became especially attractive to rural fishermen in the 1960s when those who made six consecutive voyages were exempted from military service, which at that time meant active fighting in the "Colonial Wars" in Portuguese Africa. The majority of men made many more than the required six voyages. They were lured not only by exemption from military service but also by other state incentives that included free medical care and a small family allowance—social services that would not become generally available in Portugal until after 1974. And, although the cod fishermen were paid abysmally low wages—wages that in no way remunerated their effort—they could still earn more at the Newfoundland fishery than they could fishing at home in Vila Chã. They generally invested their earnings in a small boat of their own and a piece of land on which they built a house. Once these capital investments were made, they would retire from the cod fishery and resume fishing on a daily basis from the beach in Vila Chã.[11]

Gradually the men who had worked in fisheries outside Portugal began to introduce new technology to the local fishery. The new technology included motors that enabled the boats to go out to sea during all seasons, and a variety of fishing gear that increased the size of the catches and the diversity of the species caught.

In 1959 one fisherman invested in an outboard motor. For several years he had trouble finding crew to fish with him because, as a boat owner, he wanted a greater share of the earnings from the catch to pay for the motor and gas. Crew members thought they could earn more fishing with a boat that relied only on sail and oars. Still, by the late 1960s, everyone wanted to fish with boats that had motors because they could reach more fishing grounds and at greater distances from shore; they could make more than one trip in a day if conditions were favorable; and, most important, the boats could now go out in all but the most stormy weather with a resulting increase in the number of fishing days per year. In 1985 all but one of the boats fishing in Vila Chã carried a fifteen-horsepower motor.

Boats equipped with motors became popular because they required less labor. By 1985 boats were crewed by two persons instead of the three or four that had been needed when boats were propelled by sail and oar. The boats were still of the same open design that had been used in Vila Chã since the late nineteenth century, but they were slightly bigger and longer than they used to be, and, because they were power-driven, they were fortified to carry heavier loads of up to 1,400 kilograms. All had been built by boat builders in the parish.

Fishermen who had worked in fisheries in Brazil, Angola, Mozambique, Germany, and other parts of Europe returned to Vila Chã in the late 1960s and early 1970s, bringing with them new designs for nets and the first traps. By 1985, each boat was equipped with several types of gear, and fish caught included not only the sardines, whiting-pout, and conger, but also varieties of sea bass and cod, sole, flounder, and mackerel, and several types of crabs, shrimp, lobster, and octopus. Nets were now made of nylon and no longer required the daily maintenance that cotton nets had needed. Women who had once been responsible for cleaning the nets after each use—an arduous task that required carrying the heavy wet cotton nets to the river to rinse in fresh water, and then carrying them to the beach and spreading them to dry—now spent less time maintaining fishing gear.

By the early 1970s the current system of boat ownership and labor recruitment had emerged, a system that, according to fisheries officials, may be peculiar to Vila Chã. Formerly, the labor force was divided into two groups: those who were boat owners (*donos*) and those who worked as crew. The donos were entitled to a slightly larger share of the earnings to offset their capital investment. In 1985, with few exceptions, each fisherman owned a boat, and it was customary for two donos to fish together as partners. They used one man's boat and motor for a period (usually eight days) and then used the other's boat and motor for an equal period. Each brought his own nets and traps. In this way they maintained equality because each had made an equal capital investment and both were alternately dono and crew. The wives of the two partners also worked together. They unloaded the boat, sorted and sold the fish, divided the proceeds equally between the two households, and controlled the use of the earnings.

Throughout this period of change, the Portuguese state offered no assistance to small local fisheries. The state continued its involvement in two areas only: licensing and taxation. All fishermen were required to renew their licenses each year and to pay a small fee to do so. During the 1960s, the minister of fisheries, Admiral Henrique dos Santos Tenreiro, attempted to improve the method of taxing the fishermen. Formerly, the local *Guarda Fiscal* (police and customs officers) had patrolled the beaches where the women were auctioning the fish and had attempted to collect a 10 percent tax on sales. Admiral Tenreiro designed a system of state-run auctions (the lotas) that would sell the fish for the fishermen, withhold the taxes owing (18 percent in 1985), and pay the fishermen the remainder at the end of each month. This is the system now in operation in many fishing communities, including nearby Póvoa de Varzim. In 1971, Tenreiro authorized the building of a lota in Vila Chã on the beach at the site where the women formerly had auctioned the fish. The building is equipped with two walk-in refrigerators, a weigh scale, a long table where the fish are auctioned, and a small office where the lota employee keeps his account books. In Vila Chã, however, the system does not work quite as Admiral Tenreiro had envisioned. Vila Chã women employ a number of strategies to maintain their control over the sale of the catch, to increase its value, and to receive the cash directly from the buyer. One of these strategies is to insist on selling the fish themselves and, in order to avoid taxation, to sell more than half of each day's catch, not in the lota, but on the beach directly from the boats (see chapter 7).

EMIGRATION

Since at least the mid-nineteenth century, male emigration has been an important dimension of social and economic relations in Vila Chã and a significant source of cash income to parish households. Emigration from Vila Chã follows a pattern that has been well documented for northwestern Portugal.

During the late nineteenth century, overpopulation and inheritance laws created small, agriculturally inviable plots of land, and new taxation laws placed severe burdens on the rural population, creating a situation of economic crisis that forced many people off the land and encouraged high rates of emigration (Brettell 1985; 1986). Emigration was seen by the rural population as a last resort in the attempt to avoid indebtedness, the subsequent expropriation of land and property, and proletarianization (Pina-Cabral 1986). Emigration was viewed as temporary: men "emigrated to return" (Brettell 1979). They emigrated prior to marriage or when newly married, and they went to accumulate capital that they hoped would enable them to establish their households—to build a house and buy a boat, for example. But few, in fact, secured their nest egg, and the result was a pattern of "serial migration" or "repeat migration": over the course of their adult lives men emigrated several times, often for periods of several years at a time.

At first, those who emigrated from Vila Chã were young and unmarried, the majority under fourteen years of age.[12] They went to Brazil to work as seamen on merchant vessels. After 1880, as economic conditions worsened, married men also began to emigrate. They went to work in the fisheries of Rio de Janeiro, or they worked as seamen on merchant cargo vessels. These men emigrated temporarily in the hope of earning cash that would alleviate the hardship at home. But many were away from home for periods of several years at a time, and some never returned to their families in Vila Chã. Others did return, but, when fishing became unprofitable in Vila Chã, they were again forced to emigrate, often for periods of several years. As a result, many maritime households accommodated long periods of absence of their adult male members.

This pattern of male emigration continued into the twentieth century, stopped briefly during the First World War, but resumed after 1918. By the late 1920s, there were 116 Vila Chã men and boys, married and unmarried, resident at least temporarily in Brazil. By far the majority of these were members of maritime households. Emigration by pescadores continued erratically throughout the 1930s. Many men were unable to return to Portugal during the Second World War, and wives were left without husbands and without remittances. The war period is remembered as an especially grim time for the women and children of Vila Chã. Again, emigration stopped during the war but resumed when the war ended and reached a high level again during the 1950s. Most men still emigrated to Brazil, but some began to emigrate to Mozambique and Angola to work in the large fisheries there. In the 1950s, some wives and families accompanied or joined the men. A number of Vila Chã fishermen and women and their children lived in Angola and Mozambique for as long as twenty years. Virtually all of them, however, returned between 1974 and 1976—during the independence struggles of those two countries—and took up fishing again in Vila Chã.

Emigration from Vila Chã became important again during the 1960s when emigration from the whole of Portugal reached an all-time high. In 1966 alone, more than 120,000 Portuguese emigrated to France (Serrão 1982). France was a popular destination because of its proximity and because of the possibility of returning home regularly. Women also began to emigrate. Usually they accompanied or followed their husbands, but some women did go on their own. The men went to work in construction and the women as domestics and cleaners in the large cities of France, cities such as Paris and Lyons. In the late 1960s some Vila Chã fishermen and their wives also emigrated to work in fisheries in West Germany. Emigration declined after 1978 when France and other receiving countries began to close their borders to new Portuguese emigrants, and since 1980 emigration has become increasingly difficult for members of maritime households and other rural, unskilled labor.

POST-1960: SOCIAL AND ECONOMIC CHANGE IN THE PARISH

For almost half a century the New State, through its national economic policy of "planned constraint" (Leeds 1984), maintained "stability" and poverty in rural areas. During the final years of the regime, however, Portugal began to "open up" through a set of processes and events that brought new alternatives to the rural population (cf. Aceves and Douglass 1976 on Spain). Among these were increasing urbanization and industrialization; improved roads and transportation services; increased literacy and access to mass communications media (especially television); tourism; and the introduction of new agricultural techniques at a time when farming as a way of life was declining. Extensive emigration to France and to other parts of Europe brought new cultural influences as well as new wealth to landless households and restructured rural class relations that had been based on landed wealth. The independence of the former Portuguese African colonies resulted in an estimated one million returned emigrants (*retornados*) to both rural and urban areas. After the Revolution of April 25, 1974 and the institution of democratic government, regional and municipal governments were endowed with budgets and responsibility to manage local affairs. Local government in Portugal is still in a developmental stage but offers the possibility of regional social and economic planning. Since 1974, there has also been an increase in social service programs, including old age pensions, health care, and education. In Vila Chã, in addition to changes in agricultural techniques, there have been technological changes in the local fishery and increasing wage employment in nearby factories. In rural communities like Vila Chã, "opening up" and economic development created the conditions for the structural transformation of households and of the conditions under which women work.

In the context of economic development since 1960, the socioeconomic profile of the parish has changed dramatically. In 1966 more than half the adult population (55.8 percent) were still employed in household-based agriculture or fishing. But by 1985 less than 16 percent of those employed were employed in fishing or agriculture, while 33 percent worked in factories and 29.6 percent in skilled and unskilled trades (table 1.3).

Table 1.4 presents the data obtained from the survey I conducted of 171 households in 1984–1985 in the coastal hamlets of Praia and Facho. In these 171 households, 333 people were employed. While, in the 1960s, the majority of the residents of Praia and Facho were engaged in a household-based maritime economy, by 1985 only 24.6 percent (82 men and women) of those employed worked in the fishery, while 34.8 percent were employed in industry. Skilled trades and construction employed 24.6 percent; 11.5 percent worked in services; and the remaining 4.8 percent represented other occupations.

By 1985 significant gender differentiation by occupation was also evident in the maritime households of Praia and Facho. Formerly men and women had worked together in the household maritime economy.

TABLE 1.3

Occupational Distribution, Parish of Vila Chã, 1966–1985(in percent)

	1966	1973	1985[a]
Agriculture	22.2	16.1	7.2
Fishing	33.6	22.0	8.7
Skilled[b]	14.9	21.5	15.4
Unskilled[c]	4.5	6.1	14.2
Factory	6.1	10.1	33.0
Services[d]	15.2	18.8	16.5
Other	3.5	5.4	5.0
Total	100.0	100.0	100.0
	(N = 342)	(N = 478)	(N = 851)

Sources: Electoral Censuses, Câmara Municipal do Concelho de Vila do Conde (1966, 1973); Household Survey (1985).

[a] The 1966 and 1973 voters' lists enumerate only men over 21 years of age and only women who either are heads of households or have completed a secondary education. The 1985 household survey includes all those employed, regardless of age or sex. Housewives are not included in any year.

[b] Skilled trades include, for example, carpenters, mechanics, and electricians.

[c] Unskilled trades include construction workers.

[d] Services include police, teachers, and small shopkeepers. The composition of the service category has changed significantly since 1966. In 1966, 36.5 percent (N = 19) of service workers were military officials and police; in 1985, local police represent only 4.3 percent (N = 6) of the service category. In the same period, the proportion of small businesses has increased.

In 1985, the majority (76.7 percent) of those employed in factory work were women, while all of those employed in skilled trades and construction were men. The men worked in skilled trades as carpenters, plumbers, electricians, or auto mechanics, or they worked in unskilled trades related to civil construction (*construção civil*). A profitable local building industry boomed in the 1960s and 1970s, creating employment for young men in the construction of new homes and the renovation of old homes for emigrants and retornados. By the 1980s, when emigration was becoming more difficult, the building industry began to decline, and local young men began to experience frequent periods of unemployment. During the same period, however, wage employment opportunities for women increased.

Closer examination of the female labor force (fourteen years of age and over) in 1985 reveals that the majority (61.8 percent) worked for wages in factories (table 1.4). Another 20.1 percent of women worked in the fishery, and 11.8 percent in services. Of the eighty-nine women who worked in factories, forty-nine worked in fish-processing plants,

TABLE 1.4

Occupations by Sex of Residents of Lugar da Praia and Lugar do Facho, 1985

	Female		Male		Total	
	N	%	N	%	N	%
Fishing	29	20.1	53	28.0	82	24.6
Skilled[a]	—	—	32	16.9	32	9.6
Unskilled[b]	—	—	49	26.0	49	14.7
Factory	89	61.8	27	14.3	116	34.8
Services[c]	17	11.8	21	11.1	38	11.5
Other[d]	9	6.3	7	3.7	16	4.8
Total	144	100.0	189	100.0	333[e]	100.0

Source: Household Survey (1985).

[a] Skilled workers include mechanics, electricians, and plumbers.

[b] The majority of unskilled workers are construction workers.

[c] Services include police, teachers, shopkeepers.

[d] Not including housewives.

[e] The estimated total population of Vila Chã in 1985 was 3,000. In the 1985 survey of 70 percent of parish households, the number of individuals employed was 851. The 333 employed residents of Lugar da Praia and Lugar do Facho thus represent 11.1 percent of the total parish population and 39.1 percent of the employed in the survey.

twenty-three in garment factories, fourteen in an electronics plant, and three in a plastics factory. Whereas, prior to 1966, the majority of the women of Lugar da Praia and Lugar do Facho had worked in the household fishery, by 1985 the female labor force had diversified. In 1985, women worked for the household in the maritime economy; they worked for wages in factories; and, as housewives, they worked in the home as unpaid domestic laborers. This differentiation in the occupations of women is described in chapter 7.

CONCLUSION

In this chapter I have set the stage for the discussion of women's work and lives presented in subsequent chapters. The parish of Vila Chã—and, in a more general sense, rural Portugal—is the context. Vila Chã, historically, is a community of peasant farmers; but, during the second half of the nineteenth century, the exploitation of maritime resources was developed by the landless nonheirs of agricultural households. By the turn of the century, households based on maritime economic activities constituted more than one-third of the parish's households. Until the 1960s the New State's policies of economic constraint sustained poverty in rural areas, and, until the mid-1960s, almost two-thirds of the population of Vila Chã continued to work in household-based agriculture and fishing. Throughout this period, the remittances of emigrant males were a major source of cash income to peasant and maritime households. During the 1960s, the gradual establishment of factories in rural areas on the north coast and the development of a local building industry created wage employment opportunities for young men and women; by 1985, two-thirds of the labor force was wage employed. The meaning for women of this economic transformation is the subject of later chapters. For now, we turn to the life and work of the women of the pre-1960 maritime households. The narrative of Alvina introduces us to the fisherwomen of Vila Chã.

Chapter 2

A FISHERWOMAN'S STORY

Alvina:

"Ser mulher é ser trabalhadeira."
(To be a woman is to be a hard worker.)

"I WAS BORN in Rio da Gândara in 1917. My mother had eight children. I was the third. My father was a fisherman and *pobre* (poor). My mother was the daughter of a lavrador of Fundo da Vila. They were married in 1912. My mother was one of eight children, all living. My deceased grandmother did not divide up the *casa* (the household property), and, as my mother did not inherit the casa, she had to marry a pobre, a pescador. My mother's dote was a small piece of land to build a house on in Rio da Gândara. After her marriage my mother joined the other women working on the beach harvesting seaweed. She also worked as a jornaleira for the lavradores. When I was still a child my father emigrated to Brazil. You could not earn a living fishing here on the praia in those days, and all the men emigrated to Brazil to work on boats there. But my father was always very homesick (*muito saudoso*). He missed his wife and family so much that he came home again after a year. He fished in Vila Chã for a few years, but, when fishing did not feed the family (*não dava*), he had to emigrate again. He emigrated six or seven times but never stayed away more than a year or two at a time because he would get homesick for his family again and come home.

"I went to school for little more than one year. By the time I was eight I was doing the work that all women of maritime households did: I used to go to the woods with the other women to collect kindling and pine cones. By the time I was ten I was walking to Matosinhos with my sister and a neighbor woman to buy fish—sardines and faneca. Then we would carry the fish to other villages to sell. I worked *a jornal* (as a day laborer) for the lavradores in their fields of wheat and rye. I worked with my sisters. For an afternoon's work we earned two *tostões*[1] each and were given a small lunch of bread, wine, and olives.

"I always wanted to work on the sea, and when I was fourteen and old enough I persuaded my father to take me into Vila do Conde to the Capitania for my license (*cédula*). For the test I had to swim across the Rio Ave, but I didn't know how to swim, so my father gave the man from the Capitania a coin and I got my license. After that I fished with my father and my brother, and when the weather was too bad for fishing I worked with my mother and sisters for the lavradores in the fields (*no campo*). And that was my life day in and day out until my marriage.

"I didn't marry until I was twenty-seven, and the period of my *mocidade* (unmarried youth) was the happiest time of my life. I arranged (*arranjei*) my first sweetheart (*namorado*) when I was nineteen. My mocidade is a story (*dá um romance*). It is only I who can give it value. Telling the story doesn't do it justice.

"In those days on Sundays and festival days (*dias de festa*) there was always a dance in one of the *praças* (squares) in the parish—here in Lugar da Praia or in Rio da Gândara. Everyone went. There was a guitar and accordion, a violin and a drum, and people sang and everyone danced. Everyone danced together in the open air. Not like it is today where the young people just want to go to these dance halls and dance close together in the dark. We didn't just stick to one boy the way they do today; we danced with all the boys. We used to do things together but now everything is for couples. Only at the end of the day would our sweethearts walk us home, and we would stand outside our parents' houses talking until our fathers would come out shining a lantern in our faces and say: 'Girl, it's time [to come into the house]' (*Menina, já está na hora*). The young people today are missing the fun. We used to have many namorados. We always had one that we were joking with and talking to: one to go to mass with in the morning, one for the afternoon, one for weekdays . . . But today they just find one and they stick with him. We used to namorar with many boys before we found one to marry. Now they attach themselves to one right away and they marry him.

"The lavradores came to watch but they wouldn't let their children dance with us. They didn't want their children marrying pobres. They didn't want their children marrying pescadores because the pescadores were poor and did not have any land. Those who had property also wanted to get more through marriage (*Quem tinha também queria arranjar*). In those days there were more pobres than there were lavradores. Rio da Gândara was all pobres, all pescadores. The lavradores lived where they live today in [the hamlets of] Cimo de Vila and Fundo de Vila. We, the pescadores, used to think that the lavradores were rich because they owned all the land. We used to say: 'This world is not well divided. The land all belongs to the lavradores. Some have all while others have none' (*Este mundo não fica bem partido; a terra é toda dos lavradores. Uns têm tudo e outros não tem nada*). We pescadores just wanted a little land to grow a few potatoes and cabbages, but there was not even that. We used to say: 'If I could just have a plot of land . . .' I always wanted a piece of land but there was no land to buy. For more than twenty years I have rented that small plot for my garden from a lavrador.

"In those days the lavradores had everything. Their fields were full of food to eat—beans, corn, rye, oats, wheat. They had wine. They had pigs to kill to make *chouriço* (sausage). They had houses full of food, houses full to overflowing (*casas fartas*). The lavrador had everything and the pescador had nothing. There was much hunger (*Passava-se muita fome*). When we couldn't go to sea, when the weather was bad, we would go to work for the lavradores. We would work for food, for corn to make bread, or for a little meat or wine. Sometimes women would go begging for a cup of flour. In those days the lavradores needed our help. They didn't have the machines they have now. Each lavrador had two or three or four *criados* (agricultural servants) who came from the interior, from the area of Barcelos, and, in addition, the lavradores would hire us, pobres, to work by the day. The lavradores practically starved the poor to death (*Os lavradores matavam à fome os pobres*).

"Today the lavradores have nothing. They have less than the pobres. Before, their fields were full of food. Today they only want to grow corn for their cows. They have cows for milk to sell. And they grow potatoes for sale. And they invest in agricultural machinery (*máquinas*). Today the lavradores are selling their land because they need the money. It used to be that you could never buy a piece of land, but now the pescadores are buying land. Today the pescadores say that they don't need the lavradores for anything, that they don't need the lavradores anymore. Today all the pescadores live well. God has been a good friend to today's pescadores: they all have little houses of their own (*Deus ainda foi muito amigo dos pescadores de hoje: todos têm uma casinha*).

"I met my husband at the festival (*festa*) of São Bento in Vairão in 1938. We used to go to the festas. At the festas everyone danced together in the street. I danced with him there. He wanted to talk to me but I didn't talk to him then. He was a fisherman from Póvoa de Varzim. I didn't know him. I thought he might be married. But I thought he was very handsome. Then in August I went to the festa of Nossa Senhora de Assunção in Póvoa, and I saw him again there. I went with a friend and her brother. Her brother wanted to walk with me as if we were namorados. We were walking in the crowd at the festa when I saw him. I was sorry because I didn't want him to think that I already had a namorado. I wanted to talk to him but I couldn't. We just looked at each other. Then a few weeks later I received his card. He wrote so well and he had only finished the fourth grade. He wrote: 'When I saw you, you thrilled (*supreender*) me more than any other girl (*moça*) in the world. If you already have a namorado I am very happy for you, but if you don't and you would accept my courtship (*namoro*) I would also be very happy.' I didn't know what to do! I was still worried that he might be married, that he would start coming here to visit me but that he would have someone at home too. I waited a few weeks and then I wrote back. We exchanged cards for a few months, and then he came to Vila Chã one Sunday in February to visit me. I was so nervous I nearly didn't go to the door when he came, but my sisters made me! After that we courted through letters (*namorámos por carta*), but I continued to talk and joke and dance with other boys on Sundays here in Vila Chã. Sometimes he would stop by on his way home from Matosinhos. He worked on the sardine trawlers there during the week and would go home to Póvoa for the weekend. Or he would come to visit on a Sunday afternoon. There were days when he arrived just after another namorado had left! After a year he began to talk of marrying, but I thought I was still too young. I was twenty-two. I told him that my mother had married when she was twenty-four and that I wouldn't marry before that.

"I was reluctant to marry. I had a good life then. I loved my life as a maritime woman (*uma mulher marítima*). I loved to spend nights out on the ocean. We would drift with the sardine nets attached to the boats waiting to haul them in at dawn. We sang and recounted stories. Sometimes we would doze a little; other times we would jig for faneca. In the mornings we would row the full boats in to shore where women would be waiting to unload and sell the fish on the beach. If there were a lot of fish, we would row or sail to Póvoa, hurrying to arrive while the buyers from Porto were still there to buy our fish. Then we would sail back to Vila Chã singing, still with nothing in our stomachs. We worked in the rain and the cold. If there was no wind, we would have to row. When we got home we would eat and sleep and get ready to go out again at sunset.

"I worked as hard as any man. I never had trouble finding a boat that was willing to take me on as crew. They knew I would bring in a share equal to any man's. I fished with many men on this beach and there was always respect (*respeito*). There was more respect on the sea than there was on land.

"I loved to work on the sea. We used to meet other boats and we would ask: 'Where have you been? How is the fishing there?' And so we would talk. I still love to talk with people who know the sea. Everything about the sea fascinates me. We used to say: 'The land is all owned by someone or other, but the sea belongs to no one. The sea is everyone's' (*Toda a terra pertence a alguém; o mar pertence a ninguém. O mar é de todos*). The sea has everything: the sea is rich; the sea is sacred; the sea is God's; the sea is everyone's. The sea is much richer than the land. With the land you have to prepare the soil, plant, fertilize, hoe, harvest, but with the sea you only harvest (*só se colhe*). But the life of the sea is a thankless one as well. There was much hunger and *miséria* because there were many times of bad weather when we couldn't go out in our boats and we had no fish to sell. There were pescadores who were bolder than others, who would take a chance. When they would go out [to sea] we would say, 'They went in the hands of God' (*Foram à sorte de Deus*). When someone died at sea, we used to say: 'He died at sea. His life was meant to end there. It was his destiny' (*Morreu no mar. Tinha que acabar ali*).

"I am a woman of the sea (*Sou marítima*). I love the sea and I love the work. I am a very hardworking woman, a woman devoted to life and work (*Sou uma mulher muito trabalhadeira, uma mulher da vida e do trabalho*). When I wasn't sardine fishing, I would go out jigging faneca with hook and line or I would work on the seaweed or work in the fields. To be a woman is to be a hard worker (*Ser mulher é ser trabalhadeira*). We used to say: 'A woman makes money; money does not make a woman. It is better to marry a hardworking woman who will make money than it is to marry a spendthrift woman with an inheritance who will waste it' (*A mulher faz dinheiro; o dinheiro não faz a mulher. Mais vale casar com uma mulher trabalhadeira do que com uma gastadeira com dote*).

"Pobres married pobres generally. They grew up together. They grew up together in that ambience on the beach. They knew that neither of them had anything [i.e., property], so that they were equal and could not later fight over who had brought more to the marriage, to the household. What did a girl who was pobre, a daughter of a pescador, look for in a husband? That he not be a drunkard, a gambler, a spender, and that he not be lazy. What did a boy who was pobre look for in a wife? That she not like to eat too many sweets, that she not be lazy or slovenly (*porca*), and that she not be from a *fraca família*, that is, that she not be from a family that was prone to fighting (*barulho*), that she be from a family that was hardworking.

"You did the best you could to find a good husband, but no one can be assured that they will be happy in marriage. After marriage it's what chance brings (*Mas depois do casamento é o que dá na sorte*). You try to choose a good mate and everything is fine at the wedding. In the church everyone says, 'Yes! Yes!' But afterward the fights start. In the church both are equal, but after time it generally happens that one becomes the boss, one begins to command (*manda*) more than the other. Marriage is a cross. You must pick up that cross and carry it (*carregar aquela cruz*). Some couples continue to work together, and there is nothing more beautiful in the world. The most beautiful thing in the world is a couple that gets along well together, that works together.

"Thanks be to God, I was happy in my marriage. Even after I had my children I was happy. It didn't seem I was married, I was so happy. That was the most important thing in my life: to be happy in my marriage and with my husband. I was happy in my youth and in my marriage. My sisters, all pobres, were lucky in their marriages too. We were all raised the same: to be trabalhadeiras and thrifty (poupadas). But I think most marriages are unhappy. In most marriages there is barulho. The men used to beat their wives because there was hunger. There was never enough to go around. There was no money. Now everything is luxury, everyone has food to eat, and there is still barulho, there is still beating. We used to say, 'Where there is no bread, everyone gets angry and no one is right' (Aonde não há pão, todos ralham e ninguém tem razão).

"I finally married my husband in 1944, six years after we first met. I had another suitor who was a criado de servir (servant), but he was just a diversion. I knew that I didn't want to marry a criado; I wanted to marry someone of my profession. But still I was reluctant to marry. Finally I began to think: 'This is not good. He's been with me so many years. If he leaves me one day, what will the people say?' I decided to dedicate myself to him. He was very honest, respectful, very hardworking and polite (muito honesto, respeitador, muito trabalhador e educado). People always said he didn't seem like a pescador: he was so polite and respectful, and he spoke so well. My father wanted me to marry another man, an old bachelor who had been telling people that he liked me. This man owned a small grocery shop and was rich. But I didn't want to marry him, so my mother told my father that I shouldn't leave the man I loved. My mother remembered how much she had loved my father when they were namorados and he had gone to Brazil before they were married. She would be singing and crying at the same time thinking of him as she worked in the fields and hoping he would return. And so I married the man I loved. I courted with whom I pleased and married whom I pleased. And it went well, thanks be to God! (Namorei com quem quis e casei com quem quis. E calhou bem, Graças a Deus !).

"Our wedding was simple, as were most weddings at that time. I wore a marine blue skirt that I had already worn to many festas. The skirt I wore to my wedding had been out in the rain many times before that day. On my head, I wore a black shawl belonging to one of my sisters, and I wore another sister's slippers (chinelas). Only my slip and camisole, both white, which I had made, were new. We went on foot to the church in the afternoon. My husband's mother and sister and brother came from Póvoa; only my father and mother and my god-mother came with me. Afterward, we went back to my parents' house for a glass of wine and a few sweets. It was all that my parents could afford. There was no food to give others, no food for a festa. We stayed in my parents' house in Rio da Gândara for a year and a half until a few months after my son was born. Then we moved down to this house on the praia, which we rented from a lavrador. My daughter was born here.

"I had my children at home. There was a midwife (curiosa) who came to the house. There was nothing to ease the pain and women suffered much. Nowadays there are these injections and women have a much easier time. When I had my two children, there was just my husband and the curiosa. She was the same woman who had assisted my mother at my birth. Water was boiling on the fire. The curiosa knows all the stages of the labor pains and she tells the mother that it is not time yet and to keep breathing. The mother is walking around and the pain is intense. Finally the pain is so intense and the curiosa knows that the baby is coming. The husband stands behind the woman and the curiosa is in front to catch the baby. The pregnant woman is squatting and pushing down and her husband is holding her up. I don't know how women today give birth lying down. Finally the baby comes. The curiosa cuts the cord. She bathes the baby and she bathes the mother and that is that! Today many women give birth by cesarean section (barriga aberta) in the hospital. My daughter had two cesare-ans and now she can have no more children. The cesarean makes the birth faster and less painful for the mother, but in those days women had to suffer many hours.

"All women gave the breast to their babies in those days. Today women don't want to breastfeed because they want to preserve their bodies: they want to stay beautiful. So they buy a formula at the phar-macy. But it used to be that all women breastfed. We used to say you should breastfeed for três Maios (three Mays or three years), but often women were pregnant again within the year. Women had more chil-dren in those days. But in those days many babies died. My mother had eight births; five children lived. She was one of eight living children, so her mother must have had others who had died as babies. There were none of these methods to avoid pregnancy that there are today. I was lucky, though. I only had two children. That was what God wanted (Foi o que Deus quis).

"My husband never involved himself in my business (na minha vida), because he knew that I was always a hard worker and that I was very clever with money. Once I teased him: 'You are worthless (Tu não *prestas*). You don't know anything about money. You don't know how much money there is. You leave it all up to me.' And he said, 'Because I trust you' (*Tenho confiança em ti*). He gave all his money to me. This is how it should be. A good husband is a gentleman who earns and gives the money to his wife (*um bom cavalheiro que ganha e entrega o dinheiro à mulher*). A good wife is a good manager of the household, tidy, thrifty, and industrious (*uma boa governadora de casa, limpa, poupada, trabalhadeira*).

"Do you know, a cousin of mine in Facho told me the other day that her daughter does not have a penny to her name; it is he [her husband] who runs the household (*não é dona de um tostão; é ele que manda*). I think it's a terrible thing when a husband doesn't trust his wife with the money. When she always has to be asking him for money to go to the shop, she is *mais escrava* (more of a slave, servile).

"I used to play a game with my husband like the television show 'Um, Dois, Três' where I would tease him to guess how much money I had saved. He would never be able to guess and would be very pleased when I told him. Even then, I would never tell him about all the money I had. Women didn't tell their husbands how much money they earned from the seaweed or other business (*negócios*). It was the woman's business. It had nothing to do with him (*não tinha nada que ver com ele*).

"All my life has been hard work. I was always making money, a little here, a little there, putting something in my pocket. That's what my husband liked about me: I was a fighter to make a living (*uma lutadora p'ra vida*). I was always wanting more: if I had one, I wanted two.

"For many years, my husband fished on the trawlers out of Matosinhos. He would go there in May and fish until January, coming home on weekends. I stayed here with my children for the summer to harvest seaweed and to fish and sell the fish. In September I moved with the children to Matosinhos. I left my house full of dried seaweed, and my father sold it for me when the lavradores from Póvoa came. In Matosinhos we lived in one room. The pescadores lived in one building there. Every couple had one room. The other women were from Póvoa and Vila do Conde. There were other fishermen from Vila Chã fishing there then, but none of their wives came with them to live in Matosinhos. They didn't want to live in the quarters there. Sometimes the Vila Chã women would come to Matosinhos all dressed in their finery to see their husbands, and I used to hide from them. I didn't want them to see me dressed in rags and working there. But I was there to work, not to enjoy myself. I went there to earn money. That was my life. I was always working. I used to sell fresh sardines that my husband would bring home from the boat he fished on. I would sell them at high prices, and then I would buy more, cheaper sardines of poorer quality—perhaps less fresh. These I would clean and salt and put in trays to sell at even higher prices at home in Vila Chã later in the winter. I also collected driftwood for firewood on the beach there. By Christmas, when the fishing was over for the season in Matosinhos and it was time to return to Vila Chã, I would have a hundred trays of salted sardines. I had so many sardines and so much firewood piled up that I could fill a truck. I would arrange to return to Vila Chã when there was an empty truck going so I wouldn't have to pay the freight. When I would arrive home with the truck piled high, my neighbors would be surprised and envious. For the rest of the winter I never was without firewood and we always had sardines to eat. It was the time of year when there were no fresh fish in Vila Chã, and I would sell my preserved sardines. I would sell them here on the praia or I would go to the lavradores to sell them. My neighbors used to be so envious (cheia de inveja) because I had fish to sell in the winter.

"I am a maritime woman. My happiest days were the days of my youth when I worked on the sea. I have so much nostalgia (tantas saudades, tantas saudades) for those days, for the days when I was young and healthy and able to work hard. But it's all over now."

Alvina lives today, a widow, alone in her small house, one in the row of narrow, two-story attached houses that line either side of the one street that winds through Lugar da Praia. A tiny, wizened figure, she dresses only in black—a black skirt, sweater, and kerchief—but she has lively eyes and unexpected physical strength. She maintains a ruthless pace of work even though she suffers from a variety of physical ailments, including high blood pressure, back pains, and digestive problems. Every day she walks the short distance up the hill to her rented plot to tend her garden. If there has been no rain for a few days, she makes several trips with buckets of water. She grows potatoes, three varieties of cabbages, garlic, onions, parsley, lettuce, turnips, and squash. These vegetables are for her own use and for sale or exchange with neighbors. She also grows a large variety of flowers and prepares bouquets to sell to other women each Saturday for their family graves; each Saturday she places a fresh bouquet on her husband's grave.

She also harvests from the sea. Until a few years ago she used to go out line fishing in a small boat with another fisherwoman on fine summer days. Nowadays she stays onshore and walks up and down the beach in front of Vila Chã. She cuts lapas (a small chiton) and mussels from the rocks at low tide and sells them to summer vacationers or to lavradores, who instead of giving her money might pay her with fresh eggs. Every summer morning Alvina is one of the first on the beach to see what seaweed has washed up during the night. She no longer works the way she used to—long hours wading in the shallows up to her neck in water, filling and refilling a huge, circular, wire-rimmed net with the floating seaweed and dragging it to shore. Instead, she concentrates on collecting from the rocks at low tide smaller amounts of the special types of seaweed that are sold for much higher prices to buyers from pharmaceutical and cosmetic factories in Porto. She also harvests and dries the ordinary seaweed varieties for use as fertilizer in her own garden.

Alvina's energetic pace is exhausting to observe. She never stops working but keeps going all day, *"p'ra frente e p'ra trás"* (to and fro), as she says. She is always thinking of what she can do to save a little more money. "Money saved is money in the pocket at the end of the month," she says.

Alvina receives half of her deceased husband's fisherman's pension and her own fisherwoman's pension for a total of 7,300 escudos each month (or less than $60.00 U.S.; $1.00 U.S. – 125 escudos in 1985). From this income she meets her major monthly expenses: prescription drugs (more than 1,000 escudos per month); her light and water bills (about 1,000 escudos per month); and the 175 escudos she has been paying the priest each Tuesday to say a mass for her husband, who died on a Tuesday over two years ago. Alvina tries to save as much as she can by economizing on her own daily food costs, because she lives in fear that she will become chronically ill and that she will not be able to pay for the proper medical care.

The loss of her husband two years ago was hard for Alvina, and her life without him is lonely. "It's all over now," she says. Although she lives in the center of the fishing community, over the years she has become isolated from her neighbors largely because of her self-sufficiency and her determination to be independent. Her children are now married and busy with their own lives. Her thirty-seven-year-old son, an electrician, is married to a woman from a neighboring parish, where they live with their three children. He visits his mother about once a week and invites her to his home for special occasions, such as Easter or a grandchild's First Communion. More often than not, Alvina refuses to go. Now that her husband is dead, she cannot be happy, she says. Her daughter, thirty-six, is married to a seasonally employed housepainter; she lives in two rooms in the hamlet of Rio da Igreja in the interior of Vila Chã, about two kilometers from her mother's house, where many of the young married factory workers live. She works long hours in a fish plant in Matosinhos and rarely has time to visit her mother. Her weekends are taken up with housework. Often, however, she leaves her four-year-old daughter in Alvina's care during the week, so Alvina frequently has the company of her small granddaughter as she does her work.

Alvina's life revolves around her work and her home. Her tiny house (two small rooms downstairs and two smaller rooms upstairs) is always immaculate. Her kitchen is a model of the traditional maritime household kitchen. The stucco walls are painted but are sooty from the open hearth. The floor is dark cement that she scrubs every day. A few gleaming pots hang from a shelf to one side of the hearth. There is a small refrigerator that her son bought for her a few years ago. In another corner stands some open wooden shelving built by her husband, on which she has stored masses of potatoes. Bunches of onions and garlic hang on the posts. Dried tea leaves hang in bags from a small clothesline she has strung above these open shelves and across the room. On rainy days various pieces of clothing also hang to dry on this indoor clothesline. In the center of the room, on a table, is a vase of fresh cut flowers from her garden. A second vase of flowers sits on the counter above the two-doored cupboard, also made by her husband, where she keeps her collection of mixed and chipped china. An open door leads out from the back of the kitchen to a tiny enclosed yard. Here Alvina grows a variety of green plants on shelves surrounding a cement washtub—a convenience she rarely uses because, to economize on her water bill, she carries her clothes to the river to wash. A wooden door in the corner of the yard provides for privacy in the outhouse, a single hole on a wooden bench. It was in her kitchen that Alvina told me about her life of hard work and happiness, and of her new loneliness as a widow.

Anthropological life histories and life stories are the products of collaboration between the anthropologist and the subject of study, between "the researcher and the researched" (Bertaux 1981).[2] They take the form they do because of the conjunction of a particular research problem, the particular experiences of particular individuals, and particular instances of "rapport" and "trust" (Langness and Frank 1981: 34–35). Life histories are rarely straight transcriptions but instead are pieced together from numerous interviews that take place over a prolonged period of time. The women's stories presented in this book are the products of many interviews conducted during the year I lived in Vila Chã—interviews that were formal and informal, directed and undirected, tape-recorded in a woman's kitchen and handwritten after a casual conversation enjoyed as we worked together, perhaps harvest-

ing seaweed on the beach. In the course of writing these stories, I returned again and again to the women to check with them to see if I had
"gotten it right."[3]

The women did not question my interest in their lives. They felt that
women in Vila Chã lead hard lives that deserve to be known. They have
a sense of history and a sense of autobiography—a sense of having a
"life" (Langness and Frank 1981:108–110)—and I was not imposing
upon them a new "*prise de conscience*" (Crapanzano 1977:22). Indeed,
Portuguese women appear to be good subjects for life histories (cf.
Brettell 1982). The women exhibit a strong sense of self, a directness
and independence in their self-expression, and they are skilled at the
art of storytelling. Indeed, women's conversations with one another
relating everyday events often take the form of telling stories. They are
proud of their lives and did not find it unusual or difficult to talk about
themselves. Invariably they began their stories with some statement
such as "My life is no secret." Or they commented on the form of their
lives: "My life is a novel" (*A minha vida dá um romance*), several
women said.

My purpose in presenting women's stories is to enable women themselves to describe the circumstances of their lives and to provide
women the opportunity to present themselves and their lives as they
would want them presented.[4] The life stories give us as outsiders access to women's subjective experiences and present women as social
actors constructing their lives in ways that empower them and employing strategies to achieve goals that they define within their particular
historical and social contexts. The stories of the Vila Chã women presented in this book challenge the anthropological constructions of
women that have prevailed in both the Mediterranean ethnography of
the "honor-and-shame" code and in the more contemporary analysis of
women's experience in contexts of social change and economic development. In the former, women are seen primarily in terms of their
relations with men and their reproductive roles as wives and mothers
(Peristiany 1965). Women are portrayed as "victims of their sexuality"
(Schneider 1971). But Vila Chã women do not see themselves this
way. On the contrary, Alvina tells us that women identify themselves
almost exclusively in terms of their productive work: they are trabalhadeiras; they are women who work for the household and who are
thrifty and skillful managers of the household's resources. The social
construction of women as trabalhadeiras is further discussed in chapter 5. In the women-and-development framework, external conditions
and causes of change are emphasized; the roles of rural women in the
new international division of labor are analyzed; and women invariably
are portrayed as victims of forces beyond their control (Leacock and

Safa 1986; Mies 1986; Young, Wolkowitz, and McCullagh 1981). Only in rare instances do we hear the voices of women themselves (Fernández-Kelly 1983; Nash 1979; Ong 1987; Zavella 1987). Vila Chã women's stories and their experiences of social and economic change are the subject of chapter 7.

Life histories both allow and require us to hear women themselves interpret their experiences and construct their identities. Stories like those of the women of Vila Chã remind us that individual women have their own agendas, that women's consciousness is rooted in their subjective experiences of the material and cultural conditions of their lives, and that women's interpretation and subjective expression of those experiences may not be easily accommodated by—may, indeed, contradict—macro or general theories that seek to explain gender relations and women's roles in society.

Alvina has introduced us to the themes of the chapters that follow. She has described the social opposition between pescadores and lavradores in the parish, marriage strategies and conjugal relations, property relations, the engagement of maritime women in subsistence and petty commodity production, the social construction of women as trabalhadeiras, and the impact of recent social and economic changes on the structure of the household and on the autonomy of women. We explore now the structure and character of maritime households, households like Alvina's, that prevailed in the pre-1960 maritime economy of Vila Chã.

Chapter 3

THE MARITIME HOUSEHOLD

MARITIME HOUSEHOLDS emerged in Vila Chã during the nineteenth century due to a variety of economic and social conditions, including population increases, rural poverty, and changing inheritance patterns. They came to represent both a particular way of life and a cultural form in the parish. Defined in opposition to members of agricultural households, members of maritime households—the pescadores—over time reinterpreted their experience as the poor, "os pobres," in the local social structure. Alvina has described for us, for example, how the pescadores validated the maritime woman's work in economic production through their positive valuation of the social construction of women as trabalhadeiras. We shall see in the following chapters how this gender-role construction clashed with the model held by the lavradores, who affirmed that maritime women's productive work merely signified their inferior social status.

By inverting local symbols of status, then, the pescadores redefined their way of life and asserted its superiority to an agricultural way of life. They constructed a positive social identity and cultural system of meaning for themselves from their relations of production and from the relations of everyday life. In this way they resisted the domination of the lavradores and attained a measure of autonomy over their lives. The culture of the pescadores of Vila Chã is, then, not only the system of meaning that pescadores give their way of life based on maritime production, but a "culture of opposition" (Sider 1980; 1986), a counter-hegemonic cultural form emerging in opposition to the hegemony of the local lavradores.[1]

The structure and character of maritime households are central to the construction of this oppositional culture. The maritime household was based on production through the exploitation of the communal resources of the sea—not production based on private ownership of land; a multioccupational base and a seasonal round of diverse production activities; and a gendered division of labor in which women, as producers, possessed economic authority and decision-making autonomy. Central to understanding both the constraints and the autonomy of maritime households are the relations between pescadores and lavradores, the development of endogamous marriage, local systems of

5. A lavrador's house. Woman fish vendor
with cart in foreground.

property and inheritance, and the social relations of the women members of these households.

PESCADORES AND LAVRADORES

Social relations in the parish were dominated by the opposition between pescadores and lavradores. Although the two groups shared common origins and distant kinship, the socioeconomic differences between them created relations that were characterized by conflict. Conflict originated in the two groups' unequal access to land and was embodied in their different centers of residence and in their different household economies. In the local context, fishing represented a low-status occupation, the occupation of those who lacked sufficient land to farm.

Through a process based on their different household economies and intensified by the residential separation between agricultural and fishing households, lavradores and pescadores as groups developed negative images of one another, images that persist to the present day. The lavradores maintain that the pescadores are "ill-bred," "dirty,"

6. The cemetery on the morning of Todos os Santos.

"lazy," and "drunkards" (*mal-educados, porcos, preguiçosos,* and *bêbados*). They say that the pescadores do not know how to work the land and that they do not know how to save and accumulate. In this way the lavradores deny the social reality that the pescadores, in fact, lack the capital or access to resources, including land, that would enable them to accumulate surplus. And, at the same time, they legitimate their privileged position in the parish social structure.

The lavradores object to the public life-style of the pescadores. The contrast between the two groups is evident to even the casual observer. The pescadores live on the beach or in the streets where they can be seen talking, arguing, and laughing—men, women, and children—as they work on their nets or on the seaweed harvest. Several times in the course of each day the men go to the tavern (*adega*) to drink and play cards or dominoes. The women walk around the parish selling their fish and catching up on local news. Because their houses are small and crowded and often not detached, the pescadores spend the daylight hours outside. They work on their nets, grill sardines, and often eat their meals out in front of their houses. By contrast, the lavradores live a quiet and private existence within their huge walled homes. They go to work in their fields and come home. The pescadores call the lavradores *bichos-da-terra* (earthworms) and say that they only come out in public to go to Sunday mass. Pescadores assert that the lavradores are envious (têm inveja) of them because they are freed from the responsibility of owning and working land. They describe the lavradores as avaricious (avaros) and selfish (egoístas), always saving and wanting everything for themselves. And they explain that the reason the lavradores do not drink in the adega is that they all have wine cellars of their own.

Until the late 1960s, both state and church institutions legitimated the privileged position of the lavradores in the parish. Because eligibility to hold political office was determined by taxable income, wealthy lavradores dominated in formal politics and the poorer pescadores were excluded. Similarly, the fraternal organizations of the parish church were monopolized by lavradores. The parish priests have always lived among the lavradores and have been perceived by the pescadores as their confreres. And in Vila Chã, where, until 1974, the parish priests had also effectively continued to control the parish council (although their official power to do so had ended in 1910), the unity of state, church, and local elite was both complete and transparent to the pescadores.

The relative visibility and autonomy of maritime women also contributed to the stigmatization of maritime households, as well as to the development of different marriage patterns that further separated pescadores from lavradores. Women of maritime households managed the household economy and were visible in the parish as they went about their work harvesting seaweed and selling fish. By contrast, women of wealthy agricultural households were rarely seen; they remained secluded in the home while their husbands supervised the agricultural production of the household.

The social discrimination experienced by the pescadores of Vila Chã is consistent with the reports of stigmatization of other fishing groups in complex societies. Smith (1977:8) writes that fishing peoples tend to be "a denigrated if not despised segment of the societies in which they live." Coull (1972:60) states that in many parts of Europe, fishing "has been regarded as an occupation of the lowest social classes." Describing the nineteenth-century emergence of fishing households in Sweden, Löfgren (1979:98) writes: "Fishermen were recruited from the lowest strata in the local hierarchy: the landless. They were often subordinate socially, economically and politically to the local landowning peasants." He hypothesized that "this type of unequal relations will be found in other marine communities populated by landless fishermen and landowning peasants." And Nadel (1984:104) describes the stigmatization of the Ferryden fishing community in northeast Scotland, a labeling remarkably similar in character to that experienced by the pescadores of Vila Chã. The Ferryden fisherfolk, who were separated by differences in work, residence, and social image from the rest of the town, were locally described as "inbred and weak-minded, dirty, coarse, sly, impulsive, bellicose, and inebriated. They were the objects of satire, exploitation, revulsion, and occasionally, well-meaning charity."

In Vila Chã, then, in the context of a society based on agriculture and the ownership of land, the pescadores constitute a bounded and socially stigmatized group. The nonheirs of local agricultural households, they developed an economy based on the commercial production of seaweed and pilado fertilizer and on the sale of fresh fish. By the turn of the century, they were separated from the local lavradores by their different patterns of residence, different household economy, different gendered division of labor, and different social status, all of which originated in their lack of access to land sufficient for farming.

Vila Chã pescadores, however, have chosen to interpret their social and economic separation from the lavradores as a source of cultural autonomy. They have chosen to value as the foundation of a cherished group identity the very areas upon which their social stigmatization is based—the organization of maritime production, the gendered division of labor within the household, and the construction of social images of maritime women, for example. And, over time, they have come to share a collective memory based on consanguinity and residence. In the present day, the number of people who proudly award themselves the status of pescador is much larger than the actual number of people engaged in fishing. Daughters and sons, granddaughters and grandsons of pescadores who today work in factories or construction or in professions identify themselves as "of the pescadores" and proudly distinguish themselves from the descendants of the lavradores. They use a variety of boundary-maintaining mechanisms to so define themselves and to award themselves special status. These mechanisms include the operation of an informal network for the distribution of fresh fish; a profession of knowledge and interest in things maritime, like the weather, boats, and tales of former fishing days that express their attachment to the sea; the attribution of special virtues, such as hospitality, to the pescadores—virtues the lavradores are said not to possess; and the use of personal nicknames that have meaning only for insiders, only for members of the group.

"POBRES MARRIED POBRES"

By the early twentieth century, socially and economically separated from the lavradores and tending to marry among themselves, the pescadores had become essentially an endogamous group; endoga-

mous marriage had created a web of virtually impenetrable household alliances that served as a mechanism for group closure. The lavradores acknowledged this characteristic of the pescadores by referring
to them as "very united" (*muito unidos*) and "very closed" (*muito
fechados*).

Members of maritime and other land-poor households learned as
children that "the person who is born poor, must remain poor" (*quem
nasceu pobre, pobre deve ficar*) and "the person who is born to have five
will not be able to obtain ten"(*quem nasceu p'ra cinco, não chega a dez*).
Such expressions acknowledged that social advancement beyond one's
ascribed status was rare, that social mobility was extremely difficult for
the land-poor in rural villages during the time of the New State. The
pescadores, thus, considered themselves to be a separate social group
from the lavradores. Meanwhile, in an effort to forestall intermarriage,
wealthy lavradores prevented their children from socializing with the
children of maritime households; they taught them to think that the
pescadores were ill-bred (mal-educados), dirty, lazy, and drunkards.

The separation of the two groups of prospective marriage partners
was evident in their different patterns of courtship. Fisherwomen, like
Alvina, remember with nostalgia the days of their unmarried youth.
They remember those days as carefree and happy. Although they remember their hard work as members of their parents' households
and the frequent periods of economic hardship, they also remember
the freedom from the responsibilities of marriage and of managing
households.

Fisherwomen met their future husbands walking to and from Saturday night mass at the church or at the open-air dances held on Sunday
afternoons and on festival days. On these occasions, the unmarried
youth would gather in one of the squares in the parish to dance. Someone would play the guitar, and the young men and women would
dance together in a circle singing and clapping hands as they danced.
Women remember that they danced and joked (*brincavam*) with many
young men and did not focus their attentions exclusively on one until
they had decided they would marry.

It was only the young women of the maritime and other land-poor
households, however, who would dance in the open air (*ao ar livre*)
and tease the young men. Lavradores would not allow their sons and
daughters to participate. Alvina remembers how the lavradores and
their sons and daughters would come and watch the dancing, standing
at the edge of the square, but they would never join in. In contrast with
the freedom of the young women of the maritime households, daughters of wealthy agricultural households were sheltered. They were allowed to socialize only with members of other wealthy agricultural

households and then only under parental supervision. Although not all agricultural households were wealthy, poor lavradores—those with little land—would also discourage their daughters from socializing with, or marrying, pescadores. In practice, however, daughters of poor lavradores formed part of the marriage pool of "os pobres" and married into landless households, including maritime households.

Sons and daughters of maritime households understood that they were members of the poor of the parish and that they would choose their marriage partners from among the landless and land-poor. Further, their parents accepted that they could say little about the sweethearts (namorados) of their children beyond advising them to avoid selecting marriage partners from households known for laziness, slovenliness, or drunkenness. This is to say that, among the maritime households of Vila Chã, property was rarely a factor in the choice of a marriage partner. Instead, parents advised their children that the most important attribute of a prospective marriage partner was that he or she be a hard worker. In addition to industriousness, the qualities one looked for in a marriage partner were thriftiness, cleanliness, and sobriety.

By contrast, among the lavradores of the parish the possession or expected inheritance of property was the major determinant in the selection of a marriage partner. Parents in wealthy agricultural households endeavored to marry their sons and daughters into other propertied agricultural households.

The result of these different marriage strategies was that two almost-endogamous marriage pools emerged in the parish: children of agricultural households tended to marry children of other agricultural households, and children of maritime households tended to marry children of maritime households or of other land-poor households. Tables 3.1 to 3.4 illustrate the existence of two marriage groups in the parish between 1911 and 1960 and the infrequency of intermarriage between the two groups.

Table 3.1 and table 3.2 record by decade the marriages of men— lavradores and pescadores. During the years from 1911 to 1959, of 174 pescadores who married, 114 (65.5 percent) married daughters of other fishermen; 18 (10.3 percent) married daughters of lavradores; 17 (9.8 percent) married other land-poor women; and 11 (6.4 percent) married daughters of unmarried women. By contrast, of 51 lavradores who married during these years, 41 (80.4 percent) married daughters of other lavradores; only 2 (3.9 percent) married land-poor women; only 2 (3.9 percent) married daughters of fishermen; and none married daughters of unmarried women—that is, none married women who had been born illegitimately. In the cases of the lavradores who mar-

TABLE 3.1
Marriage Partners of Pescadores by Decade, Vila Chã, 1911–1959

| | Daughter of: | | | | | |
	Pescador	Lavrador	Other Land-Poor	Unmarried Woman	N/D	Total
1911–19	13	8	1	1	5	28
1920–29	17	2	4	—	2	25
1930–39	15	6	2	2	2	27
1940–49	39	1	6	7	5	58
1950–59	30	1	4	1	—	36
Total	114	18	17	11	14	174
(%)	(65.5)	(10.3)	(9.8)	(6.4)	(8.0)	(100.0)

Source: Parish Registers

TABLE 3.2
Marriage Partners of Lavradores by Decade, Vila Chã, 1911–1959

| | Daughter of: | | | | | | |
	Pesca-dor	Lavra-dor	Other Land-Poor	Unmarried Woman	Mer-chant	N/D	Total
1911–19	—	5	1	—	1	1	8
1920–29	—	11	—	—	1	2	14
1930–39	—	11	—	—	—	1	12
1940–49	1	5	1	—	—	—	7
1950–59	1	9	—	—	—	—	10
Total	2	41	2	0	2	4	51
(%)	(3.9)	(80.4)	(3.9)	(0.0)	(3.9)	(7.9)	(100.0)

Source: Parish Registers

ried fishermen's daughters, both men were over fifty years of age (one was fifty-eight years old and the other was fifty-three), and the women were ages thirty-three and forty-five.

Table 3.3 and table 3.4 also use data from the parish registers for the years 1911 to 1959, but these illustrate the marriage pattern from the perspective of women. These two tables document whom the daughters of pescadores married and whom the daughters of lavradores married. Of 179 daughters of pescadores who married during this period, 114 (63.7 percent) married other pescadores; only 2 (1.1 percent) married lavradores; and 59 (33 percent) married other land-poor men such

TABLE 3.3

Occupations of Marriage Partners of Daughters of Pescadores by Decade,
Vila Chã, 1911–1959

	Lavrador[a]	Pescador	Land-Poor	N/D	Total
1911–19	—	13	1	1	15
1920–29	—	17	7	—	24
1930–39	—	15	16	2	33
1940–49	1	39	11	1	52
1950–59	1	30	24	—	55
Total	2	114	59	4	179
(%)	(1.1)	(63.7)	(33.0)	(2.2)	(100.0)

Source: Parish Registers
[a] It was necessary to use the occupations of fathers to determine the socioeconomic status of women at marriage because the priests who kept the parish registers did not record the occupations of women. Whether married or unmarried, women are described simply as *domésticas* ("domestics" or housewives); and even unmarried women who headed households and were, by necessity, employed in economic production, appear simply as *solteiras* (unmarried women) with no occupation. In the eyes of the church, women were wives, mothers, and daughters of men—not workers.

TABLE 3.4

Occupations of Marriage Partners of Daughters of Lavradores by Decade,
Vila Chã, 1911–1959

	Lavrador	Pescador	Land-Poor	Other[a]	Unknown	Total
1911–19	5	8	4	—	5	22
1920–29	11	2	5	2	—	20
1930–39	11	6	6	—	—	23
1940–49	5	1	6	—	—	12
1950–59	9	1	7	3	1	21
Total	41	18	28	5	6	98
(%)	(41.8)	(18.4)	(28.6)	(5.1)	(6.1)	(100.0)

Source: Parish Registers
[a] "Other" includes shopowners, police, and other service workers.

as jornaleiros, carpenters, or other craftsmen; after 1930, a few married textile factory workers in Vila do Conde. These data are recorded in table 3.3. The 2 fishermen's daughters who married lavradores are the same cited above, those who were thirty-three and forty-five years old when they married men of fifty-eight and fifty-three years old respectively.

By contrast, table 3.4 shows the occupations of men the daughters of lavradores married. Of 98 daughters of lavradores married in Vila Chã between 1911 and 1959, 41 (41.8 percent) married lavradores; 18 (18.4 percent) married fishermen; and 28 (28.6 percent) married land-poor men such as carpenters, often from other parishes. Not until the 1950s do they begin to marry factory workers, and the 2 women who do marry factory workers are both daughters of one of the poorest lavradores in the parish.

These tables document how, in a majority of cases, pescadores married daughters of other pescadores and lavradores married daughters of other lavradores. Although slightly more than one-tenth (10.3 percent) of fishermen married daughters of lavradores, these were the daughters of small landholders who could not afford to provide inheritances for all their children. Only in two exceptional cases did lavradores marry daughters of fishermen, and these men were both over fifty years of age. Sons of lavradores would emigrate or join the priesthood if they did not inherit the casa, rather than stay in the parish and marry a local land-poor woman. Daughters of lavradores, however, wealthy or poor, had little choice but to remain in Vila Chã. If they would not inherit the casa or receive a sizable dote, it was unlikely that they would be able to marry well. In these circumstances, they could remain unmarried or they could marry a poor man. Wealthy lavradores endeavored to prevent their daughters from marrying at all, and those daughters of lavradores who did marry fishermen were, in most cases, daughters of small landholders who had a large number of children and could afford neither to provide inheritances for them all nor to keep them on as unmarried members of the household.

Thus, the daughters in agricultural households more frequently married into land-poor households (including maritime households) than did their brothers. This was because sons of agricultural households could emigrate and thus avoid losing their privileged social and economic status through marriage with a land-poor woman. Daughters in maritime households were even more limited in their marriage options than were daughters in agricultural households. They could only marry men from maritime and other land-poor households.

Some cases of intermarriage between members of wealthy agricultural households and members of land-poor households are well remembered in the parish and still a frequent subject of conversation. In one case, in the 1940s, the only son of one of the wealthiest agricultural households in the parish married a poor jornaleira. His parents disowned him and refused to see him again in their house. He remained in the parish and established a farm of his own with the help of his sister, his only sibling. It has only been in the last few years that his parents have allowed him back into their home and have reinstated his inheritance, largely due to the efforts of his sister. In another case, a daughter of a wealthy lavrador chose, at age twenty-nine, to marry a fisherman rather than to remain unmarried because her parents had determined that there were no marriage partners suitable for her. Her parents disowned her, even though she was one of only two children. They never welcomed her back in their home, and they denied her any inheritance. The fishermen and women remember with pride how she took to the life of a maritime woman, worked hard, and never considered herself superior to the other women. By contrast, a daughter of a poor lavrador who had married a fisherman is remembered because she never accepted the life of a fisherman's wife. She refused to work on the seaweed or to help unload her husband's boat. She did little work for the household, and what labor she did do was agricultural work. She continued to associate with the other *lavradeiras* (women of agricultural households) and considered the women of Lugar da Praia and Lugar do Facho her social inferiors. Her husband had difficulty supporting the household of four children on his own. He eventually sank into ruin, forfeiting their small house on the beach to pay off gambling debts, and he died of cirrhosis of the liver before any of his children were married. A fisherman depended on the help of his wife in selling the fish, on her extra earnings from selling seaweed, and on her other economic contributions to the household; he knew that he could not support a household alone. Fishermen, therefore, preferred to marry daughters of other fishermen, women who had been raised from childhood to the maritime woman's life of hard work.

Age at marriage also differed significantly between the two marriage groups. Members of maritime households consistently married below the mean age at marriage for the parish, but members of agricultural households married above the mean age. During the period 1911 to 1966, the mean age at marriage for men was 24.1 years and for women 22.5 years. Throughout this period fishermen married at an average age of 22.7 years, but lavradores married at a mean age of 28.3 years. Fishermen's daughters married at a mean age of 21.5 years; daughters of lavradores married at a mean age of 25.1 years. Mean ages at marriage are documented in table 3.5 by sex, socioeconomic group, and decade.

There was also a wider difference in age between husband and wife in agricultural households than there was between spouses in maritime households. Over the period 1911 to 1966 there was an average of 1.2 years' difference in age between husband and wife in maritime households, whereas the average age difference in agricultural households was 3.2 years, with the wife in both cases being junior to the husband (table 3.5). These differences in age at marriage are important for two reasons. First, the closeness in age between husband and

TABLE 3.5
Mean Age at Marriage by Sex, Occupational Group, and Decade,
Vila Chã, 1911–1966

	Pescadores		Lavradores		All Groups[a]	
	M	F[b]	M	F	M	F
1911–19 (N = 70)	22.1	21.6	24.4	24.4	23.1	22.5
1920–29 (N = 72)	24.0	23.0	27.8	23.8	25.7	22.6
1930–39 (N = 112)	24.0	21.9	28.4	27.3	24.6	23.2
1940–49 (N = 125)	22.6	21.9	30.7	25.7	23.9	23.1
1950–59 (N = 147)	22.5	21.8	29.7	25.1	24.2	22.5
1960–66 (N = 149)	21.0	19.0	29.0	24.5	22.9	21.0
1911–66[c] (N = 675)	22.7	21.5	28.3	25.1	24.1	22.5

Source: Parish Registers

Note: All second marriages were excluded.

[a] The "All Groups" column includes not only pescadores and lavradores but all other occupational groups.

[b] For the purposes of this table, women are identified with the occupations of their husbands at marriage. Thus the women whose ages are recorded under the first column heading are women who married pescadores. This was necessary because, although women's ages were recorded in the marriage registers, their occupations were not, even though most women worked in fishing, agriculture, or some other occupation during this period.

[c] After 1966 occupations are no longer identified in the marriage registers.

wife in maritime households made possible more egalitarian relations between them than existed in the majority of agricultural households, where husbands were often noticeably senior to their wives. Second, they suggest that members of maritime households were freer to marry when and whom they pleased than were members of agricultural households. In agricultural households the choice of marriage partner and the time of marriage were constrained by factors such as the inheritance of property or the establishment of economic relations between two households.

Finally, the data presented in table 3.5 reveal that the mean age at marriage of members of maritime households decreased during the period 1911 to 1966, whereas the mean age at marriage of members of

agricultural households increased during the same period. This suggests that there was increasing concern among lavradores to keep the
casa intact to protect, or augment, its value, and that this increasingly
required delaying, preventing, or arranging the marriages of the children of the household. Once married, children would be entitled to
their share of the value of the casa for their own households, thus re-
moving those resources from the parental household (if not at marriage, then at the death of their parents). If they did not marry or if
marriage could be arranged to bring more property into the household,
the household could hope to retain its economic status in the parish for
at least one more generation. Among maritime households, however,
different changes have had an impact on the age at marriage; for, after
the mid-1960s, young people of maritime households increasingly
were entering wage employment. As unmarried members of their parents' households, they were required to give their wages to their mothers: their wages were contributed to the household as children's labor
had been in previous generations. It was only after marriage, which
signified the establishment of a new household, that they would be
able to keep their wages for their own consumption. Young people of
fishing households therefore began to abbreviate the period of courtship and to marry at increasingly younger ages after 1960.

PROPERTY, INHERITANCE, AND RESIDENCE

In some maritime societies, fisheries are truly a "common property resource" (Acheson 1981:280). That is, either there is no ownership of
fishing areas and other marine resources, or they are perceived to be
owned communally. Although in such societies people in theory can
fish where they want, in practice, a variety of measures control the
usufruct of marine resources. These measures include secrecy and information management, and allocation of temporary usufruct rights to
the boat that first reaches a fishing ground. Property rights in Vila Chã
consisted of both private property rights to movable and immovable
property, and usufructuary rights defining access to resources.

In Vila Chã, pescadores agreed that the sea and its resources belonged to no one—and to everyone. As Alvina describes it: "The land is
all owned by someone or other, but the sea belongs to no one. The sea
is everyone's . . . The sea is God's." Fishermen and women say that
they fished where they wanted to and that the places they fished varied
daily, weekly, and seasonally. However, their fishing licenses authorized them only to fish local grounds up to twelve miles offshore, between the ports of Póvoa de Varzim and Matosinhos. Within these
state-imposed limitations, then, fishing boats followed the local prac-

tice of recognizing the rights of the first boat to arrive in a fishing area to drop its nets or traps where it chose. That is, upon arriving at the fishing grounds each day, a boat would not drop its nets where another boat had already left nets, nor would its crew interfere with another boat's nets. Thus, usufructuary rights were equal for all pescadores within a state-defined local zone, and pescadores among themselves respected rights of access on a "first come, first served" daily basis.

Private property rights, however, defined potential inequality and existed within the context of the felt inferiority of the pescadores in relation to the local landowning lavradores. The historical emergence of maritime households from land-poor agricultural households and their continued social and economic interaction with the agricultural households meant that, although the maritime households were relatively propertyless, they were entirely familiar with the concepts of private property and inheritance. According to the fisherwoman Alvina, while the pescadores were committed to the economic endeavor of fishing, they all wanted to own a piece of land, but there was no land available to them. All land in the parish belonged to the lavradores and was passed on through inheritance. And the lavradores would not sell land. For the members of maritime households, inherited property included the house of residence and perhaps a small garden; the fishing boat, nets, and other gear; and in some cases a small stone hut (*casa do mar*) on the beach where fishing gear and dried seaweed were stored.

Inheritance practices and residence patterns in the maritime households of Vila Chã differed from the practices of the wealthier agricultural households of the parish and of other parishes in the county of Vila do Conde (Brochado de Almeida 1983; Moreira da Silva 1983). In fact, although under Portuguese law all children, male and female, were entitled to an equal inheritance, in practice a great deal of variation occurred. The lavradores endeavored to keep intact the casa (meaning all lands, livestock, and buildings belonging to the household) by appointing only one heir, usually a son.[2] Other siblings received their inheritance in the form of a dote that ideally would enable marriage to the heir of another agricultural household. In the households of poorer lavradores, however, it was more difficult for the heir to keep the casa intact: paying the siblings (nonheirs) often required splitting up the property itself. Meanwhile, in the maritime households of Vila Chã, as in the land-poor households of the Alto Minho (cf. Pina-Cabral 1986), daughters were favored over sons and younger daughters were favored over older daughters to inherit the household property, especially the house, boat, and fishing gear.

The most important decision was which child would inherit the parental home. Children who did not inherit their parents' house to live in (or did not marry someone who stood to inherit his or her parents' house) might never marry or might be forced to emigrate from the parish. Parents favored the child who "looked after them in their old age." In general, daughters, not sons, were preferred, both to care for their parents in old age and to inherit the house. It was felt that a daughter-in-law (*nora*) "was never as good as a daughter" to her husband's parents. It was said also that parents felt that they could control (*mandar*) a daughter (and thus see that their wishes were followed), but a daughter-in-law would mandar a son (and therefore the household). Daughters were favored over sons to inherit the house and often the boat, not only because parents favored daughters over daughters-in-law to care for them in old age but also because they feared that sons might emigrate and knew that daughters would stay in the parish.

The effect of these practices in Vila Chã was that women owned and inherited property and that a system of uxorilocal residence emerged in maritime households. At marriage, a husband generally moved in with his wife and her parents. A woman would start her married life in her parents' house, but she would move out when a younger sister married and brought her husband to reside in the house. Elder married daughters frequently moved into houses adjoining or near their parents' houses, and thereby resided uxorivicinally—that is, in the neighborhood of consanguineally related women, especially mothers, sisters, daughters, and maternal aunts (Pina-Cabral 1986:72).[3] It was generally a younger daughter (or the last to marry) who looked after the parents in their old age, who tended their graves, and who inherited the house and boat.

The daughter who inherited the property of the maritime household was still expected to pay her siblings the value of their equal share of the inheritance, but often the household was too poor to generate even the small amounts of cash needed to enable her to do so. And, until the 1970s, when social services such as old age pensions and subsidized health care were introduced, the costs of looking after the elderly couple were often great and women considered that they had more than earned their inheritances by looking after their parents. The siblings themselves were generally too poor to take the matter to court, and, in any event, their share of the inheritance would probably not cover the costs of litigation. The result was that in maritime households one child, usually a younger daughter, inherited whatever household property there was, and other sons and daughters struggled to establish households of their own.[4]

Women's property relations and their responsibility for the efficient management of the economic resources of the household contributed to relations of conflict among nonconsanguineally related women. Inheritance, for example, often created conflict in the relationship between a woman and her mother-in-law (*sogra*) although they rarely lived together. A daughter-in-law, even if she stood to inherit her own parents' house and property, would feel that her husband had not received his share of the value of his natal household because his mother (her sogra) had favored a daughter over her son. As one woman explained, she had never gotten along well with her sogra because she resented the fact that her husband "did not bring anything to the household" (*não trouxe nada p'ra casa*). She considered that her husband's sister, on the other hand, had done well for herself because she had not paid her siblings their share of the value of the parental household. Although this woman had herself inherited her own parents' house and had not paid her own siblings their share, she explained this by saying that parents preferred a daughter and not a daughter-in-law to look after them in old age.

Thus, when women were explaining why they themselves had inherited their parents' house, they would say that parents preferred a daughter's care in their later years. But, when women were explaining why their husbands had not inherited anything from their natal households and why their husbands' sisters had inherited the parents' property, they would say that their sisters-in-law were "selfish" (egoístas); they would say that their husbands' mothers had not fulfilled their duty or obligation (*obrigação*) to ensure that all children shared equally in the property; and, finally, they would accuse their husbands of having given in, of not having fought for what was their right (*direito*). They say that men are not interested enough in these things and they give in to their mothers and sisters. If I suggested to a woman that her household did not appear to be poorer than her sister-in-law's household, she inevitably would say that it was not the money or the property itself that she cared about but its symbolic value: it was "sad" (*triste*) that her husband did not have anything to remind him of his parental home; it was a violation of the way things *should* be done. Women experience conflict over property through the medium of *inveja* (literally, "envy"), and inveja in all its forms ranging from gossip to the evil eye is a strong presence in the lives of Vila Chã women. Inveja is the subject of chapter 6.

Women are closely identified with the material well-being of the maritime household, and they not only inherited property but also bought and improved property and saved money. As Alvina describes, "a good woman" was one who thriftily managed the household's resources and who saved money by intensifying her own labor. Because women feel that men do not have a concern for these things, they consider it a woman's responsibility to look out for the household's property interests. In Vila Chã, then, there is a general tendency to identify property as belonging to the woman of the household and not to the man. Sons and daughters say, for example, "The house is my mother's" (*A casa é da minha mãe*). They will not say, "The house is my parents'." This might be understandable in cases in which the mother had inherited the house from her parents, but the locution was not limited to such cases. One recently married young woman, expressing the hope that she and her husband would have a new home of their own one day, explained that the house they were now living in belonged to her mother, although actually it had belonged to her father's mother. How was it that this young woman identified the house as belonging to her mother and not to her father, who had inherited it from his mother? Her father was an only child and thus stood to inherit his parents' house. When he married, his wife had moved in with him and his mother. He, however, had emigrated several times during the first ten years of their marriage and had neglected to send home money for the support of his wife and children (in fact, he had been living with a woman in Angola and had a child with her). His wife, on the other hand, had remained in Vila Chã and, through fishing and seaweed sales, had supported herself and the children and made repairs to the house, which was badly in need of rebuilding. Through her industriousness and thriftiness, she had managed to buy other pieces of property, including another small house and garden. Even though her husband eventually returned to live again with her in Vila Chã and to fish for the household, all the property they hold is identified as hers because the household's economic well-being is perceived to be the fruit of her hard work and savings.

In addition to houses, women also owned and inherited fishing boats and gear. Two women (aged fifty-nine and sixty-seven in 1985) had bought and fished in their own boats. Other women inherited boats from their parental households. One woman, who had fished with her father since the age of thirteen and had never married, inherited the household boat on his death. She continued to fish with hired crews until she was fifty-nine, when she sold the boat. Another woman inherited her natal household's boat, and it was said locally that this was how she had "arranged" (*arranjou*) her husband, for she was lame and thought to be unattractive, while he was handsome albeit the son of poor jornaleiros. He had never fished before, but he took up fishing after they married in 1943 and was still active in 1985. He also made numerous voyages to the Grand Banks cod fishery and is considered a hardworking and good fisherman. The boat he fishes in is named for his wife, and, when asked, both he and his wife will say that it is her boat.

Women's inheritance of parental houses and property encouraged the development of a pattern of uxorilocal and uxorivicinal residence in Vila Chã. Although it has generally been assumed that a pattern of male inheritance and virilocal residence prevails in fishing communities—as indeed it does in Newfoundland and Norway (Brox 1964; Faris 1972)—there is abundant evidence that a pattern of women's inheritance of property and uxorilocal and uxorivicinal residence similar to the pattern found in Vila Chã is common in many of the world's small fisheries, including fisheries in Denmark, Sweden, Brittany, Shetland, Galicia, and in Nazaré, Portugal (Brøgger 1987; Lisón-Tolosana 1971; 1976; Thompson, Wailey, and Lummis 1983).

ILLEGITIMACY: UNMARRIED MOTHERS AND DESERTED WIVES

In Vila Chã as elsewhere in northern Portugal, high rates of illegitimacy were common until the mid-1960s and are correlated with landlessness. In this century, baptisms of illegitimate children in the parish reached a peak in the 1920s when they represented 12.7 percent of all baptisms. Illegitimacy remained significant until the Second World War, after which it decreased to represent only 2.4 percent of births by 1969 (table 3.6). This trend parallels that recorded elsewhere in northwestern Portugal by Brettell (1985) for Lanheses, a parish in the county of Viana do Castelo, and by Pina-Cabral (1986) for Paço and Couto, two parishes in the county of Ponte da Barca. In Lanheses, the illegitimacy ratio reached a high of 13.4 in the two decades prior to 1920 and had declined to 1.5 by 1969 (Brettell 1985:95). Illegitimacy reached a high of 22.4 percent in Couto and 12.5 percent in Paço around 1920 and declined quickly to less than 2 percent by the end of the 1960s. The rate of illegitimacy was consistently higher in Couto, where a higher proportion of parish residents were landless (Pina-Cabral 1986:58).[5] Increasing opportunities for wage employment after the Second World War, and especially after 1960, have provided landless peasants with sources of income that are not dependent on land ownership and that have enabled young people to marry and establish households when they choose. Also, returned emigrants began to buy land; thus, people who had been landless were no longer. Age at marriage therefore ceased to be dependent upon inheritance, and age at marriage decreased with alternative sources of income. The decrease in age at marriage after 1960 correlates with an increase in the number of premarital pregnancies that are legitimated through marriage and, thus, a decrease in rates of illegitimacy. Among the maritime households of Vila Chã, wage employment opportunities have also contributed to a decrease in illegitimacy. It is local practice that unmarried young people remain living with their parents and, as long as they are members of their parents' households, they hand over their wage earnings to their mothers. It is only after they marry, and after they establish households of their own, that they can control the consumption of their wages themselves. Access to wage earnings is becoming a primary motivation for early marriage. A premarital pregnancy is often the means by which a young couple can precipitate their marriage and thus their economic independence from their parents.

Until the 1960s, illegitimacy in Vila Chã was especially located in maritime and other land-poor households. Of the 145 illegitimate children born between 1911 and 1969, 43 percent (63 children) were born to women of maritime households, and an additional 21.4 percent (31 children) were born to women of other land-poor households, including jornaleiras and *criadas de servir* (women servants in agricultural households). A further 8.3 percent (12 children) were born to landless women who had been illegitimate children themselves. Twenty-nine illegitimate children (20 percent of all illegitimate births) were born to women whose household affiliations could not be determined from the parish registers, but it is probable that these were also women of landless or land-poor households and not daughters of lavradores, because lavradores are always identified as such in the parish registers. Only ten (6.9 percent) of all the illegitimate children born during this period were born to daughters of lavradores; five of these were born to one woman. She was the daughter of a poor lavrador and had been banished from her parental home after the first birth. She had settled in a hut in the woods at the edge of the parish and had had four more illegitimate children of unidentified paternity.

Thus, over 90 percent of illegitimate births in Vila Chã were to landless women, and almost half of these children were born to women of maritime households—a disproportionately high number, since maritime households represent only one-third of all households during this period. These data are consistent with other recent studies in northern Portugal that correlate high rates of illegitimacy with propertylessness (Brettell 1985:98–100; O'Neill 1983:69; Pina-Cabral 1986:55).

Among the maritime and other land-poor households, unmarried women and their illegitimate children were not ostracized or discriminated against as they were among the lavradores. Instead they were integrated into the community. Their integration was facilitated by three economic circumstances. First, the women could intensify their work in fishing, fish selling, and seaweed harvesting to support themselves and their children. Second, women and their illegitimate children posed little threat to the economic integrity of the maritime

TABLE 3.6

Illegitimacy Ratios in Maritime and Nonmaritime Households,
Vila Chã, 1911–1969

	Maritime Households		Nonmaritime[a] Households			Total
	Total Number of Births	Illegiti- macy Ratio[b] (%)	Total Number of Births	Illegiti- macy Ratio (%)	Total Number of Births	Illegiti- macy Ratio (%)
1911–19	121	6.6	175	7.4	296	7.1
1920–29	141	13.5	212	12.3	353	12.7
1930–39	154	9.1	246	5.3	400	6.8
1940–49	287	3.1	229	6.6	516	4.7
1950–59	226	1.3	311	2.6	537	2.1
1960–69	246	4.1	477	1.5	723	2.4
1911–69	1,175	5.4	1,650	5.0	2,825	5.1

Source: Parish Registers

[a] The data as collected do not allow a further breakdown into lavradores and jornaleiros within the category of nonmaritime households.

[b] The illegitimacy ratio is the number of illegitimate births expressed as a percentage of the total number of births. Illegitimate is the term used in the baptismal registers by parish priests to describe births of children where fathers are recorded to be "unknown" (pai incógnito); it is not a term used by Vila Chã residents themselves, who generally do know the father's identity. The women giving birth to illegitimate children include not only unmarried women (solteiras) but also widows (two births) and married women whose husbands are recorded to have been "absent in Brazil for many years" (fourteen births).

household, where it was common for one child, often a daughter, to inherit whatever property there was. Where daughters inherited the parental home, their marital status was irrelevant to their eligibility to inherit. Third, in a society in which the emigration of at least some of their children was inevitable, parents often worried about who would care for them in old age, and they may have seen the birth of an illegitimate child as binding their daughter to them to provide that care (cf. Brettell 1985:102). Marriage often meant a change of allegiances from the natal to the marital household, but the birth of an illegitimate child might bind a daughter to her natal household permanently.

Unmarried mothers often initially remained members of their parental households. As their parents aged, however, these women became acting household heads; on their parents' deaths, unmarried women with children inherited property and headed households of their own. The implications and experience of having illegitimate children then, may also be understood in the context of women's efforts and strategies to maximize their economic autonomy under socioeconomic constraints that made it difficult for some women to marry. Having illegitimate children not only offered women the possibility of establishing their own households but was also viewed by them as a form of social security, for they could expect that their children would look after them in their old age (cf. Brettell 1985). Furthermore, in the local context, there was no stigma attached to unmarried mothers or their illegitimate children. Like the women of other maritime households, unmarried mothers were evaluated more on their qualities as hard workers—their industriousness and their thriftiness—than on their sexuality or marital status. And illegitimate children grew up with the other children on the beach and, depending on their qualities as hard workers, were as free in their choice of marriage partners as were the legitimate children of the maritime households. This is to say that illegitimate children constituted part of the marriage pool of "os pobres."

MARITIME HOUSEHOLDS ARE WOMEN-CENTERED

A woman's monopoly of power in the peasant household of northwestern Portugal has long been noted. "Matricentrality," "une communauté féminine rurale," "matripotestality," and even "matriarchy" are the terms that have been used to indicate the social and symbolic expression of women's power in the household (Brettell 1986; Brøgger 1987; Callier-Boisvert 1966; Descamps 1935; Pina-Cabral 1986; Willems 1962). I prefer, however, to describe the maritime households of Vila Chã as "women-centered" (cf. Yanagisako 1977). Terms such as *matricentric* and *matrifocal* tend to emphasize the centrality and power of the mother in household relations, whereas "women-centered" acknowledges the centrality of women in general, regardless of kinship roles, which is more accurate in the Vila Chã case. The women-centeredness of maritime households manifests itself in patterns of postmarital residence, residential proximity, and mutual aid, as well as in the frequency of interaction and the strength of affective ties among consanguineally related female kin. It also manifests itself in inheritance patterns and property relations, and, as we shall see in the following chapter, in subsistence and commodity production.

The women-centered character of the maritime household has been intensified by high rates of male emigration since the last century. Male emigration created a demographic asymmetry with the result that some women could never marry. Women who never married represented between 11.1 percent and 29.7 percent of all women in Vila

Chã during the period 1911 to 1969. Although the rate of nonmarriage of women was not as high as elsewhere in northwestern Portugal, it was nonetheless significant.[6]

As Alvina tells us, emigration of fathers and husbands had an important impact on the structure of the maritime household and on gender relations within the household. Not only did women manage the household economy and, through uxorilocal and uxorivicinal residence and mutual aid, maintain strong ties with their matri-kin, but male emigration created the conditions under which a variety of women-centered household configurations developed. Although the household based on a single married couple was the cultural ideal, it was not the norm. Households comprising unmarried women and their children, or married women and children who had been deserted by emigrant husbands, were common, and in the maritime community the basic social unit was a woman, married or unmarried, and her children.

In parishes like Vila Chã, where large numbers of men were absent for prolonged periods, households headed by unmarried women were indistinguishable from those headed by married women whose husbands were absent, whether temporarily or permanently, due to emigration. Married women, for example, managed households and raised small children on their own after their husbands had emigrated and not returned. Some women who had been deserted by emigrant husbands chose to live with other men, and some had additional children with these partners. There were also women who had several illegitimate children before they eventually married the children's emigrant father years later on a long-awaited trip home. All of these women and children and these various household configurations were integrated among the other maritime households.

Households tended to be women-centered whether men were absent or present. Women's work in economic production and their decision-making authority over the use of the household's resources ensured women a central role in maritime households. Cultural preferences were for daughters to inherit household property, and these inheritance practices encouraged a pattern of uxorilocal residence that intensified women's relations with their matri-kin while diluting men's relations with their kin. Male emigration further strengthened women's ties with their matri-kin by encouraging uxorivicinality: groups of consanguineally related women lived and worked in close proximity to one another. Uxorivicinality was a strategy on the part of women both to develop mutual-aid networks in the absence of husbands and to maintain structures that reproduced women-centeredness in the household.

The women-centered character of Vila Chã's maritime households developed in the context of interrelated cultural, social, and economic conditions and cannot be attributed to any single factor. Many factors—the poverty, low social status, and endogamous marriage system of the maritime households; property relations and inheritance by women; the high rates of male emigration; the formation of households by women; and the strong ties among matri-kin, enhanced by uxorilocal and uxorivicinal residence patterns—operated together to shape the women-centered character of the maritime household, and to foster the oppositional culture of the pescadores. Most important, however, was the gendered division of labor and the role of women in the household economy. Women's work, at sea and on land, is the subject of the next chapter.

Chapter 4

WOMEN WORK AT SEA AND ON LAND

ALVINA RECOUNTS that women of maritime households were workers and that they worked alongside men in all areas of the fishery both at sea and on land. Until recently, however, maritime anthropologists have supposed that in small, nonindustrialized fisheries there was a dichotomy in the gendered division of labor, that men's work was based on the sea, and women's work was based on the land. This supposition derived from the anthropologists' own dichotomization of the world into sea and land, and their view that the sea was a male domain, the shore female territory (Andersen and Wadel 1972; Faris 1972). Recent comparative studies of women's work in fishing economies, however, support Alvina's account. These studies have found that there is not a strict and consistent division of labor in maritime societies but, instead, a great deal of variation in the work that women do. This variation stems from differences in the historical development of local fisheries (Firth 1984; Thompson 1985; Nadel-Klein and Davis 1988). Although in most of the world's fishing communities, it is the men who catch the fish and the women who work onshore, there are small fisheries in Brittany, Galicia, Sardinia, parts of Ireland, and parts of Sweden where women regularly go fishing with men. Even in Newfoundland, where strict taboos are said to exist against women's boarding boats (Faris 1972; Firestone 1967), there are communities where women regularly fish with their husbands (Davis 1983; Porter 1982).

Not only do women go to sea with men, but men often share domestic tasks with women. Like many other inshore fisheries, the Vila Chã fishery also depends on the periodic absence of men to work for wages aboard ocean-going cargo vessels or in offshore fisheries such as the Newfoundland Grand Banks cod fishery. During the long voyages, most men learn domestic tasks such as cooking, cleaning, and laundering. Many men continue to share at least some of this work, especially cooking, when at home.

In the Vila Chã fishery the household was the unit of production, and the household economy was organized around a seasonal cycle of diverse production activities. These activities included both commodity production and subsistence production, as well as occasional wage labor. Commodity production activities included summer seaweed harvesting and drying, the fall pilado fishery, the winter sardine fishery, and year-round hand-line fishing for a variety of fish. Subsistence production included gardening, collecting firewood, and keeping domestic animals. Members of maritime households also worked as day laborers for lavradores during planting and harvesting and were paid for their labor in food.

This "composite pattern" (Löfgren 1979) of organization of the household economy required the economic participation of all household members. And, based as it was on a seasonal round of activities for both subsistence and commodity production and on a delicate integration of land and marine resource exploitation, the maritime economy generated a flexible division of labor within the household. Thus, although some tasks in the Vila Chã fishery were performed primarily by men and others primarily by women, women were active in all areas of the fishery. All men went to sea, but some women also went to sea; women controlled the seaweed harvest, but, when called upon, men assisted their wives with this work; and, while domestic tasks were performed primarily by women, men also assisted with cooking and were active in child rearing. Women were able to replace men and men were able to replace women in the tasks associated with both the fishery and the domestic work of the household. At the same time, however, women were responsible for the tasks of commodity distribution and household management that defined their economic autonomy and authority in the maritime household.

WOMEN AT SEA

Since at least 1890, when the *Inquérito industrial e comercial: a pesca* was published, Vila Chã has been known on the north coast of Portugal as the only fishery where women regularly used to go to sea and fish with men.[1] Although Brandão (1923) and Lamas (1948) both mention having seen women in other communities on the north coast punting small boats near the shore as they line fished and harvested seaweed, the local view—that Vila Chã women were the only women in Portugal to go to sea—may reflect their greater involvement in fishing: they took out fishing licenses and were both boat owners and boat skippers; they went greater distances at sea and traveled up and down the coast between Póvoa de Varzim and Matosinhos; and, during the sardine fishing that took place between sunset and sunrise, women stayed out in boats overnight with male crew members who were not kin. Vila Chã women were seagoing as early as 1876, when eight women were shipwrecked (and two drowned) returning with a load of pilado. It continued to be common for women to fish at sea until at least the late 1960s, and in 1985 two women were fishing occasionally.

In the late nineteenth century there was effort on the part of marine authorities to prevent Vila Chã women from going to sea, but the women resisted any restriction of their activities. In a letter dated 1897, the marine commissioner solicited the aid of the administrator of the concelho of Vila do Conde.[2] He reported that the women continued to fish although it was against marine regulations; whenever officials had gone to Vila Chã to enforce this regulation, they had met with "hostile manifestations" by the women. Archives of the Capitania do Porto in Vila do Conde have no record of there ever having been a regulation prohibiting women from fishing, and officials there in 1985 suggested that this 1897 reference to "marine regulations" probably reflected the unofficial attitudes of the male marine authorities. These authorities, as civil servants and members of the bourgeoisie of the city of Porto, subscribed to the ideology that a woman's work should be centered in the home. In their minds, Vila Chã fisherwomen violated this ideal. The women, however, continued to go to sea.

Between 1920 and 1940, fifty-four Vila Chã women took out their fishing licenses from the Capitania in Vila do Conde. These women, like Alvina, had begun fishing as young girls, and when they reached the age of fourteen they took out licenses and became professional fisherwomen (*pescadeiras*) and crew members. Another fisherwoman, Lucília, explained:

> There wasn't anything special about it. It was either work on the sea or go to work for the lavradores. I wasn't going to do that and leave my parents alone down here with the younger children and all the work to be done on the praia. Besides, the lavradores paid almost nothing—just a little something to eat. And they worked at all hours. A lot of their work was done at night. It wasn't like it is today—all done by machine. At that time all the work was done by hand. It was hard work and all day long. My father had no sons. We were five girls. There was only one boy but he died when he was only eleven months old. My father had no sons so we went with him. This way he didn't have to pay someone from outside the family [to crew], and what we earned was our own [the household's]. But it wasn't anything special, my dear. In those days many women in Vila Chã worked on the sea.

Lucília took out her license in 1923 and fished for thirty-six years. She never married. She inherited her natal household's boat, and, when she retired from active fishing in 1959, she retained her license for ten more years, during which time she employed others to fish for her. Her sisters also fished at various times. One sister, Ana, started fishing in 1928 at age thirteen and continued to fish with Lucília and her father after she married and until the seventh month of her first pregnancy. When her child was seven months old, Ana's husband emigrated temporarily to Brazil, and she began fishing with Lucília and her father again. She stopped going to sea later, due to seasickness during her second pregnancy, and did not return to active fishing again; instead she assisted with the work onshore.

Girls began fishing as crew for a father or a brother. Once married and managing their own households, women sometimes found shore work too time-consuming to permit them to continue fishing on a regular basis. Some married women, like Alvina, however, continued to fish after marriage and throughout their lives. Women deserted by emigrant husbands often returned to fishing in order to support themselves and their children. Other married women fished when they could because they enjoyed the work and because it was always a way of earning money for the household. And it was not uncommon for women, like Lucília's sister, Ana, to continue to go to sea well into pregnancy. Veiga de Oliveira, Galhano, and Pereira (1975:129) recount the story of a Vila Chã woman who was out pilado fishing when she went into labor and had to be rushed to shore to give birth. Women's role in human reproduction was not perceived to be a hindrance to their fishing alongside men.

Women fished with men. They fished with their fathers and brothers. A few women fished with their husbands, but this was generally considered unwise: in the event of marine tragedy, children could be orphaned. But women also fished with men who were no relation to themselves. That women fished with men who were non-kin suggests that women's sexuality was not a consideration when they fished: they became "like men." Indeed, a Vila Chã fisherwoman describing her work at sea invariably will say, "I fished as a man." Thus, although fishing was culturally constructed as masculine work, the work of fishing could be, and was, performed by individuals of either sex.

A few women took the examination for the skipper's license (*carta de arrais*) authorizing them to skipper boats along the coast between Póvoa de Varzim and Matosinhos. In 1979, Maria, the last of these women skippers, retired. She describes the circumstances under which some women continued fishing throughout their lives, the relative economic independence this work offered to women, and the self-image of the fisherwoman.

The Story of a Woman Skipper: Maria

"I was at the same time *dona de casa* (housewife)
and *pescador* (fisherman)."

"I was born in 1926, the third of four children. We had no father.[3] I was raised in Lugar da Praia by my mother who worked as a jornaleira,

7. Woman spreading seaweed to dry on beach. Laundry drying.

8. Women harvesting seaweed in nets.

9. Emptying nets. Sorting fish. At right, woman selling fish.

10. Auctioning fish in lota.

harvested seaweed, and sold fish in order to feed us. But often there
was no food and we had to beg for food from our neighbors.

"In my childhood girls used to collect seaweed both from the beach
with a hand net (ganha-pão) and from boats, using a type of rake (gan-
chola). It was also common for them to accompany relatives fishing.
When only ten years old I began to accompany neighbors when they
went fishing. When I was fourteen I took out my license and I continued to fish on boats owned by neighbors. These men are all dead now,
but it was they who taught me this work.

"I married when I was only twenty years old and I think this was too
young. My husband was a pescador from a neighboring parish. He
came to live with me and my mother and grandmother and took up
fishing in Vila Chã. I continued fishing whenever I could, and after my
daughters were born I left them in the care of my mother in order to go
out on the sea. I also worked at the seaweed harvest, often going out
alone in the boat to collect seaweed.

"From the beginning my husband was selfish. He never helped me
with my work but would instead go off to attend to his own affairs (a
vida dele). I married too young. We had two daughters and, when I was
pregnant with the third, my husband emigrated to Brazil. He was gone
for almost four years, during which time I heard nothing from him and
he sent no money. I decided to go to Brazil to find him. In 1955 I went
by ship with my sister-in-law who was going to join her husband, my
brother, in Brazil. I found my husband involved in a life of women and
drink (amigas e bebidas), and after a few months I returned to Vila Chã
alone. I wanted to make my life in Vila Chã and I missed my daughters.
I took up full-time fishing and harvested seaweed when I wasn't fishing, and in this way I supported my mother and my children. In 1961,
I bought a boat of my own and took out my skipper's license.

"I like my profession but I fished because I was forced to. My marriage had become difficult. My husband went away to Brazil, leaving
me in the street (deixando-me na rua) with three children, and I had
to face life on my own. Fishing was not as productive then as it is now
(a pesca não dava o que dá agora), and the life of a pescadeira was
difficult. But I had to turn to what I knew. First I fished in a boat belonging to another pescador, and then for eighteen years I owned and
fished in my own boat Três Marias. About fourteen years ago I managed to buy a small house, which little by little I have fixed up, and
that's where I live now.

"Although in recent years I have been the only woman skipper
(mestre), there have been no difficulties for me at all, because I know
my profession very well—as well as any of my comrades (camaradas).
Men used to like to fish with me because they knew I was strong. C.,

one of my partners, used to say that I was stronger than he. Fishing holds no secrets for me and, besides, I think that women have the right to face life beside men (*acho que as mulheres têm o direito de enfrentar a vida ao lado dos homens*). What suits men, suits women (*O que serve para os homens serve para as mulheres*). I am respected by everyone, men and women. I have many friends, and when the weather prevents fishing we all stay here on the beach working on the nets and conversing. I have always enjoyed my work on the sea. I was never one who liked to stay at home (*Nunca gostei de estar em casa*).

"When my daughters were small I used to be at sea day and night—whenever there were fish. They stayed at home with my mother. Later, when they were older and I was fishing, my daughters assisted my mother harvesting seaweed, and in this way they contributed to the maintenance (*o sustento*) of the household. As soon as I returned from fishing I would start the housework. You see, I was at the same time housewife and fisherman (*Olhe, eu era ao mesmo tempo dona de casa e pescador*).

"I retired in 1979. I sold my boat and I gave my fishing gear to my son-in-law. I sold my boat to a fisherman in Matosinhos because I could not bear to see it anymore here on the beach. In 1982 I bought a piece of land in [Lugar do] Facho, and two of my daughters are building a duplex there now. My third daughter and her husband and three children live with me in my house. I have helped all of my daughters establish their households. I have been very good to them. Now that I am old and my heart is not good, they are looking after me. When I returned from Brazil leaving my husband there, I could have found another man to live with. I couldn't marry but I could have lived with another man. But I never wanted to do that because, if things didn't work out with us, I worried that he would take it out on my daughters because they were nothing to him. I preferred to have my daughters (*Antes quis as minhas filhas*).

"Recently, my husband has begun writing to me from Brazil. He wants to return to Portugal and he wants me to take him back. He needs someone to care for him now in his old age. But I won't take him back. It's not right at all (*Não tem jeito nenhum*). I liked him once but that's all over now. The best part of the life of a couple is passed. I'm not interested in his returning. I'm not an object to be put away and then picked up, dusted off, and used again (*Não sou um objecto p'ra deixar e depois retornar e limpar e usar mais uma vez*). I am not an object. I am a human being. I have the right to be a human being, don't you think? I managed to make a life for myself here, but he has arranged nothing for himself there, nothing (*não arranjou nada lá, nadinha*).

He arranged nothing here, but he also arranged nothing there. He has nothing. He has never done anything for me or for my daughters and now he wants to come back. Who does he think he is? I am not crazy (Não sou tola). He has no right whatsoever (Ele não tem direito nenhum)."

Maria's narrative illustrates women's economic autonomy and women's strategies in the maritime households. Maria could support herself, her mother, and her three children without the help of her husband or of any other man because fishing was locally perceived to be an occupation suitable for women as well as for men. Having been left by her husband "in the street" with nothing, Maria recognized the importance of owning property. Maria bought her own boat and gear and later a house and a piece of land. She solidified her economic security by investing in property and in her relationship with her daughters. When she made the decision to raise her daughters on her own, Maria consciously invested in her relationship with her daughters to provide for herself in her old age. And, having supported herself and her children, she is clear about her rights as a person and as a woman. Maria has worked side by side with men all her life; she has earned the respect of the pescadores of Vila Chã, and she will not now subordinate herself to a man. This is why, now that her estranged husband is trying to claim her services to care for him in his old age, she is refusing. Her reasons are found in the strong self-image she developed through a life of hard work and independence. As she sees it: "I am not an object to be put away and then picked up, dusted off, and used again. I am a human being."

Maria's story further confirms the existence of a local understanding that such vocations as those of fisherman or skipper were masculine roles but could be filled by women as well as men. Maria's case illustrates how gender, rather than being static or predetermined, is on the contrary negotiated through social roles. Maria has drawn on existing gender ideas in local society and manipulated them. She adopted a masculine self-image: she is the only woman of her generation who wears trousers. Maria wears the typical dress of a maritime woman—a skirt, apron, slippers, wool socks, a head scarf, and a wool shawl—but she also wears trousers under her skirt. She is large and muscular and walks with a masculine stride. Maria speaks with a man's self-assurance and lack of restraint (although it must be said that women of maritime households generally are outspoken and assertive). Maria's presentation of self and her assumption of masculine rights (exemplified in her refusal to take back her spouse) suggest that she has negotiated a masculine gender identity or perhaps a third-gender identity in the local context.[4] Certainly, her self-perception and behavior do not resemble the stereotype of women in the code of honor and shame.

Thus, in Vila Chã, there existed cultural definitions of men's work and women's work: men fished and women worked onshore. The social reality of the division of labor, however, was that both men and women fished. Women who fished described themselves as "like men," but, as Lucília explained, "there wasn't anything special" about women fishing. Fishing was socially constructed as a masculine role, but either sex could, and did, do the work. Women like Maria and Alvina manipulated social constructions of gender in order to maximize their economic autonomy, that is, their decision-making authority, access to resources, and control of their own labor. Fishing "like men" was one strategy that some women employed.

WOMEN'S WORK ON LAND

Women's work on land was indispensable to the local fishery and gave women control over the management of the household economy. Women were responsible for looking after the nets, unloading the boats, sorting the catch, and selling the fish. As well, they controlled the harvest and sale of seaweed fertilizer, kept the subsistence gardens, managed the domestic work of the household, and kept account of household income and expenses.

Maintenance of the nets was heavy work. The sardine nets (*peças*) were made of cotton and when wet were extremely heavy. Women working in pairs rinsed the nets in fresh water after each use, then carried them on their heads from the river to the beach, where the nets were spread to dry. Once the nets were dry, the women rolled them up and carried them, ready for use, to their boats. Both men and women were responsible for making and mending the nets, and also the sails. Boat maintenance was considered a man's task, but women assisted.

The women were responsible for the sale of the fish and for management of the household earnings from fishing. They unloaded and sorted the catch, and they auctioned the fish on the beach or carried their wares inland to neighboring parishes for sale door-to-door to lavradores. The women received the cash from the sale of fish and kept accounts of the earnings and expenses associated with the operation of the household boat.

Women managed all the income and spending for the maritime household, and the job of making ends meet was their responsibility. And, because no household could survive on earnings from the fishery alone, women engaged in a variety of other income-generating and subsistence production activities.

All women of maritime households harvested seaweed. They spent long hours on the beach during the summer months. They waded in the shallows, often in water up to their necks, and harvested the loose seaweed in their hand nets. Or they collected the seaweed as it washed onshore with the incoming tide. They carried the heavy wet seaweed to the high water mark to be spread on the beach to dry for a few days. Once it was dry, they rolled it into bundles, which they carried on their heads up the beach to a larger pile ready for sale to lavradores. It was the women who made the necessary contacts to sell their seaweed and they who received and controlled the earnings. Seaweed provided a source of income for women that was independent of the household earnings in the fishery and therefore independent of the work they shared with their husbands. The economic autonomy of Vila Chã women and their managerial role in the household economy were in large measure due to their monopoly of the sale of seaweed.

The women also kept small gardens where they grew potatoes, several varieties of cabbage, turnips, and onions. Men and women would work together and exchange labor with other maritime households during the peak times of soil preparation and planting in the spring, but at other times the garden was a woman's responsibility. Women would also keep hens, for their eggs, and chickens and rabbits for meat. And when times were hard it was a woman's responsibility to beg from a lavrador a cup of flour to make bread. Each woman was careful to develop and maintain a special relationship with one or two lavradores, whom they referred to as "amigos" (friends). They would offer their labor to these lavradores during peak times in the agricultural cycle, and it was these households they would go to for food during the hungry winter months when the stormy sea beached the fishing boats.

Housework was of little importance to maritime women. They spent little time on meal preparation and laundry and housecleaning because, unlike fish selling, seaweed harvesting, and gardening, these tasks did not directly generate income for the household. And they were relatively simple chores, not time-consuming, and usually shared among household members. A woman could direct other members of the household, including children, to prepare the basic meals: cabbage soup, grilled sardines and bread, or boiled fish and potatoes. There was less laundry to do then than there is now, because people wore the same work clothes every day (only changing and washing underclothes), and they owned only one change of clothing for Sundays and festas. Houses were small and household furnishings simple, and there was little effort expended in either decorating or cleaning homes.

Alvina laughed when I asked what her house was like when she was a young wife and what was involved in work such as cooking and cleaning. She said:

> In those days [the 1940s] houses were nothing like they are today. They were only huts (*barracas*). God has been very good to the pescadores today, for they all have nice houses (*casas boas*) of their own. But in those days we lived in barracas. We were crowded into two rooms. At the end of the summer I always had one room full of dried seaweed ready to sell. There was only a dirt floor so it was nothing to clean. And meals were simple. We had little to eat. We often went hungry (*Passava-se muita fome*). Life was a misery (*uma miséria*) then. Usually we had a cabbage broth—a few cabbage leaves boiled in water. Sometimes my husband grilled sardines. We cooked on an open fire. We didn't even have a table. We ate standing up or sitting on stools, and there were no dishes to wash because we didn't own any dishes to speak of—just a few bowls. We ate with our hands. My grandchildren all know how to eat with a fork, but we ate with our hands. Today the pescadores all eat well. They always have milk and fruit for the children and they eat meat every day. But in those days we often went hungry.

Child rearing also took place in the context of household production. Children were raised on the beach. They trailed after their parents and grandparents, aunts and uncles, and, as the adults went about their work, all watched out for the children. At an early age children were recruited to help with tasks such as firewood collecting, seaweed harvesting, and meal preparation. Veiga de Oliveira, Galhano, and Pereira report that in Vila Chã, where both parents were often out at sea, young children prepared the meals for the entire family (1975:129). Children were recruited early to work for the household and assist the adults in their work.

In maritime households, then, there was flexibility in the gendered division of labor, so that most tasks could be, and were, performed by either sex. Women were active in masculine work on the sea, and women worked onshore in commodity and subsistence production, and in domestic work. Women controlled the sale and distribution of the commodities—fish and seaweed—that the household produced, and they managed the income generated. This economic control gave women relative autonomy and decision-making authority in the household. At the same time, women manipulated the flexibility in the gendered division of labor in order to maximize their economic autonomy and in order to negotiate their gender identity and social relations.

Chapter 5

WORK AND SHAME:
THE SOCIAL CONSTRUCTION OF GENDER

WORK AND SHAME (TRABALHO E VERGONHA)

UNTIL RECENTLY we have been able to view women in Southern European societies only dimly, through the shadow of the anthropological construction of men embodied in the code of honor and shame. The honor-and-shame code was conceived by male ethnographers in the early 1960s and embodied British views of what were then known as Mediterranean societies (Campbell 1964; Caro Baroja 1965; Peristiany 1965; Pitt-Rivers 1965). In this view men are the subject, women are the "other." A preoccupation with honor was thought to rule men's lives, and men's honor was protected, in part, through control over the behavior and destinies of their wives and daughters—especially their sexuality and fertility—and achieved by imposing a moral code of shame on women.

In the code of honor and shame, women are "victims of their sexuality" (Schneider 1971). Mediterranean societies are conceived of as comprising small equivalent units—households—competing for scarce resources, and households have been thought to be male-centered or "male-headed." Honor is understood as esteem, respect, prestige, or some combination of these attributes. The literal Portuguese translation is *honra*, a term never heard in Vila Chã; instead, in Portuguese, *honor* probably best translates as *respeito*, or respect. Honor and shame, according to anthropologists, are components of a system of male prestige that served as a mechanism of social control, defined social boundaries and loyalties, substituted for physical violence, and provided some cohesiveness to otherwise fragmented societies (Schneider 1971). Women, or, rather, women's sexuality and fertility, constituted the one universal resource that provided a focus for honor, and women's sexuality and fertility were constructed as evil, threatening, dangerous, and requiring control. Control was achieved through the domestication of women's sexuality and fertility—through the social construction of women as wives and mothers—and through the conflation of women with shame (and men with honor). For their part, women exhibited respect for male honor through their deference to the moral code of shame and through their virginity and chastity.

Women were victims of their sexuality not only in the honor-and-shame conceptualization of local gender systems, but also in ethnographic writing that generally saw women through their reproductive roles as wives and mothers and neglected their roles in economic production—which, as we have seen, are primary in Vila Chã women's perception of themselves.[1]

Recently, the concept of honor and shame has undergone some scrutiny, but anthropologists also continue to shore up and elaborate the paradigm (Gilmore 1987). Pina-Cabral maintains that the delineation of a code of honor and shame was the British ethnographers' way of coming to terms with their own feelings about the agonistic tendencies of the Southern European societies they were observing. He has also recently suggested that the apparent ongoing propensity of Anglo-American anthropologists to be fascinated with the concepts of manhood embodied in this code may stem from the fact that "they are so ignorant of working-class behavior in their own countries of origin" (1989:402). Fernandez (1983:170) has pointed out that "there is now a long tradition of giving our deepest psychological impulses a Mediterranean embodiment." Similarly, Herzfeld (1984) has suggested that when ethnographers, following the code of honor and shame, simultaneously attribute to women both "virginal purity and diabolical sexuality," their own culture may be the source of the underlying stereotypes. Brandes (1987) also refers to the "Anglo-Saxon" ethnocentrism and androcentrism of the anthropological concept of honor and shame and sees the code as deriving from an "Anglo-Saxon" perception of the agonistic tendencies of Mediterranean societies as "deviant" and requiring explanation. Lever (1987) considers the code ethnocentric and, more importantly, class-blind and sex-blind, in that it denies the stratification and conflict based upon class and sex differences that prevail in Mediterranean societies.[2] Corbin (1987) considers that, because of the androcentrism of the concept of honor and shame, the anthropology of Southern Europe does not represent women in their own terms and is "incomplete and demeaning." Corbin says that "a truly stereoscopic view" would have to recognize that "women may not regard themselves as inferior or dominated, may not consider their own activities less valuable than men's, may be as ambivalent about men as men are about them." Recently, anthropologists such as Kertzer (1987) have suggested that although the honor-and-shame code was once the "bread and butter" of Mediterranean anthropology, "we are now ready for a richer diet." And, Pina-Cabral (1986) and O'Neill (1987), without systematically addressing the question of a code of honor and shame, dismiss its utility in their respective ethnographic cases by saying that northern Portugal, unlike southern Portugal, is not "Mediterranean."[3]

In the following discussion, I illustrate why it would be entirely inappropriate to employ any notion of honor and shame to conceptualize the gender system in Vila Chã.

In this chapter I argue that the anthropological conceptualization of honor and shame mirrors the ideology of family promulgated by the Roman Catholic church and the fascist states in power throughout the Mediterranean (including Portugal) at the time the first anthropologists of Mediterranean societies were writing. I argue that, in practice, gender is actively constructed and negotiated at several levels and that local gender systems do not merely mirror the hegemonic constructions of church and state. If we are to understand how men and women negotiate and manipulate gender, it is particularly important that we understand how gender construction operates at the levels of household and community. If we take the approach of looking at different levels of gender construction, we are able to see the ambiguities and contradictions that allow, and even require, that men and women negotiate their gender identities and gender relations. In Vila Chã we find that, at the level of the household, women are defined as productive workers and managers, yet an ideal of partnership between husband and wife exists. At the level of the community we find that a myth of male dominance is manipulated by both men and women, but that, as rural communities under the Salazarean New State had no political representation and were essentially powerless, it was the level of the household that was most important to rural people. At the state level we find that male dominance is legislated (and contrary to local practice). And we find that the church advocates the servility of women.

The honor-and-shame code emphasized women's roles in human reproduction and obscured their roles in economic production. That is, women were understood primarily in terms of their sexuality and fertility and less in terms of their work. Images of women as mothers, as wives, and as daughters prevailed. Mothers were fertile and nurturant, wives were chaste, and daughters were virgin. Men—fathers, husbands, sons—were authoritarian and independent. As we have seen in previous chapters, however, Vila Chã women see themselves more in terms of their roles as productive workers and household managers than in terms of their reproductive—or potentially reproductive—roles as mothers, wives, and daughters. They present themselves as workers and see themselves as *governadoras* of their households. Nonetheless, shame (vergonha) is important in their lives; by problematizing the social construction of gender, we can reach a greater understanding of shame than was possible when we saw shame as opposite to honor and woman as man's other. We learn that shame (vergonha) and work (trabalho) are both central to the social construction of women in Vila Chã.

Gender Role Socialization

Having children was positively valued by both women and men in Vila Chã. People say, "A couple without children is like a tree without branches" (*Um casal sem filhos é como uma árvore sem ramos*). Both women and men, however, had strong opinions about family size. A family of two or three children was thought to be ideal: an only child was too risky because the child might die, leaving a couple with none; but having too many children was thought to be improvident, for children "bring poverty" (*trazem pobreza*). Actually many couples had more children, and those couples with two or three children were admired. At the opposite end of the spectrum, couples with large numbers of children were disdained. One couple who had had twenty-two children, sixteen of whom lived through childhood, was looked down upon by other couples and considered "undisciplined" and deserving of their poverty.[4]

As to the sex of the child, boys and girls were equally desired by their parents. In general, both husband and wife wanted to have at least one child of each sex: "If your first child is a boy, then you want your second to be a girl; if your first is a girl then you want your second to be a boy." If there were several children in a household already, women often preferred to have more daughters than sons, because daughters would help them with their work. Both husband and wife also preferred a daughter to look after them in their old age and welcomed the birth of a girl for this reason.

Although children of both sexes were equally desired, once a child was born, different treatment of the sexes began. Attitudes toward the sex of a child originated in the parents' view of the contributions children would make to the household as they grew up and married. Many parents assumed that daughters would make longer-term contributions to the parental household than would sons, because of the prevalence of male emigration and the residence patterns of uxorilocality and uxorivicinality that had developed in maritime households. Parental attitudes were complicated, however, by their perception of differences in male and female sexuality, and this perception led to different behavior toward children of different sexes.

Girls in maritime households were socialized to the role of the trabalhadeira. The term *trabalhadeira* translates literally as "hardworking woman" and represents a woman who was industrious, thrifty, and skillful at the management of household resources. Girls were raised to a life of hard physical work and instilled with those character attributes that firmly established the female self-image of the trabalhadeira. At the age of seven or eight they were already following in the footsteps of their mothers, aunts, and grandmothers working on the beach and collecting their own small piles of seaweed to dry for sale or exchange. By the time they were ten they were accompanying mothers and grandmothers on their fish-selling expeditions, carrying small loads of fish in wooden trays on their heads like the older women, and walking long distances to neighboring parishes. Similarly, a girl learned agricultural work either in her mother's garden or working alongside her mother for a lavrador in his fields. By the age of eight or ten, girls were also effective workers at the domestic tasks associated with keeping the home: preparing the simple meals, cleaning the house, or washing clothes at the river.

Girls learned that the woman in a maritime household was responsible for managing the household economy. In order to do this well and under conditions of resource scarcity and economic hardship, she must be "very hardworking, thrifty, and [must] struggle constantly" (muito trabalhadeira, poupada e lutar p'ra vida). A woman's job was "to make a livelihood" (fazer a vida). She was to make ends meet in order to ensure the economic well-being of the household. Girls learned that the job of the woman of the household was to be "the manager of the home" (a governadora do lar). As Alvina tells us, "There was always the idea that a woman had to learn to be thrifty, to be a good manager of the household." Girls from the land-poor maritime households also learned that the possibility of their finding a good husband depended on their capacity for hard work. Alvina says: "A woman makes money; money does not make a woman. It's better to marry a hardworking woman who will make money than it is to marry a spendthrift woman with an inheritance who will waste it."

The image of "woman as worker," the social construction of women as trabalhadeiras, was extremely important. The reproduction of the maritime household depended upon a woman's skillful management of household resources and on women's central role in economic production. It was, therefore, essential that young girls develop the skills and character of a trabalhadeira. Girls learned, as Alvina puts it, that "to be a woman is to be a worker," and that "a woman is like an ant: she toils and toils, making a livelihood" (a mulher é como uma formiga: arrasta, arrasta, faz a vida).

Girls were disciplined and taught to be hardworking, but parents tended to be more lenient with boys. Boys were taught the virtues of a hardworking, sober life-style, but they also learned that as adult men they would be allowed certain vícios (vices). These vícios included drinking, gambling, and passing time in the adega (tavern) in the company of other men and away from household responsibilities. Girls, meanwhile, learned that as adult women and wives they would be expected to make allowances for the vícios of the men of the household. This emphasis on instilling virtue in women and allowing vícios in men derives in part from the local perception that women, as managers, were central in the household economy and that men, as emigrants and fishermen, might be absent from both household and community for long periods.

Differences in the rearing of boys and girls also stemmed, however, from local perceptions about sexuality. Girls were taught to have vergonha—a Portuguese concept without direct English translation. Although commonly translated as "shame," it covers a wider range of meanings, including virtue, modesty, decency, restraint, and propriety. Vergonha can also be translated as "reputation" or "embarrassment." It is by no means evident that people use the term in conjunction with or in opposition to an equivalent term for "honor" (whether honra or respeito in Portuguese). Indeed, the term vergonha by itself seems to encompass the range of behaviors anthropologists have placed within the honor-and-shame code.

"Honor and shame" essentially refers to a system of social control characteristic of virtually all face-to-face societies that function as moral communities by evaluating their members according to a single set of relatively unambiguous standards (Peristiany 1965; Brandes 1987). In Vila Chã (and throughout rural Portugal) invoking vergonha is a means of social control; the target is usually either disrespectful behavior that scorns public opinion and basic social obligations, or hapless circumstances that evoke pity. Vergonha can operate as a mechanism of social control because rural Portuguese communities are face-to-face societies in which people know one another in multiple capacities as neighbors, relatives, work companions, and friends, and in which gossip is the prevalent means of social control.

A person who exhibits a lack of shame, decency, modesty, restraint, or propriety is said to be sem vergonha. This term can be used fondly to refer to children, who, prior to their First Communion, cannot be expected to control "shameless" behavior. Or it can be used to express mild to strong moral condemnation and social disgrace in reference to adults. The predicament of a woman who is unable to pay her bill at the local grocery shop is described by her neighbors as uma vergonha—an embarrassment, and pitiable because she is falling short of the trabalhadeira ideal. A woman whose husband works in construction and has not received pay from his employer for months will say that the employer's behavior is uma vergonha—a disgrace, because he has not fulfilled a basic obligation. I used to wear a heavy cotton madras skirt, and one day a neighbor told me of another neighbor's indignation: it looked as if I did not wear a slip under my skirt—"did I not have any ver-gonha?" My informant reportedly replied to her that stealing hay from a neighbor's field is "not having vergonha," not failing to wear a slip. The husband of the critical woman was renowned for stealing hay from others' fields. Nonetheless, I went to market in Vila do Conde that Friday and bought a slip.[5]

Expressions about vergonha are used daily to refer to both men and women, except in the area of sexuality, where vergonha is expected of women but not of men.[6] A girl was taught to have vergonha because she must maintain control over her fertility. Should she become pregnant, it was she who would assume responsibility for the child's needs or become a burden to the parental household. A boy, however, could be allowed greater freedom because, at least in theory, he could choose when and under what circumstances he would assume social responsibility for his sexuality. Thus, female sexuality was conflated with fertility, but male sexuality was not seen in the context of fertility and human reproduction.

Pina-Cabral, writing of rural northwestern Portugal, refers to the antisocial threat of female sexuality (he, too, conflates sexuality and fertility) that requires domestication through marriage and the formation of households. He argues that female sexuality is threatening and antisocial because it can lead to reproduction outside the boundaries of the household, the primary social unit. In rural Portugal, where women have such a central social and economic role, their natural control over biological reproduction presents, he says, "a real threat to the social structure." The power over human biological reproduction must, then, be transferred from women alone to women and men within the household through marriage. Pina-Cabral asserts that marriage is a "necessary support" for the household as the primary social unit, and a "necessary support" for the "power of men." And he maintains that "any interpretation of the local conceptions of sexuality, gender roles and human reproduction must take this into account" (1986:82), but he then goes on to describe local constructs of female sexuality as "natural" and does not explore the ideological or political origins he alluded to initially. I argue that constructs such as vergonha are used to "socialize" female fertility (cf. Boddy 1982:687) in order that marriage will continue and households will be formed, and not because female sexuality is, by nature, "antisocial" and "threatening." The perception of female sexuality as "antisocial" and "threatening" is a social construction. Indeed it is precisely because women's sexuality is socially constructed and precisely because marriage is a politically sanctioned institution (and not a "natural" condition) that gender constructs are not static and gender identities are negotiable. The adult maritime women of Vila Chã, such as Alvina and Maria, are continually negotiating their social, economic, and sexual identities. As we have seen, in their work fishing, for example, they choose to identify themselves as "like men."[7]

Vergonha is idealized in the socialization of girls, but, in practice, parents also encouraged their sons to be sexually responsible, and, when they did have premarital sexual relations, boys would generally marry these girls. Nonetheless, a theoretical difference remained in the local perception of male and female sexuality, and this difference gave rise to differential treatment of boys and girls. In Vila Chã, this difference was understood less through the negative construction of female sexuality that anthropologists have described than through a pragmatic consideration of the social and economic consequences of women's fertility.

Different perceptions of male and female sexuality and fertility were evident in the expressions parents used to acknowledge the sex of their child at birth. When a boy was born, his mother would say, "I don't have to worry" (Ando à vontade) or "At least he won't come home to me pregnant" (Ao menos, olhe, não me aparece grávida em casa). When a girl was born, however, parents were quiet. They knew that she might one day fica grávida em casa (become pregnant while still resident in the parental household).

Boys and girls achieved adulthood in different ways. When a girl began to menstruate, people would say, "Já é mulher" (Now she's a woman). A woman achieved adulthood when she became fertile. A boy, however, became a man (um homem) only when he married. A man who never married was known as a "boy" (um rapaz) throughout his life. Adulthood, therefore, began when the individual assumed responsibility for the reproductive consequences of his or her sexuality. A woman assumed responsibility for her sexuality as soon as she began to menstruate, for it was she who would raise any children she had while unmarried; a man assumed this responsibility only when he established a household of his own (through marriage) and acknowledged children as his.

Girls began to menstruate around sixteen or seventeen years of age,[8] and soon afterward they began to have namorados. A son was said to be able to "have sex freely" (pode trabalhar à vontade), but a daughter should not have sex freely and should show restraint (ter vergonha) in the expression of her sexuality. Again, a woman's sexuality was defined in the context of her fertility. People in Vila Chã say, "Guard your little she-goats [i.e., daughters], for my billy goat [i.e., son] runs loose" (Guardem as vossas cabrinhas, que o meu bode anda à solta).

Parents may have appeared to concern themselves more with the sexual activity of a daughter than with that of a son, but they would also discourage a son from intimacy with a woman they would not want him to marry; a son would, in all probability, marry a young woman he was intimate with if she were the daughter of a neighbor maritime household of Lugar da Praia, Facho, or Rio da Gândara and therefore a suitable mate. Parents generally considered that it was difficult to control the sexual activity of both sons and daughters, and premarital sex was common and widely assumed.[9] And, if it should become known that a young unmarried woman was pregnant, other parents with daughters still unmarried would be slow to criticize. They would say, "I can't talk because I have three daughters at home [i.e., still unmarried]" (*Não posso falar porque tenho três filhas em casa*).

When a woman reached menopause people would say: "She is no longer a woman. She can have sex freely" (*Já não é mulher. Pode trabalhar à vontade*). This did not mean that menopausal women were more sexually active than other women, but it supports the argument that premenopausal women were to be guarded (ter vergonha) in the expression of their sexuality because of their fertility and not their rapacious and threatening sexuality.

It is interesting to note that older women use the verb *trabalhar* (literally, "to work") for "to have sexual intercourse," suggesting that they see themselves as sexual actors in the way they see themselves as economic actors, and that they perceive women, like men, to be active (if cautious) in sex. Younger married women, however, apparently think of sex as a service performed for husbands. They say, "*O meu homem serviu-se de mim*" (literally, "My husband used me"), implying female passivity in intercourse.[10]

Thus the socialization process differed for females and males, and contradictions existed between socialization for gender roles in economic production and socialization for gender roles in human reproduction. On the one hand, dominance of women was prescribed in household production and constructed through female socialization for the role of trabalhadeira. On the other hand, restraint (vergonha) was required of women in human reproduction and in the expression of their sexuality.

Fertility was associated with femininity, while sexuality without the consequences of pregnancy was associated with masculinity. The ideology tried to fuse female sexuality with female fertility. The contradictory social reality, however, allowed their separation. High rates of illegitimacy, for example, suggest that women manipulated their fertility and their sexuality and that women's fertility, regardless of social deference to "vergonha," could be a source of power and autonomy for women. Thus, in the social construction of gender, the contradiction appears to be between the definition of women in production and the definition of women in human reproduction, but, at the level of daily life, there is also contradiction within the sphere of human reproduction. These contradictions allow women (and men) to negotiate their gender identities even while deferring to local social and political constructs about gender.

CONJUGAL RELATIONS

Conjugal relations within the maritime household were also defined in terms of both sexuality and the gendered division of labor, and both arenas presented contradictions to the local ideal of partnership and mutuality in marriage.

In the maritime households of Vila Chã, both women and men sought marriage partners who were hardworking, and egalitarian relations between husband and wife were the ideal. A man needed to marry in order to leave his parental household and to set up a household of his own. And a man needed a wife to do the shore work related to the fishery, including household management.[11] For her part, a woman benefited from marriage because the labor and economic contribution of a husband increased household prosperity and made her task of household management easier. The characteristics both men and women sought in a mate were that he or she be hardworking, thrifty, sober, and clean. After marriage a husband considered that a good wife was one who worked hard for the household and who was a skillful manager of the household's resources; a wife considered that a good husband was one who was a hard worker, who turned over all money to his wife, and who "trusted his wife" (*tinha confiança na mulher*) to manage the household without his interference.[12] Elaborate efforts were required, however, by both partners to make relations within the household resemble the egalitarian ideal.

Women, as trabalhadeiras, were culturally constructed as thrifty hard workers and managers of the household economy. Women sold the fish and received the cash, and they took on a variety of other income-generating and subsistence production tasks. Whereas wives were thrifty and saved (*poupava*) the household's resources, husbands spent (*gastava*) household resources. Women's household management included budgeting for men's vícios, primarily gambling and drinking. Because wives managed the household economy, husbands daily were required to ask their wives for money to buy beer, wine, and tobacco in the adega. Wives budgeted for these expenses, but inevitably there were times when they were required to tell their husbands that there was no money for their excursion to the adega. These were times of maximum tension in marital relations, and husband and wife both often resorted to tears and violence to express their mutual frustration. Wives would regret the situation but try to remind their husbands of the rights of their children. Husbands recognized that their wives were right to manage the scarce resources in the best interests of the household but resented the powerlessness they felt because, in the division of labor, women had control over the allocation of household resources. Periods of male emigration further intensified the dominant managerial role of women in the household. When husband and wife were living together, however, while a woman managed the economic resources, she did so in a way that respected her husband's right to be an equal partner in the household enterprise. For women, this sometimes required playing a fictional role of submissiveness: women selectively employed submissive behavior in an attempt to equalize gender relations within the household (cf. Rogers 1975).[13] For men, their invisible role in the efficient operation of household affairs led them to develop ritualized behavior outside the household. In Vila Chã, men's ritual behavior was located in the men's society of the adega.

A variety of popular expressions were used regularly by both men and women in Vila Chã to manage tensions stemming from contradictions in the gendered division of labor in the maritime household. Among them are the following:

A. *Na vida da casa quem manda é a mulher* (In the business of the household, it is the woman who rules);
   O mundo da mulher é a casa; a casa do homem é o mundo (The world of the woman is the house; the house of the man is the world);
B. *Quem manda é as calças* (The one who wears the pants rules);
   Os homens é que têm sorte (It's men who have luck);
   Ao homem tudo é permitido (For men, everything is allowed);
   Ao homem nada lhe fica mal (Nothing is unbecoming of a man);
C. *Eh pá! Não es tu quem manda em casa?* (Hey, man! Isn't it you who rule the household?);
   Entre marido e mulher não metes tu a colher (Don't interfere between husband and wife).

These popular adages (*adágios*) were among the many used in Vila Chã to describe gender relations and the distribution of power within the household. The frequency with which they were invoked and the contradictions they reveal suggest that the allocation of power between husband and wife was being negotiated constantly and was never assumed.

When we examine these expressions we can identify at least three categories: the first set (A) identifies women as the controlling power within the household; the second (B) suggests that men are in a more privileged position than women; and the third set of expressions (C) suggests that people recognize that gender relations are problematic and not ideal.

The first two expressions (A) recognize that women control the household but assert that power in the household does not have value when viewed in the context of the external world. These expressions endeavor to denigrate the structure of gender relations in the household and to enforce the view that relations outside the household are more important, that is, a greater source of power, than those within the household. Through the use of these expressions a dichotomy between household and extrahousehold spheres, between private and public, is created. This dichotomy implies a hierarchy of relative importance: the public sphere (*o mundo*), where men are said to rule, is defined to be of greater importance than the household sphere, the domain of women. The dichotomization is, however, ideological. The two spheres are not separate but are integrally connected. Furthermore, in rural parishes like Vila Chã during the Salazarean New State (i.e., until 1974), the local structures of the extrahousehold sphere—such as the parish council, which was dominated by men—had no decision-making authority or political power.

The second set of expressions (B) appear to state in straightforward terms that it is men who are lucky and, by implication, that it is women who are unlucky in their lot. There are no similar expressions idealizing the experience of women. Yet one must wonder why, if men's superiority and privilege is unquestioned, it needs to be asserted so frequently. It would seem that men's privileged position is not secure or guaranteed; rather, it must be decreed and enforced ideologically.

And, finally, the third set of expressions (C) suggest that men and women recognize and experience the contradictions between the ideology of egalitarian relations and mutual dependence between husband and wife and the social reality of women's dominance in the household. Third parties are advised not to interfere in the business of a husband and wife, because gender relations in the household are fragile and potentially violent. Gender relations are particularly fragile because they are negotiated relations.

In the rhetorical question, "Hey, man! Isn't it you who rule the household?" the fishermen in the adega use humor to dispel the tension generated when the society was forced to recognize publicly that male dominance was not absolute. This occurred, for example, when a woman came into the adega to retrieve her husband, reminding him in front of the other men that he had been there long enough, that it was time he was home, that he was wasting time and money, and so on. This was not an uncommon event. When the social fiction of male dominance was maintained, a woman would not show such public dominance of her husband. In the social fiction men have luck and everything is allowed (*tudo é permitido*). Men go to the tavern, fraternize with their male friends, and, among men, construct the world in a way that upholds their power not only within the household but also in the community and beyond. To maintain this social fiction, however, men knew the limits of the time and money they could afford (and that their wives would allow), and they came home when they reached that limit. If they abused or crossed that boundary, their wives would be forced to come and remind them. This was embarrassing for all of the men and especially for the husband involved. The other men, however, did not ridicule the woman who had entered male territory to retrieve her husband; instead they taunted the errant husband. They pretended they were surprised that, in this man's household, it was his wife and not he who ruled (*Eh pa! Não es tu quem manda em casa?*). Through humor they dissipated the tension and embarrassment at the same time that they legitimated the woman's authority and the gendered division of labor in the household. On the way home, however, the husband might endeavor to salvage his fictional position of dominance through physical violence toward his wife.

Elements of a "myth of male dominance" therefore were present in conjugal relations in Vila Chã maritime households, but the phenomenon was not as well developed as has been reported for European peasant agricultural societies (S. Rogers 1975). Women may say, "It's men who have luck" (*Os homens é que têm sorte*), but it is difficult for them to act in a manner of deference or subordination to men. Fundamentally, women believe that men and women are equal. "*Somos iguais*" (We are equal), they say. Meanwhile, men say that it is their wives who "rule" (mandam). Men and women appear to employ different constructions of gender, and this adds further complexity and contradiction (cf. D. Dwyer 1978).

Although there was no public display of physical affection between husband and wife, sexual relations were an important part of a marriage for both men and women.[14] As one married woman said, "Who is there who doesn't like sex?" (*Quem é que não gosta?*). There was no hesitancy on the part of either men or women to talk about sex, although women talked more publicly about sex, including their own sexual lives, than men did. Invariably, when fishermen and women worked together on the praia unloading boats or sorting fish or mending nets, the conversation turned to sex. Men and women joked freely, the women often taking the lead in making lewd jestures or teasing the men. Sexual banter was a favorite pastime for both men and women as they went about their work. Women were not sheltered from sexual knowledge or passive in their sexual activity. Indeed, as noted earlier, women refer to sex as "work" (trabalho), implying action and not passivity on their part.

Despite this apparent egalitarianism in the expression of sexuality, sexual relations ultimately were viewed in the context of human reproduction, and within marriage, as prior to marriage, there were greater limits on the expression of female sexuality than there were on the expression of male sexuality. Women were required to remember the possible consequences of their sexual activity, but men could choose to pretend that their sexual activity was without consequence. Women, therefore, experienced their sexuality as a source of tension and conflict: on the one hand, they enjoyed sex; on the other hand, they wished to control the possible reproductive consequences. This tension led to contradictions in the way that women presented their sexuality: for example, they did not shrink from being sexually explicit in conversation, but they were careful to be modest (ter vergonha) in their dress by wearing somber colors, heavy shawls, woolen skirts and socks, and head scarves.

Women learned sexual restraint, but they also learned that they possessed power in their capacity for human reproduction and they manipulated this source of female power. Having illegitimate children was one way that some women used their fertility as a "resource" (cf. Lambek 1983). Female fertility represented a source of power for women, and this contradiction enabled women to manipulate their sexuality and fertility for their own strategic ends. Women selectively employed what might be called the "myth of female virginity" to assist them in manipulating their sexuality. For example, a woman might say that her baby was born "too soon" if not quite nine months had passed between her marriage and the birth of her first child.[15]

Biological virginity, however, is not a dominant theme in local gender relations, and the relative unimportance of virginity is a further contrast between the gender system of Vila Chã and the gender systems described by anthropologists as characteristic of Mediterranean societies (Campbell 1964; Peristiany 1965; Pitt-Rivers 1971; Schneider 1971). In the maritime households of Vila Chã, a woman's deference to the appearance of virginity and to the restraint of female sexuality serve to control female fertility; they do not protect male honor. They show a woman's respect for social order and her assumption of adult responsibility. Virginity in Vila Chã is a social construction and it

11. Women waiting on beach for return of fishing boats.

12. Three sisters-in-law wait for the return of the boats.

13. In the adega.

14. Two retired fisherwomen,
now widows, chat on the street.

is manipulated by women. Deference to a cultural ideal of virginity signifies respect for social order but has little to do with preservation of biological virginity. As earlier noted, high rates of premarital sex and illegitimacy exist among the maritime households and are acknowledged locally. Premarital pregnancies are a common way of bringing a courtship to marriage, and women are often pregnant when they marry. They may show respect for the ideal of virginity by suggesting that the baby came "too soon," but what matters far more to the local society is a woman's comportment after marriage, the kind of household she runs, and her industriousness as a trabalhadeira. Where marriage is not a possibility and illegitimate births result, unmarried mothers, as we have seen, establish households of their own and are fully integrated into the community through their deference to the two ideals of femininity: trabalho (work) and vergonha (shame). There is little moral outrage surrounding the question of virginity. In Vila Chã, virginity is a "woman's accomplishment" (Clark 1987); it is not a resource controlled and protected by men.[16]

In a successful marriage, a husband and wife would respect (respeitar) each other's sexuality and not engage in extramarital relations. Women, however, perceived that men were sexually freer than women. While ideally a husband would remain sexually faithful to his wife, it was recognized that, at least in theory, he could engage in extramarital relations with relative impunity (although people would talk). A woman, on the other hand, would be criticized by both men and women if an extramarital liaison should be discovered. She would be seen as a woman "without shame" (sem vergonha) because she had not exercised the restraint expected of women. The frequency with which extramarital relations actually occurred cannot be known, but the knowledge that men could not be punished while women could had the effect of a double standard whether or not men took advantage of it. Women, however, did not blame men. They said, "It's a stupid man (literally, "an ass") who doesn't take advantage [of his freedom]" (Burro o homem que não se aproveitar), implying that they would if they could. The happily married woman, however, would be proud to say in her old age: "My husband was my good friend. He always respected me" (O meu homem foi muito meu amigo. Sempre me respeitou)—meaning that he never had sexual relations with other women (that she knew about).

The contradictions generated in gender role socialization created the conditions that required daily negotiation of conjugal relations. Conjugal relations within the maritime household were characterized by the tension between the egalitarian ideal and the actual dominance of women in household production, and the tension between the cultural expression of women's sexuality through the idiom of vergonha and the social reality within which women manipulated and controlled their fertility. As a result, Vila Chã maritime women were neither "alienated" from their reproduction (cf. O'Laughlin 1974:312) nor subordinated in their work in economic production.

STATE AND CHURCH

State and church defined gender relations in a national context that removed them from the everyday relations of the household. Rural men and women, however, held the view that the national gender ideology was also negotiable, and in this way they considerably moderated the influence of state and church in defining gender relations at the local level. Gender relations were mobilized by the people as part of a general, if silent, resistance to state intervention in daily life and as part of a long tradition of anticlericalism in Portugal.

The ideological construction of gender by the state was embodied in legislation and was subject to change. During the first Portuguese Republic following the fall of the monarchy in 1910, legislation was introduced that legalized divorce and declared husband and wife equal before the law. This progressive legislation was revoked in 1933 in the Constitution of the New State (*A Constituição Política do Estado Novo*) that had attained power following a military coup in 1926. The Constitution was revised once in 1966 but was not changed significantly until 1976, following the institution of democracy after the Revolution of April 25, 1974.[17]

The New State was authoritarian, militantly nationalistic, Christian, anticapitalist, and anticommunist; it was strongly influenced by Italian and Spanish fascism and later by Nazi Germany. The rise of fascism in the form of the New State in Portugal, as elsewhere in Europe, was related to post–World War I fears of liberalism, democracy, populism, mass society, and industrialization. The particular strain of fascism, known as "corporatism," that developed in Portugal between the wars was one impact of the world depression on the most economically underdeveloped country in Western Europe and was strongly influenced by its first prime minister and primary spokesperson, Oliveira Salazar.

In frequent speeches, Salazar outlined the principles of the regime and its view of the nature of society, the importance of the family and work, and the virtues of tradition and rural life. Society was an organism with each segment in its proper place. To keep each segment in its place, the regime developed sophisticated measures of social and political control that included strict censorship of all media; an authorized curriculum and education system operated by the Roman Catholic church for the state; a labyrinthine bureaucracy that permeated daily life; omnipresent police in the form of the civil guard (the *Guarda Republicana*) and a highly trained national secret police force, the *Polícia Internacional e de Defesa do Estado*, the P.I.D.E.; corporate organization of all sectors of the economy that united employers and employees in associations, denied the existence of different class interests, and instead instituted a concept of "class harmony"; an economic policy of "planned constraint" (Leeds 1984) that endeavored to control industrialization and keep the majority of the population rural-based; and an appeal to nostalgia and the traditions of the past that became a denial of the poverty of rural life and a romanticization of what the regime preferred to call its "stability" and "order."

The New State's concept of order and harmony rested on a view of society as a metaphorical "family" and of the family as a unity of shared interests—a model that denied the existence of different interests and of inequalities between husband and wife. The interests of the family were, in the state's view, coincident with those of the husband, whose authority within the household was legitimate. This model reflected Salazar's own views of the importance of paternal authority in the family and derived from his strongly held Catholic Christian principles. A deeply religious man, Salazar early in his life had studied to enter the priesthood. He remained celibate throughout his life and has been described as an "asexual patriarchal figure" who represented the values of "austerity, frugality, humility and chastity" to the people; he was "the ideal father and not the desired husband" (*o pai ideal e não o marido desejado*) (Fiadeiro 1984). The institutionalized paternalism and the monolithic bureaucracy of the New State were justified in Salazar's claim that "like a great family or a great concern, the nation, for the protection of its common interests and the attainment of its collective aims, requires a head to control it" (as quoted in Leeds 1984:17). The legal and administrative prescriptions for gender relations during the New State derive from the regime's model of the family and its representation of the state as "one great family with a father [Salazar] at its head" (Leeds 1984).[18]

The 1933 Constitution of the New State asserted the equality of citizens "except as concerns the woman [due to] the differences resulting from her nature and in the interest of the family." Under the Civil Code (*Código Civil*), only marriages in the Roman Catholic church were legal, and divorce was, once again, illegal. Legal separation was possible, but different requirements applied to husbands and to wives. A man could be granted a legal separation if his wife had committed adultery, but a wife could apply for legal separation only if her husband's adultery had created public scandal, if he had completely abandoned her, or if he had brought his mistress to reside in the married couple's home. In other words, a woman's adultery was in itself subject to penalty, but a husband's adultery was only illegal under certain conditions. The husband was the "head of the family" ("*chefe de família*"),[19] and a wife was her husband's legal dependent. A wife could not legally contract debts or acquire or alienate goods without the authorization of her husband. The administration of the couple's goods, "without exception of the property of the woman, pertain[ed] to the husband," and a wife required "the authorization of the husband . . . for each act in which [she] intend[ed] to engage" (Riegelhaupt 1967:113). The Civil Code also established a husband's right to insist that his wife remain in the home. Women under the New State were, then, according to the law, restricted in their economic activities and in their access to property, and household economic decisions were seen to rest with men as husbands.

The New State further supported the authority and dominance of men by declaring that men and women had different electoral rights and by prohibiting women from holding public office on district, municipal, or parish councils or acting as judges or diplomats. In the election of the local parish council, the junta de freguesia, only heads of families could vote. The "heads of families" category included all married men and only widowed women of "recognized moral fitness" who supported dependents (Riegelhaupt 1967:114). Criteria for eligibility to vote for the National Assembly were slightly different. A man was eligible to vote if he was the head of a family, if he could read and write, or if he had paid an annual tax of at least one hundred escudos. A woman was eligible if she was the head of a family *and* could either read and write or had paid a tax of one hundred escudos or more. A woman who was not the head of a family could vote only if she had a secondary education. Needless to say, a secondary education was extremely rare for rural women under the New State. Until 1960, only three years of education were compulsory, and the majority of rural women left school at age eight or nine. A married woman could vote only if she knew how to read and write and, in addition, had paid a personal tax of not less than two hundred escudos. These prescriptions effectively disenfranchised the entire female Portuguese population (Brettell 1982; Riegelhaupt 1967).[20] In practice, voter participation was extremely low. Electoral registration was never encouraged, and the literacy requirement effectively disenfranchised a significant proportion of the rural population, both men and women. Officially, over one-third of the population was illiterate; unofficially, an even higher proportion of the population was functionally illiterate, and illiteracy rates in Portugal were the highest in Europe.

Legal and administrative definitions of gender relations, then, prescribed a dominant role for men both in the household and in the larger community. These state prescriptions, however, bore little resemblance to the local gender ideologies and actual household relations in Vila Chã that we have described in earlier chapters. As we have seen, maritime women owned property, made independent household economic decisions, and did not defer to a concept of paternal authority in the family. In order to understand this divergence, we need to understand the relationship of rural men and women to the state under Salazar.

Under the New State there was no effective way to communicate local parish needs to the government; instead, administrative decrees were instituted from above, and local bodies at the concelho (and not the parish) level enforced them; parish councils were dependent upon initiatives taken by the concelho administration. State administrative structures in the form of an elaborate bureaucracy permeated almost all areas of rural life in Portugal. Peasants were required to visit the town hall (Vila Chã residents going to the câmara in Vila do Conde) for marriage certificates, payment of local taxes, license applications, and payment of fines, and to fill out the myriad "papers" that a Portuguese citizen was required to have. The list of licenses required was endless—licenses were required for everything from owning a radio to repairing a house—and no Portuguese could avoid the process of petitioning for licenses or paying fines when caught without the proper license (Riegelhaupt 1979).

The response of rural men and women to the overpowering presence of the state in their daily lives and their powerlessness to influence state policy was to avoid contact with the state and its representatives as much as possible, and to restrict social and economic transactions to the level of the household and hamlet. They labeled all people with whom they did not have face-to-face dealings as "Them" (*Eles*), not to be trusted—indeed, to be avoided; among "Eles" were those who represented or had access to the state system (Riegelhaupt 1979). This local strategy aided rural communities in resisting the cultural hegemony of the state and enabled them to maintain their own systems of social interaction, including gender relations.

Resistance to the pervasiveness of the state in everyday life was played out on the local stage in the context of local systems of social stratification, and in Vila Chã through the oppositional culture created by the pescadores. Resistance was the strategy of the landless class within rural communities and was an extension of their antagonistic relations with local landowners, whose interests they rightly saw as protected by the New State. Local landowners—the lavradores of Vila

Chã—were seen by the pescadores to be closely allied with the state. Lavradores dominated the parish council and had close relations with the priest, who, until 1974, effectively controlled the council. The representatives of the state at the local level—the *regedor* (a kind of parish administrator) and the secret police (P.I.D.E.) officer, for example— were both appointed officials of the New State and were both prosperous local lavradores.[21] Furthermore, lavradores chose to emphasize the coincidence of their interests with those of the state by modeling their social relations as closely as possible on state ideals and by thereby serving as local representatives of these ideals. Gender roles and relations served as a metaphor for the divergent social and economic interests present in local communities, and were a focal point of the counter-hegemonic cultures of resistance the poor constructed against the power of the local landed elite. Landowning households aspired to reproduce the gender relations prescribed by the New State in order to legitimate their elite status; the landless and land-poor, however, negotiated gender relations on the basis of their experience of everyday life. The result was that gender relations among the land-poor bore little resemblance to state prescriptions. In Vila Chã, wealthier agricultural households were male-headed, men had decision-making authority over agricultural work, and wives did not engage in productive work outside the home. In maritime households, women, as we have seen, could not be said to defer to their husbands in economic matters, nor was the husband viewed as the household head.

Vila Chã maritime women and men resisted state control over family and household life in the context of a local struggle, the antagonistic relations between landed and landless, between lavrador and pescador. They also mobilized a long tradition of "popular anticlericalism" to undermine the influence of the Roman Catholic church in the life of family and household, and in the determination of gender relations.[22]

Church and state had been officially separated in 1910 under the First Republic but were united again under the New State, and the Concordat of 1940 reestablished the Catholic church as the most important national institution at the local level. The Concordat reaffirmed that only a Catholic marriage was legal and that divorce was illegal, and granted the church full control over education in the country. Through its teachings the church inculcated the values of discipline, humility, sacrifice, and the acceptance of authority in the Portuguese population, and endorsed the state's image of the family as based upon paternal authority.

During the New State the central conflict between the people and the church involved the people's view that religious ritual was communal ritual, set against the church's teaching that the goal of religion was personal salvation (Riegelhaupt 1973). In the people's view, religion defined community in a society that was otherwise fragmented and characterized by competition between households, and where balanced reciprocity and avoidance were the primary mechanisms for reducing conflict and hostility. Community festas with fireworks, dancing, and processions were, in the people's view, synonymous with religious practices and took place in the context of the intense rivalries that existed between neighboring hamlets and parishes. For the priest, however, religious practice was ritual that took place within the church and that he controlled.

Thus, under the New State, parish priests in Vila Chã and elsewhere actively tried to discourage festas and to encourage worship inside the church. Following directives from the national church, they also endorsed pilgrimages to supralocal, national shrines—especially to Fátima, but also to other regional shrines—a strategy that undermined community festas and encouraged people to view religion as an individual endeavor that takes place under the guidance of priests and within the bounds of churches (Riegelhaupt 1984). In Vila Chã in the post-Salazar period, such festas are fondly remembered more than they are actively celebrated. The festas celebrated by the greatest number of people in Vila Chã are the state-sponsored festa of São João in Vila do Conde, the festa of Fátima in the parish on the eve of the twelfth of May, and the processions and celebrations associated with the children's First Communion. The rivalries between hamlets, especially between the coastal hamlets of Facho and Praia and the interior hamlets where the lavradores live, now take the form of competition among women to create the most beautiful carpet of flower petals (*tapete*) along the route the procession is to follow. Other unauthorized festas such as São Martinho, São Pedro, Carnaval, and the parish's own São João festa are today halfheartedly acknowledged by a few but clearly were much more extensively celebrated in the not-too-distant past. All Saints' Day (Todos os Santos), however, continues to be one of the most important events in the ritual calendar in Vila Chã—and the most cherished moment takes place outside the church when, unauthorized by the priest, men, women, and children visit the graves of dead family members in the cemetery.[23]

The persistence of anticlericalism in Vila Chã is, however, particularly evident in the manner in which local residents disregard church prescriptions for gender relations, and in the way women appropriate the Virgin Mary for their own. Here we are concerned more with the land-poor maritime members of the parish than with the wealthier landowning households, among whom church prescriptions tend to be more respected as ideals. Maritime women are aware, for example, that the model of marriage held by the Catholic church prescribes the obedience and submission of wives and upholds the authority of husbands. At the marriage service, the priest counsels women that it is their wifely duty to serve (servir) their husbands. But the maritime household—past and present—depends upon the managerial role of women, a role that both husband and wife accept, and there is little that is servile in the way that a wife interacts with her husband.

In rural Portuguese society, as in much of Western Europe, religion is considered the woman's domain.[24] In Vila Chã, women participate in and give meaning to religious activity as an extension of their role as managers of the household. That is, they manage not only the economic affairs but also the spiritual life of the household, including the masses for the dead, the children's religious education, and the negotiations ("petition prayers" or promessas—literally, "promises" or "pledges") with important divine figures (cf. Christian 1989:119, 134). Their fundamental concerns are the prosperity and status of their households within the larger community, the health and well-being of family members (including the souls of dead family members), and the problems of being a woman. The women are active in constructing religious experience to meet their own needs, and the women's view of the role of religion in their lives does not coincide with the goals of the parish priest.

Vila Chã women, nonetheless, are faithful in their attendance at mass and consider themselves to be deeply religious even though they differ from the church in their views on the nature of marriage and the structure of the household. The women explain that their apparent piety stems not from respect for the teachings of the church as presented by the parish priest but rather from the personal relationship each woman has with God, the Virgin (Nossa Senhora), and one or more healing saints. The women explain that they could not have suffered all the hardships of their lives if they had not had this divine help. Further, the women express a strong antipathy for the priest. "We do not need him. We need Him," they say.

Vila Chã women are devoted to the Virgin. During the month of May a prayer service devoted to worship of the Virgin is held each night in the parish church, and maritime women are faithful attenders. On the night of the twelfth of May, the image of Nossa Senhora de Fátima is taken out of the church by the people and carried through the parish along the colorful and fragrant flower tapetes prepared by the women. A crowd of women, men, and children falls in behind the image and, carrying lighted candles and singing, follows the image back to the church. The priest does not accompany the procession but waits in the church to lead a prayer service when the saint's image is returned—by which time most people have left the procession and made their way home. The festival is entirely organized by the parishioners, who want to bring the Virgin into their community, and the procession is disapproved of by the priest, who wishes to localize religious behavior inside the church under his control and authority. In this way, although the festa of Fátima was introduced to the parish and encouraged by the church as a way of detracting from other festas that celebrated communal identity, the people have appropriated the visible and, in their view, most important, part of the festa for their own purposes. Bringing the image of Nossa Senhora de Fátima out of the church and carrying it past their homes and along their streets, the people are acting to ensure that their households and community are renewed and blessed. A relatively new and church-authorized festa is being put to old communal purposes by the people.

The devotion of the women to Nossa Senhora also represents a different understanding of the meaning of Mary from that held by the Catholic church and taught by the parish priest. The church employs the image of the Virgin to sacralize the reconciliation of the contradictory values of virginity and maternity, to conflate sexuality and fertility. Clergy maintain that these are the values women respect when they worship Mary. The women of Vila Chã, however, do not identify the Virgin with virginity and maternity. Instead, they see her as a womanly friend, as a woman who understands women's experience. She is both divine and human. They turn to Nossa Senhora for assistance, advice, and consolation in meeting the trials of daily life, especially those concerning the health and material well-being of the household—hunger, debt, poverty, illness, marital unhappiness. Prayers to her are concerned with everyday problems and as such are like conversations. Vila Chã women turn to Nossa Senhora for comfort in times of infant death, and unhappily married women are even said to pray to her for the death of their husbands. Many Vila Chã women make an annual pilgrimage to the national shrine at Fátima, where they fulfill their promessas and make votive offerings to thank the Virgin for her assistance.

Lisón-Tolosana's observations on Marian devotion in Spain may also be applied to Portugal: "The emphasis that has been repeatedly put on the relationship between religion and sexuality, especially virginity . . . isolates perhaps only one of the ingredients of the Marian devotion and probably not the most important. . . . The cult and devotion to our Lady constitutes one of the essential characteristics of popular religiosity. It is both a result of Catholic teaching, and a projection of social feminine values, values which are not necessarily linked with the theme of virginity" (1983:306–309). Lisón-Tolosana describes the number and variety of Marian images and invocations and discovers that none of them has to do with virginity. Instead, they are all reflections of a woman's role in the household. "The Marian cult is characterized by the projection of woman's state to Mary as Mother of God; it is not to God, not to the Holy Sacrament to whom they resort most frequently in their needs, when their husbands or children fall ill or in any emergency whatsoever." It is to Mary they turn. "They turn to Mary as woman to Woman" (308).[25]

Thus, while the parish priest and the Catholic church conceive of the Virgin as representing maternity and the denial of female sexuality, Vila Chã women see Mary as a friend who understands the trials of being a woman. The priest can have little control over the form that individual devotions and promessas take, and, in Vila Chã, it is women who define the nature and basis of their relationship with the Virgin. In this way, they construct the meaning of their religious experience.

State and church definitions of gender during the New State were directed toward defining relations between men and women within marriage. Under the Civil Code, the husband was the head of the household, and a wife was her husband's legal dependent. In the Portuguese Roman Catholic church, the family was defined as based upon paternal authority, and a wife's duty was to serve her husband. The maritime women and men of Vila Chã, although aware of state and church definitions of gender, negotiated gender relations on their own terms and in the context of relations of production in the maritime household. They employed a strategy of avoidance to resist state intervention in household affairs, including gender relations, and they mobilized a strong tradition of anticlericalism to impede the realization of church doctrine in local gender relations. The Vila Chã maritime woman found her gender identity in her role in the household's economic production, and she employed her religious experience—especially her profound relationship with the Virgin—to meet individual and household needs associated with that role.

CLASS AND GENDER: WOMEN DIVIDED

Social stratification in Vila Chã divided parish women. It also created the conditions that gave rise to the fragmented consciousness of maritime women: on the one hand, maritime women were proud to identify themselves as workers, trabalhadeiras; on the other hand, they knew their productive work denoted their membership in the lowest social class of the parish.[26]

In earlier chapters we have described how lavradores and pescadores expressed their antagonistic social and economic interests in the parish through their different centers of residence, different strategies for marriage, and different household structures, and how differences in the gendered division of labor reinforced the division between agricultural and maritime households. Maritime women and men mobilized their gender system in their creation of a culture of opposition, part of a general resistance to the power and status of local lavradores in parish life. Once again, gender is a metaphor for the expression and negotiation of other social relationships and other levels of identity (cf. Herzfeld 1986). Whereas lavradores were proud to assert that women in their households did not have to work in the fields, pescadores were proud to validate maritime women's identity as industrious and productive workers responsible for the economic well-being of the household.

In the gendered division of labor in the maritime household, women worked outside the home in economic production, and they were managers (governadoras) in their households. They moved freely about the parish, barefoot and in ragged work skirts, as they sold their fish and seaweed, or sold their labor as agricultural day workers. They worked side-by-side with men in the fields, on the beach, or at sea. Their productive work left them with few hours each day within the walls of their houses; they returned home only to sleep and eat.

By contrast, the wives of wealthy lavradores never performed manual labor in the fields and would never want to be seen in public in work clothes. They did not move about the parish because, unlike the fisherwomen, they had no work requiring them to do so. And they did not manage the economic resources of the household. In the wealthiest lavrador households, the husband ruled (mandava); the wife was a dona de casa (housewife) confined to the house, where she supervised domestic servants and passed her time with crochet or embroidery (Lino Netto 1949:60; Brochado de Almeida 1983:12).

Pina-Cabral (1986:83ff.) has described the gendered division of labor in Paço and Couto, two agricultural parishes in the interior Alto Minho; the description resembles the ideal held by lavradores in Vila Chã and contrasts with the division of labor in the maritime households. In the Alto Minho households, men look after the cattle and the *produtos do ar* (literally, "products of the air"): the fruit trees, the vines, the olive trees, and the pine woods. And men undertake any business external to the household, such as bureaucratic tasks and wage employment. Women are concerned with the *produtos da terra* (things that grow in or near the soil), the maize, beans, potatoes, pumpkins, the kitchen garden, and the pigs and poultry; and women devote the greater part of their time to housekeeping—to being donas de casa. Women are thought to be more rooted in the ground and the home and therefore less mobile; jobs that involve leaving the home are allocated to men. Because men traditionally have controlled the products destined for the market and men have emigrated to earn wages, men have had greater control over the sources of cash income to the agricultural household. The division of labor in these households clearly contrasts with that in maritime households, where women traditionally have controlled the main sources of cash—the sale of fish and seaweed fertilizer—and where new wage employment opportunities in factories are opportunities for women. In agricultural households, it is understood that men should be household heads and should have more power and authority than women. When, in practice, agricultural women often do have real power, this contradiction with the ideal is, according to Pina-Cabral, a source of conflict that is experienced profoundly and generates a high level of hostility between men and women within the household. He writes: "For the peasants of Minho, there is no doubt that women as a group are weak and impure. The fact that they hold so much power is . . . problematical" (1986:88).

The contradiction between real and ideal gender relations is less perceptible in the maritime households of Vila Chã, where women's social and economic power has been integrated into the prevailing gender ideology, an ideology that idealizes the partnership between men and women in marriage, and where the cultural construction of women as trabalhadeiras legitimates the power and autonomy of maritime women. The pescadores are able to construct a gender system that—in its recognition of women's power—clearly contrasts with that held by local agriculturalists because the agriculturalists consider the pescadores their social inferiors, and because the pescadores perceive themselves to be living in opposition to the lavradores.

The cultural legitimation of women's power in the maritime household has, however, a double edge: as it cuts for a woman, it also cuts against her. On the one hand, women within the maritime community are recognized to possess economic autonomy and decision-making authority; on the other hand, pescadores recognize that maritime women have this power because their households are among the poorest and have the lowest social status in the parish.

In the context of the local status system, then, a woman ideally centered her work in the home and was dependent upon her husband. Although, in practice, there were few agricultural households in Vila Chã wealthy enough to keep a woman in the home as a dona de casa, lavradores nonetheless endeavored to maintain their privileged status in the local social structure by conforming as much as possible to state and church prescriptions for gender relations, including the servile and subordinate role of the wife. Women who had to work outside the home in order to maintain it therefore received no social benefit from their work. For, in this context, to be a trabalhadeira was a stigma, an indicator of low socioeconomic status. The fisherwomen of Vila Chã chose to value positively their identity as trabalhadeiras, but they also valued positively the role of dona de casa—not because of its content (which restricted physical movement within the community and resulted in economic dependence upon husbands) but because, for them, it was associated with wealth and status. The positive evaluation of the dona de casa role introduced further contradictions to the experience of the women of maritime households, because male dominance within the household was ideologically coexistent with the dona de casa role for women. The positive evaluation by maritime women of the role of dona de casa holds contradictions that lead to even greater conflicts in the lives of maritime women's daughters who in the mid-1960s begin to enter the factories in the hopes of escaping both the poverty of their mother's lives and the stigma of being trabalhadeiras. The conflict between the trabalhadeira and the dona de casa roles for women is further discussed in chapter 7.

THE SOCIAL CONSTRUCTION OF GENDER IN VILA CHÃ

The social construction of gender is a historical process of giving cultural meaning to sex differences. It is the production of gender ideologies within particular social and economic contexts and cannot be divorced from the material conditions of a particular place and time. But gender ideologies are not mere epiphenomena of the material conditions in a society. On the one hand, ideological construction is bounded by material conditions in society; on the other hand, ideology possesses a "relative autonomy" within those limits, and the historical process of constructing meaning is a process of negotiation and often selective manipulation by individuals and groups. Women and men often maintain definitions and perceptions of social reality that are distinct from ideologies forged by local power structures, and women's implicit ideologies often differ from men's (D. Dwyer 1978). Through their behavior, women and men interpret, modify, and construct ideology.[27]

In this chapter we have found that gender is actively constructed at different levels and that layered systems of meaning operate. We have found that individuals negotiate their gender identity through manipulation and reinterpretation of varied, and often contradictory, gender ideologies according to their own experiences and socioeconomic conditions. When we look at different levels of gender construction, we see how the anthropological code of honor and shame is a representation of official gender ideals, those propagated by state and church and upheld by the landed and powerful social classes, but that this code is not an accurate representation of the gender systems operative among the landless and powerless of rural Portugal—in our case, the pescadores of the rural parish of Vila Chã. Among the pescadores, women are valued for their industriousness, thriftiness, and management capacities and are rarely regarded solely in terms of their roles in human reproduction or their social roles as wives and mothers. Work (trabalho) is primary in the social construction of maritime women, and partnership—not hierarchy—is the ideal in conjugal relations. At the same time, shame (vergonha) is also important. But, contrary to the code of honor and shame, vergonha is a resource that women manage, not one that men control. Vergonha is a construct that originates not in a perception of female sexuality as evil and rapacious, but in local recognition of the desirability of controlling fertility. Where anthropologists have tended to conflate sexuality and fertility, residents of Vila Chã have not. The tension between fertility and sexuality was also the root of a contradiction that women were able to manipulate: women's fertility needed to be controlled, and this was achieved partly through the valuation of vergonha. But women's fertility was also recognized as a source of power for women. Women's power, then, was legitimated in the trabalhadeira ideal and through local recognition of women's roles in both economic production and human reproduction. The term *trabalhadeira*, however, also connoted the maritime woman's low social status, and women's awareness of the stigma created for them a fragmented consciousness, a locus of conflict that became a motor for change in local gender roles and ideals in the post-1960 period of economic development.

Honor and shame, a gender system that defines women in terms of their sexuality and in a context of male prestige, cannot, then, be invoked as the gender system of the pescadores of Vila Chã. In this chapter, we have analyzed gender as a layered system of meaning, and we have examined gender relations from a women's point of view. The inappropriateness of honor and shame as a model of gender relations in the Vila Chã case makes one wonder how valid it is as a model of gender relations elsewhere in Mediterranean or Southern Europe. Nonetheless, the social construction of the region's women in terms of their sexuality continues to dominate the anthropological literature (Brandes 1981; Gilmore 1985; Giovannini 1981; Schneider 1971). I suggest, as O'Brien (1984) does for another part of the world, that the ethnography of the Mediterranean area has emphasized women's roles in human reproduction and ignored women's economic roles, and that this portrait derives from the androcentric bias of anthropologists and their categories—not from the social reality. As we have seen, an emphasis on women's sexuality fails to represent the way Vila Chã maritime women (and even men) perceive their gender roles and relations.

In the next chapter we find that a system of social control more powerful than honor and shame is in operation in Vila Chã, and that it is less directed to controlling women's sexuality than it is to monitoring women's economic production and relative social and economic success. Moreover, this system of social control, inveja, is enforced more by women than it is by men.

Chapter 6

INVEJA: WOMEN DIVIDED?

STORY OF AN EMIGRANT'S WIFE: LAURA

Sou a comandante da família.
(I am the commander of the family.)

"I WAS BORN in Rio da Gândara in 1928, the youngest of nine children. My parents had married in 1917 and my mother had had the children one after another. Four children died as infants, so I was raised as one of three daughters and two sons. My father was a boat builder. He had learned the trade as a boy working with my mother's father who was one of the few carpenters in the parish who built the small boats used in sardine and pilado fishing. My father also owned two boats of his own and went fishing when there was no work boat building.

"My mother worked in the fields. From her parents she had inherited a small field and, over time, she managed to buy another and to rent a third. As well, she looked after the garden at the house in Rio da Gândara that she and my father rented and eventually bought. She did not work on the seaweed because she had too much agricultural work to do. But when my father fished she would come down to the beach to unload the boat, sell the fish, and clean the nets and spread them to dry on the beach.

"My mother's mother was the daughter of a lavrador, but he was only a small lavrador and poor. Only the child who inherited the casa could be considered a lavrador; the others became pobres. They might inherit a small field or sum of money, but they would probably have to emigrate or take up fishing and marry a pobre.

"My father's father was a lavrador-pescador. He owned and cultivated fields, and he owned two fishing boats and fished for pilado and for fresh fish. My father's mother was also the daughter of a small lavrador-pescador. For her dote she inherited her father's casa do mar, the small stone hut on the beach that each household owned for storage of their nets and boats, and dried seaweed and pilado. That casa do mar became my dote from my parents.

"I left school when I was nine years old in the middle of grade 3. My brothers had finished the fourth grade, which at that time was considered finishing school. People thought it was more important for boys than for girls. My brothers worked with my father in the boat-building trade before they emigrated to Angola. At nine years old I began to accompany my aunt and my sisters on their rounds buying sardines from the Vila Chã fishing boats and carrying them in trays on our heads to sell in Gião, a parish a few kilometers away. I also began to harvest seaweed with the other women each summer. I helped my mother with the agricultural work and fed the cows and the pig we kept. I went on expeditions with the other women into the nearby forests to collect firewood. This was my work until I married.

"I began to namorar when I was eighteen. We met boys at mass on Saturdays and Sundays or at the evening prayers during May, the month of Nossa Senhora de Fátima, or the daily prayers during Lent. We would talk to each other, and sometimes the boy would continue to talk with us and sometimes he would disappear, never to be heard from again! It was like this [singing]:

> Vamos à feira
> ver o que vai.
> Porcos e homens
> é o que sai!
>
> Let's go to the market
> to see what's going on.
> Pigs and men—
> that's what's we find!

"I was free to namorar and marry whom I pleased. My parents didn't interfere. Parents might say that so-and-so (*fulano*) was from a 'weak family' (*fraca família*)—meaning that they were lazy or drunkards—and they would try to discourage a daughter or son from marrying into such a family, but generally *o pobre era pobre; era como um cão* (a poor person was poor; s/he was like a dog). Only the lavradores tried to arrange marriages to join their lands (*juntar terra*). There was one lavrador who, in order to join lands, married all his daughters to men who were ten years older than they were. He even married one daughter when she *ainda não era mulher* (was not yet a woman [i.e., premenstrual]).

"I began to namorar with my husband when I was eighteen. I danced with others and used to enjoy a good time at the festas, but I never had another sweetheart (namorado). It was always him. I knew him because he fished for my father. He had no father of his own. Although his mother was a hard worker, often she could not feed the children, and they had to beg for food to eat. The neighbors always found some food to give him because he had no father. At age eleven he and his sister started fishing as crew for my father. We became namorados when we were both eighteen and we married in 1951 when we were almost twenty-three. He was a pobre but then so was I. But he was a hard worker, determined not to remain poor. And he was very handsome!

"In my day, weddings were not like they are today—*tudo luxo* (all luxury). We went on foot. Everyone did. To the church. João, his mother and grandmother. I with my father and mother. We returned to my parents' house. There were more people there—brothers and sisters—a few cakes, wine, and that was it! Not like today. Today the pescadores spend more than the lavradores on weddings. They spend a fortune on the festa and the gown and the photographs. Some of them even have the wedding feast in a restaurant in town.

"We married in March 1951. We lived with my parents after we married, and João fished that summer with my father. I sold the fish they brought in and I harvested seaweed. In November João went to Brazil. He was young and there were no fish here. He thought he could make a better life for us there. He went alone but there were other Vila Chã fishermen there. Many went to Brazil in those days. There were very few fishermen left here in the 1950s. They went to Brazil to earn money fishing there so they could buy their own boats here in Vila Chã—so they could be donos (owners). Before, there used to be donos and *camaradas* (crew) and the donos took a larger share of the fish.

"Our first child, a daughter, was born in December but she died when she was ten months old. My husband never saw her.

"I did not see João for three years, during which time I stayed with my parents and continued to work on the seaweed and to sell fish in Gião. In 1955 João's sister wanted to go to Brazil to find her husband and I decided to go with her. We went by ship.

"I joined João and we lived together in Rio de Janeiro for almost seven years. João was a fisherman there and I was a dona de casa. We lived in a Portuguese community near Rio but not with people from Vila Chã. We thought we were going to make our life there forever. There my son was born and then my daughter. I was pregnant again when I got sick. It was colitis. I was so sick I thought I was going to die, and I didn't want to die in Brazil. I wanted to die at home. So, we all returned to Vila Chã. It was in 1962. My son was born a week later. But I didn't die. I recovered. At first we lived with my parents in Rio da Gândara, but then we moved down to the casa do mar that I had inherited from my mother. I couldn't always be going back and forth from Rio da Gândara to the beach. João was fishing and I was helping him, unloading the boat and selling the fish, and I was working on the seaweed (*ajudava na praia e andava na sargaço*).

"We had three more children. One daughter died when just fifteen days old. But still we had five growing children to raise. Fishing in Vila

Chã could not support us. Life was *uma miséria* at that time. There was much hunger (*muita fome*) and João resolved again to emigrate in search of a better future for the family. He first went to France but returned after less than a year. Another man from Vila Chã was going to Mozambique and João decided to go with him. It was 1969. In Mozambique he worked for a while in construction but he didn't like it. Then, already forty years old, he resolved to return to school to complete grade 4 and to join the merchant marine. This he did and he has been working on cargo ships ever since, sailing throughout the world.

"When João went to Mozambique in 1969, I stayed behind in the casa do mar on the beach with the five children. The house was not like it is today. It was just a hut (barraca) that had been used to store dried seaweed and fishing gear. I cooked on an open hearth. There was no bathroom. I slept with the smaller children in one bed and the bigger children slept together in another bed. João sent money home and I, with the help of the children, harvested and sold seaweed and kept a vegetable garden. We lived that way until 1973, when my husband said that he wanted to move the whole family down to Mozambique. He felt that his children didn't know him, that they didn't love him. He couldn't afford to fly home very often to see them. They were all studying then and he thought they could have a better life in Mozambique. It's hard for fathers to be away from their children. *Têm muitos saudades* (They are very homesick). So, I and the five children, then ages five to seventeen, flew to Mozambique.

"I loved Mozambique. I was amazed at the Portuguese there. They were more human (*Fiquei admirada com os portugueses lá. Eram mais humanos*). I was surprised at how different the ambience was there among the Portuguese. In Brazil it hadn't been so different. But in Mozambique the people were much more *humanos* than they are in Vila Chã. There wasn't the inveja. There's so much inveja here. People helped each other. They talked to one another even when they didn't know each other. I used to meet people in the line for rationed food and they would say, 'You know where you can get carrots cheap?' or potatoes? or sugar? Instead of keeping the information to themselves, they would tell each other, help each other. In Vila Chã people try to get all for themselves so that others will have none.

"In Mozambique my life was the same as it is here. *Sou a comandante da família* (I am the commander of the household). My husband earned the money and I managed it. The job of the husband is to give the money to his wife (*entregar o dinheiro à mulher*). My husband hands the money over to me and I do the shopping, cooking, and washing—I manage the life of the household (*fazer a vida em casa*).

"I liked it better in Mozambique—the ambience. This is why I'm encouraging my niece to leave Vila Chã, to go to the United States. Her husband has a contract to fish for a company there. She's miserable here. She's sick with *nervos e barriga* ('nerves' and stomach problems). She's very like me in that the same things upset her in the same way and she has the same health problems. She'll be happier and she'll have a better life if she goes away.

"It's the atmosphere of inveja that's so hard for her here. And for me. Here, I don't know why, people are full of inveja of me. I don't have inveja of anyone but people have of me. I don't know why. Perhaps it's because I put my children to study, I don't know. But when I walk down the street people don't even say *'Bom dia'* or *'Boa tarde.'* So why bother going down to the beach or even out in the street when people are so invejosos and only want ill to happen to you? People say things deliberately to upset you, and afterward you become sick with nervos and things go 'round and 'round in your head and you have nightmares. Better to stay at home with my family and to make our lives. It's tiring to have people always saying mean things about one another and wishing one another ill and criticizing one another. It gives a person nervos, and then you can't sleep and you get sick.

"People have inveja of me because I put my children to study, but we made many sacrifices for this. This is what my husband wanted for his children and why we have worked so hard and why he has been away so much. We have never exploited our children (*não os explorámos*). Our children can do what they want with their education and the money they earn because of it. But these people put their daughters in factories when they're only fourteen years old. Is that not exploiting them? And women say to me: 'My son doesn't need to study. He's working.' He's working but he's ignorant. These people are even worse when they get a little money. They have a nice house and good clothes, but they are stupid and ignorant. In the old days people didn't send their daughters to study because they felt they didn't need it as much. My brothers finished the fourth grade, but no one felt that we daughters had to. But I think that daughters should be educated as well as sons. I am illiterate (*analfabeta*), but I know that knowledge is not a burden (*o saber não pesa*), that education is valuable, that it means rising out of ignorance. And I know that many parents here exploit their children.

"We lived in Mozambique for only fifteen months. We arrived in 1973, but by 1974 the War for Independence was sending many Portuguese home. João was worried about our safety, so we all, except him, flew home to Portugal again in 1974. And that was no joke (*Não era brincadeira*). It cost a lot of money. João didn't return to Portugal until 1976. He stayed there working on the ships. When he returned, he arranged work on Portuguese cargo ships and has been working on ships ever since. He is away from Vila Chã on voyages for months at a time. But he has his own fishing boat and motor and nets here in Vila Chã, and he fishes when he is home on holidays.

"Returning to Vila Chã was difficult for me. Life here was not as it was in Mozambique. There we had a flat, but here we had only the barraca on the beach with no modern conveniences and no space. My son found it hard to study. In Mozambique we had a flat. Here we had nothing. We started over again. We lived in that barraca for almost ten years. Eventually we bought a small piece of land and built this new home, but it's not all paid for. We moved here just two years ago. My husband earns well and we live well, but we have many expenses. Life is very expensive these days. We are many at home, many to feed. And books and transportation to school are expensive. My husband earns well, but we never know when his next voyage will be or how much he'll earn. We live well but things are never certain.

"This is why I believe in God. Because one has to be very persistent (*teimosa*). One has to struggle, to continue, to never give up, to go forward and lift up one's head in order to make a living (*andar p'ra frente, levantar a cabeca, p'ra fazer a vida*). You can't stop for a minute. You have to keep on going always, keep on trying, keep on working for the future, and you need God's help. This is why I believe in God and why I go to mass. Not because I listen to the priest. We don't need him. We need Him."

Laura elaborates upon many of the themes Alvina discussed in chapter 2 and that we have described in earlier chapters. She describes relations between pescadores and lavradores and their impact on women's work and women's marriage opportunities. She describes the acquisition of property by women—her mother and herself—and the practice of uxorilocal residence after marriage and during the absence of emigrant husbands. She documents women's experience of emigration both as wives left behind to raise children and manage households on their own—like Maria in chapter 3—and as emigrants themselves accompanying their husbands and establishing households in faraway places, in Laura's case in the large cities of Brazil and Mozambique.

The life stories of Laura, Alvina, and Maria contribute importantly to our understanding of the processes involved in the social construction of gender and present women as actors in these processes. The stories open a window onto the terrain of women's consciousness and illustrate how women, through their behavior, construct their identity and their social world. The stories document how women negotiate their gender identity by manipulating the range of roles and tasks available to them. Both Maria and Alvina, for example, took up fishing, locally perceived to be a masculine occupation, and thereby negotiated for themselves a gender identity that was independent of their female sexuality and that accorded them the respeito (respect) and comradeship of men. And, as Alvina noted, "There was more respeito on the sea than there was on the land."

Laura also identifies herself in terms of her work and her role in the household economy, but her work is located more in the context of home and family. She describes herself as a dona de casa, but she, like other women of her generation, defines a dona de casa within the context of the cultural role of trabalhadeira. In this context the work of the dona de casa is that of household manager, or "comandante," as Laura puts it, implying a position of decision-making authority and autonomy. Laura's work as a dona de casa includes subsistence and commodity production but also management of the consumption of her emigrant husband's wage. Like Alvina, who says, "A good husband is a gentleman who earns and gives the money to his wife; a good wife is a good manager of the household—tidy, thrifty, and industrious," Laura says, "The job of a husband is to give the money to his wife." His job is to earn the money; hers is to manage it. Laura chooses to interpret this as an equitable division of labor and not to recognize her economic dependence on her husband. She defines herself as the "comandante da família," affirming that her husband works for her and the household. She uses to her advantage the model of women's traditional role in maritime households to define her status as an emigrant's wife. She is able to define her role and her identity in this way in part because the absence of her husband requires that she single-handedly make decisions and manage the household, but also because this perception of herself and of her role is an extension, under changed circumstances, of the women-centered character of households and of the trabalhadeira role to which she was raised.

Married women like Alvina and Laura manipulate the gendered division of labor in the negotiation of their conjugal relations and their gender identity. And the ways that the women define their roles as wives illustrate how gender relations are negotiated relations and are never static or unilateral.

INVEJA

Laura's story also introduces us to, and highlights, the role that inveja plays in Vila Chã women's lives. *Inveja* translates literally as "envy," but this is only one meaning of the term. *Inveja* also refers to "harm caused by envy" and incorporates a wide range of behavior, including gossip (*falar mal* or *má língua*), sorcery (*feitiço*), and the evil eye (*mau olhado*). And, according to Pina-Cabral (1986:176), in northwestern Portugal inveja is not only an emotion—the emotion of envy—it is a principle of evil.

Laura is the object of inveja because her household is supported through the wages of her emigrant husband, and because she herself emigrated and lived outside Vila Chã for seven years in Brazil with her husband and children and for a shorter time in Mozambique. The emigration experience removed Laura and her husband from the local social and economic constraints on maritime households, and it showed them the necessity and benefits of education for mobility in the larger world. Their respect for the value of education is uncommon in contemporary Vila Chã, where most parents are anxious to send their children to work for wages for the household as soon as they complete the now-compulsory six years of primary schooling.

The education achieved by her children is indeed extraordinary in Vila Chã. Laura's eldest son is a doctor in the parish, and his success and superior social position constitute the single most important reason for her neighbors' inveja. When people in Vila Chã talk about Laura, they inevitably preface their remarks with "Laura, the one whose son is a doctor . . ." The doctor, his wife, and their small daughter live in an apartment that Laura and her husband built in the basement of their new house to provide a place for their children to live when they first marry, and until they can buy or build houses of their own. Laura's daughter-in-law commutes into Porto, where she is studying languages at the university, and Laura cares for her granddaughter during the day. Laura's eldest daughter completed high school and now works at Texas Instruments. Her second son works in a plastics factory and is finishing his high school courses at night. Her third son is studying computer science at the university in Porto and commutes there each day. And her youngest child, a daughter, is finishing high school in Vila do Conde and plans to study law. They all live at home. Laura prepares their meals, does their laundry, and budgets for their books and supplies, transportation, meals, and other school-related costs.

One reason that few parents encourage their children to continue in school is that after the sixth grade they must bus into Vila do Conde for junior and senior high school or take the train into Porto to attend the university. The costs of books, meals, and bus and train fares are all expenses that many households feel they are unable to sustain. But for Laura the education of her children is an expense she puts before all others. Budget management has assumed primary importance in the division of labor in Laura's household, and Laura affirms her role as manager—comandante—of the household's resources. Her husband is away at sea for long periods during the year. His wage is deposited monthly in a bank in Vila do Conde, and Laura controls its expenditure. Laura uses her husband's wage to meet the household's two major expenses—paying off and maintaining the new house, and educating the children—and she herself works to meet other household expenses. She keeps a large vegetable garden and chickens for household consumption, and she is a shrewd bargainer for fresh fish at low prices. Despite headaches, back problems, and colitis, she harvests and dries seaweed on the beach during the summer months. Her hands are never idle: when she is indoors on stormy winter days, she sews and knits clothing for her children. She washes clothes every morning in her washtub in the yard and irons daily in order to ensure that her childen are well dressed. And she has renovated the small house on the beach (the casa do mar that she inherited from her parents) to rent out to summer vacationers from the city at exorbitant monthly or weekly rates during the months of June, July, and August. Finally, she is extremely careful with all cash expenditures for the household and keeps a mental record of all moneys spent and accounts owing.

Laura is offended by her neighbors' inveja because it denies the sacrifices that she and her husband have made and the perseverance required of them in difficult times. She says that she and her husband escaped the poverty of their childhood only through hard work, discipline, and her skillful budgeting. Her neighbors' refusal to recognize her sacrifices and, indeed, their outright antagonism to her and her success are, she says, the cause of her illnesses, both psychological (nervos) and physical (colitis). Laura attributes the prevalence of illness among Vila Chã women to the pressures of their lives and to the social and economic constraints on them.

In Laura's case, inveja targets the emigrant experience and the education achieved by her children, but inveja is a dominant force in the lives of most Vila Chã residents and takes a variety of forms. The cases presented in the following paragraphs offer some additional examples of the contexts in which inveja is invoked.

Ana, a widow in her late sixties and a retired fisherwoman, explained that she has to be careful because her neighbors are *invejosas* (full of inveja). According to her definition, inveja is operating "when someone has something that you don't have and you want it. It's having *raiva* [literally, "hatred," but here derived from a combination of anger and envy] of people who can pay cash at the shop and don't have their names go down in the shopkeeper's book of accounts owing. It's having raiva of people who don't owe anything." She maintains that she has always paid cash, even during the sixteen years her husband was ill, when they were making frequent and expensive trips to doctors, *bruxos* (white witches, curers), and saints' shrines: "All the years of my husband's illness and we never borrowed a cent. We paid for everything and my neighbors had raiva of this. I never asked for anything from these people during all those years of sickness and we paid for everything, and I still work and save and pay cash for everything. Although I don't have raiva of anyone, no one likes me (*ninguém gosta de mim*)."

Ana feels that her neighbors wish her ill, and she takes measures to protect herself. Like many women, she wears a *figa* and a small horn on a chain around her neck, which she says are to protect her from the inveja, the evil eye (mau olhado), of her neighbors. The figa is an amulet in the form of a clenched fist with the thumb placed between the index and middle fingers. She also has a six-pointed star (*signo-salomão*) carved on her cement washtub. These are all ancient symbols that are held to have strength to ward off the evil eye (Elworthy 1895). She keeps a productive garden and is careful to protect her produce from the inveja of her neighbors. She piles dried brush on top of her garden wall so that people walking by on the road cannot see what she has in her garden and will not rob her or cause harm to her flowers and vegetables. When returning home from the garden, she carries her produce in a bucket that she covers with dark plastic or newspaper. She explains that she does this to prevent her neighbors from knowing what she has in her house. She takes the same care with purchases she makes in the shop.

Ana's neighbors are, indeed, critical of her and especially of her relentless pace of hard work and her independence and self-sufficiency. Although Ana's behavior might also be seen as that of a trabalhadeira par excellence—a sort of "culture hero"—her neighbors describe her as selfish (egoísta). As is often the case, each party sees the other as "full of inveja." In this sense, inveja describes—is a metaphor for—the character of relationships between households and is not simply an emotion of envy. Ana feels that her neighbors have inveja of her, but they, because she seems to have such control over her economic well-being, describe her as intensely invejosa, as "wanting everything for herself."[1]

Fátima, a young woman married for less than two years, says that her husband's sister (her *cunhada* or sister-in-law) has inveja of her and is trying to cause problems between her and her husband.[2] The sister-in-law does this by independently telling Fátima and her husband things that are untrue about one other, for example, that he is spending time with other women or that she has been seen with a man in town. Fátima and her husband fight, and only in the course of argument, after many hurtful things have been said, do they realize that the lies originated with the sister-in-law. By this time, they are mistrustful and angry with one another.

Fátima explained that her sister-in-law has inveja of them because they live on their own (in a house they rent from Fátima's mother), while the sister-in-law and her husband have to live with his parents, and also because Fátima's husband is doing well with his own small construction contracting business—well enough to hire his brother to work for him. On one occasion her husband was so anxiety-ridden about the unhappiness of their marriage and got "such a case of nervos" that he asked Fátima to go to the bruxo for a cure. The bruxo is a local man known for his "seeing" capacities and cures. When she went to see the bruxo, taking with her a piece of her husband's clothing, he told her that she and her husband were suffering from a bad case of inveja. He advised her, using holy water, to make the sign of the cross and say a blessing in each room of their house for five days. The cure seemed to work: her husband relaxed and relations between them improved. She, however, is avoiding any interaction with her sister-in-law. And, for protection from inveja, she wears around her neck a locket containing a picture of Nossa Senhora de Fátima.

Fátima says that inveja is a general problem in the community: "Sometimes when you're walking down the street you can just feel inveja all around you, and you arrive home full of nerves (*cheia de nervos*). You can't really be friendly with your neighbors. '*Bom dia*' or '*Boa tarde*' is enough to say when you pass them in the street because they smile to your face and cut you down behind your back. I can talk to no one here. I trust no one."

Carlos, a young fisherman, says that fishermen are especially invejosos: "They never want you to know how much fish they've brought in. They want to have the most fish. They always want to bring in more fish." He and his wife are experiencing financial difficulties. Their difficulties are due, he says, to his wife's prolonged illness (apparently related to her second cesarean section, which left her unable to bear more children). She requires frequent trips to doctors and expensive medications, and she is often unable to help him on the praia by unloading the boat and selling the fish as other wives do. Carlos also says he has poor luck (*sorte*) as a fisherman. He explained why he is not a successful fisherman:

> If I were more invejoso, perhaps I'd have been able to make a better life. If I'd pushed harder, been more invejoso, I might not be so poor. But I never worry about what the next person has got. I figure that what [fish] I catch is what God gives me, and that's good enough for me. Also I know that there are people in my own family who wish me ill, who don't want

me to do well in life, who want things to go badly for me. My wife went to a bruxo and took a piece of my clothing with her and told him that someone was making things go badly for us. The bruxo said it was true and he identified a couple in my own family—my brother and sister-in-law—but there is little we can do about it.

Laura's experience and these three additional examples of inveja have a number of common features. First, all concern a household's material well-being—the level of economic production of the household and its social status relative to other households in Praia and Facho. Ana's economic self-sufficiency and Laura's recently acquired economic resources, with which she has chosen to educate her children, make them feel themselves to be targets of inveja. Fátima, whose husband has started a small business of his own and who does not have to live with her in-laws or parents as most young couples must do, similarly feels that she and her husband are the objects of inveja because they are more economically independent than other young couples. And Carlos blames inveja for his inability to earn a living fishing. In the first three cases, the women consider that their relative material well-being makes them the target of inveja. In the last case, a man explains his economic misfortune as the result of inveja. Inveja, then, is experienced both by those who have and by those who have not. And, although it is more commonly experienced by and attributed to women, men can also experience inveja.

Second, household reproduction is also subject to inveja: marriages and children are targeted. Fátima feels that her sister-in-law is trying to introduce marital problems between her and her husband because of her inveja of them. Laura feels that others have inveja of her because her children are educated and well employed.

Third, inveja is seen as a cause of illness. Laura and Fátima talk of inveja's causing nervos. *Nervos* translates literally as "nerves" and refers to feelings of anxiety, frustration, anger, or a lack of power or control over one's life or over an immediate situation. It is believed that nervos also can lead to physical complaints and illnesses, especially high blood pressure, stomach ulcers, digestive problems, headaches, and insomnia. Nervos is, then, both a cultural metaphor for the expression of emotional distress and a description of real pain or sickness. Vila Chã residents clearly link their nervos to the stresses, both economic and social, of parish life. The experience of relative poverty and the perception of social inequality are identified as primary causes of nervos, or of the inveja that causes nervos.[3]

Fourth, people use amulets for protection from inveja and consult bruxos for advice and cures for inveja. *Bruxo* translates literally as "witch," but when Vila Chã residents speak of bruxos they are referring to white witches—specialists, male or female, who may be diviners, sorcerers, faith healers, mediums, exorcists, or even a certain type of priest. These are people "endowed with supernatural powers to annul the effects of antisocial forces and, at times, to counter-attack these" (Pina-Cabral 1986:189–190).[4] Although in special cases Vila Chã residents may travel some distance to consult a bruxo, they usually visit the local bruxo, the son of a pescador, a man they describe as "one who sees." They seek his aid especially to identify and discuss cases of nervos and inveja. For purely physical and medical ailments, nowadays, they consult doctors and pharmacists. In Vila Chã it is more commonly women, not men, who make the trip to the bruxo. Fátima's husband sent her to the bruxo for a cure for his nervos, and Carlos, the fisherman, sent his wife to the bruxo to find out who was causing their misfortune.

Finally, inveja can be experienced in a general form from all of one's neighbors, or it may be attributed to a particular individual or category of individuals. Fátima and Laura say one can "feel" the inveja in the street; Carlos and Fátima identify sisters-in-law as the sources of the inveja that is bringing economic or emotional distress into their lives.

Gossip, envy, and competition—the behavior inveja incorporates— were early recognized by anthropologists to be characteristic of the social relations of face-to-face societies (Colson 1953; Foster 1972; Gluckman 1963; Paine 1967; Radin 1927), including European peasantries (Bailey 1971; Campbell 1964; Cutileiro 1971; Dionisopoulos-Mass 1976; du Boulay 1974, 1976; Herzfeld 1981; Pina-Cabral 1986). Some of these explanations of inveja have focused on the evil eye, also known as the "envious eye," and attribute the evil eye to the emotion of envy (Elworthy 1895; Maloney 1976). These have tended to be symbolic, psychological, or psychoanalytic explanations (Dundes 1981; Foster 1965, 1972). Inveja, including the evil eye and gossip (má lingua, or "evil tongue") is also frequently interpreted as a form of social control (Cutileiro 1971; du Boulay 1976; Harding 1975, 1984). Herzfeld has recently written of the evil eye as a symbol for transgression of social boundaries and a form of insider-outsider discrimination ("kin" versus "friends") in an endogamous community in rural Greece. He argues that "indigenous concepts of inclusion and exclusion" are key to cross-cultural understanding of the meaning of the evil eye in diverse ethnographic contexts (1981:570). Du Boulay (1976), Spacks (1985), and Gluckman (1963) write of gossip as a means of establishing group membership and an important channel for the reaffirmation of shared values. Further, some anthropologists have argued that gossip represents women's "informal power" and women's "control of information"

(Friedl 1967; Harding 1975, 1984; Riegelhaupt 1967; S. Rogers 1975). This latter approach is, however, ultimately limited in explanatory power because it defines a separate sphere for women rather than integrating the analysis of women's relations with that of the social, economic, and political relations of the society as a whole.

Economic and political approaches to understanding the evil eye (and other forms of inveja) offer an alternative avenue to interpreting the meaning of inveja in Vila Chã. A cross-cultural survey of the occurrence of belief in the evil eye, based on a sample of 186 societies, found a close correlation between the presence of social inequality and the elaboration of the evil eye concept, and a close association between authoritarian states and belief in the evil eye (Roberts 1976). More recently, Galt (1982), writing of southern Italy, has argued that the evil eye is manipulated to control one's position in the local system of social stratification. And, writing of the peasants of interior northwestern Portugal, Pina-Cabral (1986:176ff.) argues that the concept of inveja is used to explain the existence of evil, in the form of misfortune and conflict caused by social inequality, in their society—a society that holds egalitarianism as an ideal. For the peasants of Alto Minho, inveja is an evil force and an unfortunate attribute of social relations. According to Pina-Cabral, inveja is related to awareness of differences in wealth and is "one of the central concepts of the peasant worldview" (176). Whereas the inveja of poor people manifests itself in their wanting what belongs to others, rich people are accused of "wanting everything for themselves," and thus of being envious.

In Vila Chã, inveja is a metaphor for the political nature of interhousehold relations; it is also a barometer of those relations. To understand the meaning of inveja, then, we need to take a diachronic or historical view of household relations. There is no doubt that, in a small face-to-face community like that of the pescadores of Vila Chã, competition is inevitable, and interhousehold relations have always contained ambivalence and some degree of tension. Like all social relations, however, they are subject to change. Interhousehold relations (and relations between women) have been, and are, undergoing change in the context of larger forces of social and economic change. Change, however, rarely occurs rapidly and instead comes about through a dialectical process: a contradiction is introduced; a struggle ensues to identify the contradiction; and a resolution is found, one that is itself transitory and subject to change. One force that has had a particular impact on the quality of interhousehold relations in Vila Chã is, as Laura has experienced, emigration—and emigration has been more important at some points in the parish's history than at others. A second force has been the increasing commoditization and industrialization of the post-

1960 period that is the subject of chapter 7. Although it is difficult to reconstruct historical emotions (cf. Behar and Frye 1988), it is probable that the intensity of inveja has waxed and waned in the context of changes in social and economic conditions.

In the 1980s, inveja was certainly pervasive in daily life and an important part of my own experience as a resident in Vila Chã. People frequently asserted to me, "We're all *como família* (like family) here." At the same time they reported to me countless experiences of inveja not unlike the four examples given above. It seems that the definition of who is família and who is not is a flexible one—expanding and contracting with the perception of the relative availability of social and economic resources. Família are people among whom resources are shared, and relations among família are relations of love and trust. By contrast, relations with people who are not família are based on competition and distrust. In Vila Chã, where households are women-centered, where patterns of uxorivicinality are strong, and where women control household resources, it is women who define the família. And, in the 1980s, they rather narrowly defined família as a constellation of consanguineally related women. Inveja was the metaphor by which they affirmed their trust of consanguineally related women and their distrust of other women.

In Vila Chã women are considered to be more invejosas than men, and women's inveja is considered to be more powerful than men's (cf. Cutileiro 1971; Pina-Cabral 1986). A Vila Chã man explained to me why this is so: "Women are the *contabilistas do lar* [literally, "accountants of the household"]. Women are more aware of the value of things than men are. Women are more aware of who's got what and of what they themselves haven't got. Whereas men's inveja concerns only themselves, women's inveja extends to a wider area and includes the household and the children. Women's inveja concerns every aspect of daily life."

Inveja, then, is a metaphor for talking about political relations within the community, especially relations among women. Inveja describes the opposition between households that perceive themselves to be competing for resources, both social and economic. Because it is women who are ultimately responsible for managing the household's resources in order to ensure its survival, inveja is a powerful presence, and a source of stress and illness, in the lives of women.

There is evidence, however, that in the not-too-distant past the character of interhousehold relations enabled women to define the boundaries of família more broadly, in a way that, at times, incorporated the entire community. The evidence suggests that increasing commoditization and industrialization have introduced new divisions and intensified competition among maritime women.[5] In this process, the opportunities for women to cooperate with one another and the possibilities for offering one another mutual aid have been undermined.

For example, women remember how, before the bakery was built in Rio da Gândara in the late 1960s, they used to share the *fermento* (leaven, fermenting dough). Each house had an open hearth and a bread oven, and women made their own bread. Half a dozen women, often neighbors, would rotate the fermento among them. Laura's daughter-in-law recalls how when her mother wanted to make bread she would ask the children, "*Onde está o fermento?*" (Where is the leaven?). And one or other would answer, "Está na casa da Ti' Laura ou Ti' Norte ou . . ." (It's in the house of Auntie Laura or Auntie "Norte" or . . .).[6] Her mother would go and get the fermento, make her dough, and set aside a portion of fermenting dough of the same size for a neighbor who would come to her—probably the next day—when she wanted to make bread. Through this network of interdependence and this independence from external bread production, each woman ensured as much as possible that there was bread for her household. By 1985, however, all women in Vila Chã were buying their bread, and they used their old wood-fueled ovens only to make bread for festas, especially at Easter, Christmas, and sometimes for weddings. The cooperative structure of bread making—this mechanism that enabled women to help one another—had fallen into disuse.

Another ritual by which maritime women supported one another and renewed their interdependence used to occur on the birth of a daughter but has also disappeared. Nowadays babies are born at hospitals in Vila do Conde or Porto, but when babies were born at home with the assistance of a local midwife (*parteira*—or curiosa, as Alvina calls her), they were immediately bathed. And, when the baby was a girl, the women of the community—kin and non-kin—would put their gold jewelry into the bathwater and wish the girl wealth during her life. In this way women affirmed their common identity (and that of the new female member of the community) as trabalhadeiras, responsible for the economic well-being of their households.

In the recent past, it would seem that ample opportunities for cooperation among women existed—at childbirth and with child care; in subsistence production, such as firewood collecting and seaweed harvesting; in times of illness; in widowhood; and so on. These were also opportunities to affirm the ties of shared experience that linked women. But, in 1985, almost the only time that these ties seemed to express themselves was at death, especially when a person died at home. Then, the women of the household prepared the body for visitation by other members of the community.[7] They would take turns grieving at the bedside of the deceased, and other women—kin and non-kin—would come and go, keeping them company during a vigil that usually lasted about twenty-four hours. At the end of this period, male relatives carried the coffin out of the house—to the intensified weeping of the women—and the men of the community accompanied the coffin through the streets of Facho and Praia to the church in the interior of the parish. The visiting women remained at the house with the grieving household women. It seems death is still a leveler in the maritime community.

In the post-1960 period relations among women (those who are not consanguineally related) tend to be stressful. Inveja is painfully experienced and women feel divided. Women see themselves as responsible for the economic well-being of their households and perceive themselves to be in direct competition with other women who hold this same responsibility for their own households. They experience and describe this competition as inveja, and they manipulate inveja in all its forms, ranging from gossip to the evil eye, in their negotiation for social and economic resources for their households. They engage in the politics of inveja in their role as producers and managers in the maritime household, and because of the political, social, and economic constraints to household production and reproduction in rural Portugal. The net effect of these constraints and the force that inveja holds in their daily lives is to divide women and to leave them with little possibility of offering each other mutual aid.[8] To ignore its political and economic basis, and to interpret inveja as women's "informal power" or women's "control of information" is to deny that these are stressful relations (Laura tells us they lead to real illness for women), and that they are detrimental to any collective organizing by women to bring about change in the social, economic, and political constraints in their lives. The need for solidarity among rural women becomes even more critical in the contemporary period, for women are finding themselves increasingly overworked, underremunerated, and isolated from one another. In the following chapter we examine the processes of social and economic change that have introduced new divisions among women, reduced the extent to which women share their daily experience, and thus further undermined the possibilities for women to help one another.

Chapter 7

FISHERWOMEN AND FACTORY WORKERS:
NEW WORK FOR WOMEN

THE NEW STATE's economic policy of constraining capitalism and controlling industrialization delayed the development of alternatives to household agriculture and fishing in northern rural Portugal, and, until the 1960s and 1970s, the only escape from rural poverty was emigration, both legal and illegal. Beginning in the 1960s, an almost unchecked proliferation of factories in rural areas occurred due to a combination of factors that included the economic and human drain of the Colonial Wars in Africa, the influx of entrepreneurial retornados from Mozambique and Angola, the investments of emigrants, the absolute poverty of the rural population and the clear need for new and local sources of household income, and the declining health and eventual demise of Prime Minister Salazar. The rapid industrialization of northwestern Portugal after 1960 has meant a relatively recent and radical immersion of rural households in a wage economy. Although, through emigration, these households have long been engaged in the international economy, the advent of factories in rural northwestern Portugal has required new structural changes in household and gender relations. The factories that were established in the coastal zone north of the city of Porto where Vila Chã is located are garment, food-processing, and electronics factories—transnational industries that, based on their international experience, employ a primarily female labor force and actively seek out rural populations throughout the world from which such a labor force can be extracted and poorly remunerated. Thus, it is not only the recent industrialization of rural areas but also the nature of the industries involved that has generated the impact on women and the household in rural northwestern Portugal.

The burgeoning of an anthropological and feminist literature on the experience of women and economic development in the 1970s offers one avenue to interpreting the experience of Vila Chã women after 1960, but it is only a partial interpretation. This literature began with Boserup's (1970) liberal argument that women need to be "integrated" into economic development and was advanced during the decade that followed through a socialist feminist critique of development itself. The feminist critique derives its impetus from the Marxist debate on the

international economy and the "underdevelopment" of the so-called
Third World but introduces a gender consciousness to the debate. The
essence of the critique is that as small-scale societies become engaged
in the international economy, and as economic production is removed
from the household, women lose economic autonomy and decision-
making authority over their time and labor (Beneria 1982; Beneria and
Sen 1981; Etienne and Leacock 1980; Fernández-Kelly 1983; Leacock
and Safa 1986; Mies 1986; Nash 1979; Young, Wolkowitz, and McCullagh 1981). Harris (1981:57) summarizes the argument and the general consensus of these anthropologists. The model targets the nature
and role of the household as the mediator of women's economic and
social authority: "As many studies have shown, shifts from household
production for subsistence to household-based petty-commodity production, to an economy based on the sale of labor-power, affect radi-
cally the structure of households, power relations within them and the
resulting changes in the power to command the fruits of one's own
labor."

Furthermore, depending upon the kind of development taking
place, the introduction of capitalist relations of production has been
understood either to remove women gradually from economic production and enable men to control new sources of cash income, or to util-
ize women as a pool of cheap labor as, for example, in the "Free Trade
Zones" of Southeast Asia (Ong 1987), the Mexico–United States frontier (Fernández-Kelly 1983), and, as we shall see, in northern coastal
Portugal.[1]

By the late 1980s, however, this now-voluminous literature on
women and development had itself become the subject of critique. The
new critique argues that this analytical framework constructs rural
women as "victims of development." It argues that the framework allows rural women neither a voice in the interpretation of the development process nor the possibility of constructing their own gender identity in terms that originate outside the frames of reference of feminist
scholars from advanced industrial societies (and often in terms that
may contradict the analytical constructions of those scholars; see
Behar 1990b; Phillips 1990; Mohanty 1984; Sen and Grown 1987).

In this chapter I interweave an analysis of women and economic
development in Vila Chã with an analysis that views the economic and
attendant changes from the perspective of Vila Chã women rooted in
their subjective experiences of local history, society, and culture.

VILA CHÃ

In 1966, 55.8 percent of households in Vila Chã had economies based
in agriculture and fishing. By 1973, this proportion had decreased to

38.1 percent, and in 1985 only 15.9 percent of households were engaged in agriculture and fishing. During this same period, the percentage of parish residents earning wages in skilled and unskilled work increased from 25.5 percent to 62.6 percent. Households based on wage employment have come to dominate the parish. The relatively recent dependence of Vila Chã households on permanent wage employment (as opposed to seasonal, periodic, or sporadic emigrant remittances), the engagement of women in factory work, and the resulting changes in household and gender relations are not atypical of the impact of economic development on rural women and communities throughout northwestern Portugal. In 1985, the women of the maritime households of Lugar da Praia and Lugar do Facho were employed in a variety of different kinds of work. Some women assisted their husbands in the fishery, others worked for wages in factories, and still others worked in the home as full-time housewives (donas de casa).

WOMEN IN THE FISHERY

In the post-1960 period, the maritime households of Vila Chã have become based upon diverse sources of income, and women's work now revolves around the management of these sources of income. In 1985, the term *maritime household* denoted those households that owned fishing boats and had at least one member who worked at least part-time in fishing. All of these households, however, had other sources of income in addition to their income from fishing. These included women's seaweed sales, rental income from summer vacationers, and wages earned by teenage sons and daughters.

Changes in women's work in maritime households followed the technological and organizational changes that took place in the Vila Chã fishery during the 1960s. These changes included the introduction of outboard motors, new types of nets and traps, and the dono system of partnership and boat ownership described in chapter 1. Women were less needed to work as crew on the boats, and it became rare for women to go to sea. By 1985, the gendered division of labor in the maritime household more closely resembled the dichotomization that Andersen and Wadel (1972) had described for maritime societies generally: men's work was on the sea; women's work was on land. Now when women describe their work they say, "*Ajudamos na praia*" (literally, "We assist on the beach")—meaning that they help their husbands with the work in the fishery. The retired skipper, Maria, laments that women no longer know what it means to be pescadeiras (fisherwomen). She says: "To be a pescadeira is to make decisions; to know where the fish are and to know how to get them. These women today don't know how to bring home a boatload of fish."

In 1985, women's primary tasks in the fishery were unloading the boats, selling the fish, and keeping the accounts. As women had done in the past, women keep the accounts of fish caught and sold each day; they pay for the gas and the maintenance of the household boat; they give their husbands money for beer and cigarettes; and they control all other household spending.

Although women continue to have responsibility for sale of the catch, there have been important changes in the way that women sell fish, especially with the intrusion of state control over fish marketing. When formerly women had auctioned the fish on the beach or carried the catch inland for sale to lavradores, women now sell fish in the state-run lota (fish auction). Built in 1970, the lota is a state mechanism for greater control over fish selling and over the taxation of maritime households. Under the original plan, a fisherman was to bring his fish to the lota, where a government employee would handle the sale of the fish, deduct 18 percent in taxes, and pay the fisherman his earnings at the end of the week or month. This is the system now (in 1985) in operation in neighboring Póvoa de Varzim. But Vila Chã women objected that this system ignores the fact that fish selling is women's work, and they have modified the lota system to meet their own ends. They insist on selling the fish themselves and on collecting the money from their buyers. The women say they do not trust the lota and that by selling the fish themselves they know exactly the value of their boat's catch and the value of their household's share. The lota employee is forced to follow the women around as they auction and weigh their fish, and he can only estimate the total value of their sales. Furthermore, in order to avoid paying taxes on all fish caught, the women always sell a part of the catch outside the lota, and it is impossible for the state employee to monitor the quantity of fish sold in this way. This is called the *fuga da lota* (flight from the lota), and regional fisheries authorities estimated that as much as 50 percent of the fish sold in Vila Chã is sold in this way. Finally, although state officials have tried to hire an employee of their own choosing to work in the lota, Vila Chã pescadores have demanded that they be empowered to select the employee. In the fifteen years since the lota opened, there have been three employees, and all have been sons of local pescadores. As one Vila Chã resident explained, the pescadores choose the lota employees based on their willingness to *fechar os olhos* (literally, "to close their eyes" or "to wink at"), that is, to collaborate by not reporting the fish sold illegally outside the lota. In this way women have been able to retain a measure of control over the marketing of fish.

Women also continue to earn cash for the household through the harvest and sale of seaweed. As did women of previous generations, the women of contemporary maritime households work long hours on the seaweed harvest from June through September. A woman who harvests seaweed watches each high tide to see if there will be seaweed to collect. She works on the beach morning and evening and every moment she can during the day to collect the wet seaweed, carry it up the beach, spread it to dry, roll it up when dry, and stack it in huge piles ready to sell to the lavradores who come from north of Póvoa de Varzim to buy Vila Chã seaweed for fertilizer. A market has developed for different types of seaweeds, such as francelha (*Gelidium sesquipedale*) and botelho (*Chondrus crispus*), used in the cosmetic and pharmaceutical industries; thus women now harvest several new varieties of seaweed, which they sort and sell at higher prices than the seaweed they sell for fertilizer. Women who devoted themselves to the 1984 summer seaweed harvest earned an average of 50,000 escudos (50,000$00, or about $400.00 U.S.).

The women of Lugar da Praia and Lugar do Facho also rent out their houses during the summer months. Since the 1960s, an increasing number of vacationers have come to Vila Chã (and other coastal communities) from the interior cities of Braga, Guimarães, and Amarante, and from the city of Porto. They come to enjoy the healthy sea air during the months of June through September, and Vila Chã women are happy to rent them their homes. A woman will either move her family into a small outbuilding behind the house, or she and her family will move in temporarily with her mother, a married daughter, or a sister. For the month of August, some women are able to ask as much as 50,000$00 rent; rents for other months are slightly lower. The average rental income a woman earns for a season falls between 10,0000$00 and 125,000$00 (between $800.00 and $1,000.00 U.S.). This is an important cash contribution to the household, given that the minimum monthly wage in Portugal (and the average wage of a factory-working daughter) is 15,000$00, or about $120.00 U.S. To earn additional cash, the women also sell fresh fish and vegetables from their gardens to their summer tenants. Reinvesting in their homes is the way most women spend the rental income. Earnings from summer house rentals have provided many maritime households with the extra cash they have needed to furnish their homes, to install bathrooms, or to buy new appliances.

There is competition among the women to rent their houses early in the season and for a good price, and access to rental income is a new object of inveja. City families begin to come to Vila Chã each year on Easter weekend to arrange to rent a house for a few weeks or a month during the summer. The arrival of prospective summer tenants has changed and intensified women's preparations for Easter. For at least three generations, preparing for Easter has involved extensive house-cleaning—the biggest cleaning of the year, and taking more than a week's time—in anticipation of the annual visit of the Holy Cross (*o compasso*), when the priest brings the Cross into each home on Easter Sunday. Nowadays, since Easter is also associated with the arrival of prospective house renters, the house must be looking its very best. On Easter Sunday the houses are immaculate and especially decorated. Easter is the day that women display their handiwork: each bed is covered with a crocheted bedspread, and tables and other surfaces are decorated with cloths and doilies all made by the women of the household. After Easter Sunday they are put away again until the next special occasion, which may be the next Easter or perhaps a daughter's wedding, a child's First Communion, or the festival of Nossa Senhora de Fátima.

In 1985, women's household management also included managing the wages earned by teenage sons who work in construction and by daughters who work in factories. In maritime households it has become common for sons and daughters to go out to work as soon as they reach the legal age of fourteen and have completed the compulsory six years of formal education. When daughters approach the age of fourteen, their mothers canvas the nearby garment factories to speak with the owners and arrange employment for their daughters. At about the same age, sons make the choice between taking up fishing and apprenticing in a trade; the majority are choosing wage work over fishing.[2] Unmarried sons and daughters deliver their wages to their mothers, who pool them with the other economic resources of the household and use them to meet cash needs. Sons keep a small amount for cigarettes and for spending in the café, and, by working overtime on Saturdays, they can earn the extra money needed to buy and maintain a small motorcycle. An unmarried daughter, however, gives all her wages to her mother on the understanding that her mother is saving money for her wedding dress and for her kitchen furnishings after she marries.

Women's work in the maritime household has, then, changed significantly from the days when women went to sea with men, and when women devoted themselves to making ends meet by intensifying their own subsistence and commodity production. In 1985, women's work in maritime households consisted primarily of managing the diversity of sources of cash income that have come to be more important to the household than earnings from the maritime economy itself. New sources of income have also modified women's work so that women spend increasing amounts of their time seeking additional cash income—for example, by arranging wage employment for their sons and daughters, or by renting out their homes in the summers. The increased emphasis on cash income also encourages household consumption and increases the household's cash needs. There has been a growing emphasis on women's consumer role over their role, so important in the pre-1960 maritime household, in economic production. These changes in women's work have begun to erode women's economic autonomy as women become dependent on sources of income controlled outside the household, rather than on income they generate through their own time and labor.

WOMEN ENTER THE FACTORIES

As early as the 1930s, a few Vila Chã women were walking the eight kilometers to work at the textile factory in Vila do Conde or the fifteen kilometers to Matosinhos to work in sardine-processing plants.[3] Local women did not, however, begin to enter factory work in significant numbers until the mid-1960s. By 1985, more than half of parish residents who worked for wages were women employed in factories, and more than three-quarters (76.7 percent, $N - 116$) of factory workers were women.[4] They worked in garment factories, food- and fish-processing factories, and at a transnational electronics plant.

In the 1960s new factories in the area surrounding Vila Chã actively began to recruit women workers, and older factories in Matosinhos and Vila do Conde began to provide free transportation to bring in women from the villages. Women had become attractive as industrial workers in part because there was a shortage of male labor, due to high rates of male emigration and the draft to the Colonial Wars in Africa, and in part because of the nature of the industries that were being established in the industrial zone north of Porto. Fish processing had been important in the area since at least the mid-nineteenth century, but the processing of other types of food, including chocolate and dairy products, had become increasingly important. These processing industries preferred to hire women workers. During the mid-1960s and early 1970s, numerous small garment factories opened up, and these factories hired women as seamstresses. And in 1974 Texas Instruments opened an electronics factory in Maia, about ten kilometers south of Vila Chã. Based on their international experience and the low wages that could be paid to women workers, Texas Instruments sought to hire almost exclusively women workers. Food processing and garment and electronics manufacture are perceived, both locally and internationally, as jobs for women. These are jobs for women because they are perceived to be extensions of women's tasks in the home, such as sewing or cooking, and are thought to require the same skills; in addition, in the social construction of women in industrial capitalism, women are seen as more tolerant of tedium, better able to work under supervision, and naturally endowed with the "nimble fingers" required in these kinds of manufacturing (Elson and Pearson 1981; Safa 1981). Furthermore, these jobs are defined as unskilled and are remunerated with low wages. Low wages for women factory workers are justified by a model that portrays the household under capitalism as based on a male wage, a model that assumes a woman's earnings are supplementary to her husband's.

Images of women factory workers have changed during this period of industrialization. Formerly, women who worked in factories were women of the poorest households. Stigmatized by their low social and economic status, these women were already morally suspect. Factory work similarly stigmatized women, not only because the women were poor but also because they conducted their work outside the purview of village mechanisms of social control (like vergonha). These women left the parish each day, worked among strangers, and could meet and socialize with men about whom the village knew nothing. Middle-aged Vila Chã men recalled that they had not wanted to marry factory workers precisely for this reason. They preferred a hardworking maritime woman whose virtues were locally known.

The image of the factory worker as a woman of questionable morality also complemented the New State's attribution of respectability to the woman who stayed in the home, meeting the needs of her husband and children. As we have seen, the Salazarean regime promulgated a model of the family based on male authority and a male wage. Salazar's speeches, state legislation, and schoolbooks all promoted the image of woman as virtuous wife and mother and reinforced the local view of the promiscuity of the early women factory workers in Vila Chã and elsewhere.[5] The attribution of sexual depravity to factory workers also had the effect of denigrating industrial work in the eyes of the rural population and thus complemented, at the local level, the state's national policy of constraining capitalism.

By 1985, however, women factory workers, especially those who worked in the clean and relatively well-paid jobs at Texas Instruments, had high status in the parish. They were envied by other women for their jobs and were desired by men as wives. Because the household has become dependent upon wage earnings, factory work can now be understood as an extension in an industrial context of the trabalhadeira role for women: by entering factories, working long hard days, and contributing their wages to the household, young women are trabalhadeiras like their mothers and grandmothers before them. But this attribution is contingent. Young factory workers, in order to be worthy of the local respect accorded the trabalhadeira, must be seen to be industrious and respectful of family and community values, and not to be seeking self-gratification. And the morality of young women factory workers, particularly their sexual mores, is still in question.[6]

Factory workers themselves, however, are less concerned with being respected as trabalhadeiras than they are with actively challenging and resisting local gender constructions and village morality—vergonha—especially through the negotiation of their sexuality and of sexual images. They use cosmetics and wear fashionable, colorful, tight-fitting jeans and sweaters, in stark contrast to the modest skirts and drab colors their mothers and grandmothers wear. This new presentation of the female self is a deliberate mechanism by which young women seek to distance themselves from the rural community and to gain acceptance in the increasingly urban context of their lives (cf. Collier 1986). They frequent the cafés that have sprung up in all rural parishes, including Vila Chã; there they smoke cigarettes and consume alcohol with women and men friends. They practice birth control and are knowledgeable about a variety of methods. They enjoy conspicuous consumption not only of stylish clothing but also of other consumer goods—a direct contradiction to the thriftiness and self-deprivation of the trabalhadeira ideal. The consumer needs of unmarried daughters are a new source of conflict with their mothers, who endeavor to hang onto their daughters' wages for household needs. At root is the conflict between the claims of family and household, and the young women's claims to new rights as wage workers.

The degree to which young women workers explore a new image of female sexuality and challenge existing household and gender relations is proportional, however, to the wages they are paid and the status their job is awarded locally, and Vila Chã residents hierarchically rank the three manufacturing industries that employ parish women. The oldest industry, fish processing, is considered work of the lowest status and is the most poorly remunerated; the most recent industry, electronics, is considered the highest-status work and is also the highest paid. Women who work in fish processing tend to remain more rooted in the values and self-image of the trabalhadeira, whereas women who work in the electronics industry tend to explore new gender images and social relations.

Women fish-plant workers are paid the minimum wage (15,000$00, or about $120.00 U.S. per month), and they experience the worst working conditions. The majority of Vila Chã women employed in fish processing work in one sardine cannery in Matosinhos. Of 120 workers at this cannery, 100 are women. The twenty men operate and maintain the machinery, operate the steam ovens, supervise distribution, and manage the office. The women process the fish. Fish processing is divided into several tasks, and each woman spends her day repetitively performing one of these. About twenty women stand at a long table leaning over a tank of water to wash the fresh or frozen fish; the workers then place them on racks on an automated line that takes the fish to the steam oven for cooking. Once cooked, the fish are transported to a table where another twenty women sit cutting off the tails and packing the cooked sardines neatly into tins. Two women then place the tins in vats of olive oil for a few minutes, and two more women take the tins to a table where women feed them into a machine that presses lids onto the tins. The closed tins come out on a belt and are run through hot water and then into steam ovens again for sterilizing. From the steam ovens the tins are taken to a dry warehouse where more women check the tins for flaws, wrap them with paper labels, and pack them in cardboard cartons ready for shipping. Except for those who work in the warehouse, where it is dry and relatively quiet, the women stand on wet floors and work amid the continuous loud clatter of machinery. The damp air and the incessant noise, along with the stress of constant supervision and the pressure to work quickly, combine to make the conditions of fish-plant workers formidable.

Seamstresses in garment factories work under slightly better conditions than do fish-plant workers, but their work is also repetitive and poorly remunerated. The factories are small, family-run operations employing between thirty and forty workers, all women. They manufacture jeans, blouses, jackets, suits, and other women's clothing, mostly to fill orders for export. The factories are located in small rural communities, and the workers come from the surrounding area. Some factories provide transportation in the back of a covered truck, but others require women to arrange their own transportation by bicycle, on foot, or by train.

The majority of women who work in the garment factories are unskilled, perform repetitive tasks, and are easily replaced. Like the fish-plant workers, most are paid the minimum wage. Only a few workers are paid more (up to 20,000$00) per month. These are the women the management considers to be the fastest and most skilled seamstresses, and they are charged with responsibility for the meticulous detail involved in finishing the garments.[7]

Each stage of a garment's production is performed by a different woman. The women take their place at one machine and sit working at that machine from 8:00 A.M. to 6:00 P.M. daily with a one-hour break for lunch. Each worker performs one task only; workers are dependent on the workers preceding them, and all must endeavor to work at the same pace. Two overseers, one for quality and one for speed, walk around the shop floor checking the work of the women. There are daily quotas to meet, and if a worker is not maintaining a high enough level of production, she is let go and replaced: almost every day someone is sent home.

There is a continuous and abundant supply of young girls from Vila Chã and other rural parishes lining up for factory jobs, and some garment factories have established what they call an apprenticeship system to exploit this labor supply and to reduce production costs. Under this apprenticeship system, girls are hired at half the minimum wage (7,500$00, or about $60.00 U.S. per month) for a set term (six months, one year, even eighteen months). At the end of this so-called training period, when the girls expect to be hired on at full minimum wage, they are instead let go and new "apprentices" are hired, again at half the minimum wage.

Women who work at the Texas Instruments factory are considered to be the most fortunate. The company is a multinational, pays the highest local wages to women (30,000$00, or about $240.00 U.S. per month—double the wage of a fish-plant worker), and offers numerous benefits to its workers. Women workers at "Texas" enjoy the use of a recreation center for themselves and their families; they attend parties sponsored by the company to celebrate national holidays throughout the year; and they are provided with free transportation in air-conditioned buses to and from Vila Chã each day. The women work on one of three eight-hour shifts that keep the factory operating twenty-four hours daily. Work at the electronics plant is repetitive, as it is in the other factories, but there is greater opportunity for women to advance, and salaries are scaled according to seniority and task. Conditions at Texas are also relatively clean, so the women can go to work in clothes of the latest fashion, in contrast to the fish-plant workers, who wear their oldest clothes and always smell of fish. Employees of Texas Instruments also have a higher level of education than women who work in other factories. When Texas Instruments first opened in 1974, it had hired women regardless of their level of education, probably because few rural women in northwestern Portugal had a high school education. Gradually, the company increased its education requirement, and in 1985 only applications from women with a completed secondary education were considered. This education requirement has increased the status and desirability of these jobs in the eyes of local people. In Vila Chã, women who work for Texas Instruments have high status because they earn the highest wages of all women factory workers, they have a higher level of education than most people, and they receive benefits that other factory workers do not receive.

THE LIFE OF A FACTORY WORKER: ADÉLIA

Women factory workers are not only young, unmarried women but also married women with families. In 1985, more than two-thirds (67.1 percent; $N - 82$) of young married women in Lugar da Praia and Lugar do

Facho worked for wages. They had started factory work as unmarried members of their parents' households and had continued to work for wages after marriage because a majority of their husbands were construction workers and often were unemployed. Few households could afford to keep a woman at unpaid work in the home after marriage. A household needed the wage, however low, that a woman factory worker could earn. The majority of young wives and mothers, therefore, continue wage work after marriage, although they may leave the work force to have, or to care for, their children and later return to employment. The story of Adélia illustrates the life of a woman raised in a maritime household, trained to be a trabalhadeira, who at age fifteen went to work in a fish plant and who, now a wife and mother, faces the dilemmas of the woman factory worker.

Each morning at seven o'clock, Adélia stands with the other women at a corner in Rio da Gândara waiting for the truck that drives through the parish to pick up the workers and take them into Matosinhos to the fish plant. The truck returns them at seven o'clock each night. But Adélia's day begins long before seven in the morning, and she is rarely finished with her day's work before midnight. She is up by six to do laundry outside in the washtub and to hang it on the line to dry before she goes to work. And in the evenings she washes dishes, irons clothes, and cleans the house. On weekends she shops and cooks and does laundry and tries to spend time with her children.

"My father was a fisherman and my mother was a fisherwoman. I was born in Vila Chã in 1949. I have one older brother. I left school in the middle of grade 4 when I was ten years old, and I worked helping my mother with the seaweed and selling fish. When I turned fifteen my mother arranged a job for me at a *conserva* (a fish-processing plant) in Matosinhos. I continued to live with my parents, and the wages I earned I gave to my mother. That was in 1964 when the company started to provide transportation for the workers. The company sends a truck around to the villages each morning to pick up the women and brings us back each night. I've been working at that same fish plant for twenty-one years now.

"When I was twenty-five [in 1974] I married Manuel, but we stayed on living with my parents because we had nowhere else to go. Manuel was a pobre but then so was I. He had no father. His mother was a jornaleira, but she died when he was only fourteen. He works as a housepainter, but he has never been able to earn very much. Sometimes he has no work. And in the winter they can't paint houses because of the humidity. But you can't afford to miss a day's work here; life is so expensive. He talks about emigrating. Those [i.e., families of emigrants] are the only people who can have a good life here. But he has never had luck in getting work outside Portugal. Besides, he'd miss the children so much.

"Our son was born in 1977 and our daughter was born in 1980. That's when we left my parents. It was getting too difficult. After we married, what I earned was my own. We paid the light bill at my parents' house, but we cooked and ate on our own. My wages were my own but my mother was always criticizing how I spent them. She thought the food I bought was too expensive. She had always made only cabbage soup and fish and potatoes, and she thought I should do the same. She said I was wasteful and a big spender (*gastadeira*) because I bought meat and because I gave the children fruit and milk each day. Finally, when I bought a set of china her words were more than I could take anymore, so we decided to move out. The only place we could go was to my husband's sister. She was a widow and we could move into the buildings behind her house and fix them up. So we have two rooms here, and this is where we eat our meals and where we sleep.

"My dream is to have a house of my own one day. We are trying to save but it is very difficult. Manuel often has no work so we depend on my wage. I earn only 15,000$00 per month, but I almost never bring home that much. I always have to miss a few days each month because of illness or because of the children or because I am tired, and I don't get paid for the days I'm sick. Sometimes I have to stay home to catch up on my housework. So, often I bring home only 10,000$00 or 12,000$00 for a month [$80.00 to $100.00 U.S.].

"Working at the fish plant is the worst work there is. It's the most dirty (*suja*) and it's cold. Some garment workers get paid more than we do, but we should be paid more because our work is so cold and hard and dirty. One month I missed ten days because of my back. I have back problems and bad rheumatism in my legs. It's because at the fish plant I have to stand all day. I have to stand all day on the wet floor, and sometimes we work with frozen fish from the Soviet Union, and they dump the fish on the floor beside us to defrost. So it's always humid and damp. They shouldn't do that, because we're all full of rheumatism and illnesses (*doenças*). I've been doing that work for over twenty years. The doctor says I need to rest, that I should not be on my feet, but what can I do? I can't stop work. We need the money.

"I worry about my children. My son is lazy at school because he has no one to encourage him. It's hard on the children. My husband does what he can. When he has no work, he looks after the children. And he always has the evening meal ready when I come home. He's a better cook than I am!

"But our life is very difficult. I don't know how we're going to manage. Everything is so expensive these days (*A vida é muito cara hoje*).

And it's only going to get worse. Someday I want to have a house of my own. But for now we live in these two rooms. Our life is very hard."

In Adélia's narrative we see many of the conflicts that face married women factory workers in Vila Chã: the disparity between her aspirations and her economic circumstances; the new conflicts between factory-working daughters and their fisherwomen mothers over the structure and management of the household, and their different constructions of women's identity; the daily struggle to manage the double day of wage work and domestic work; and an increasing inequality in the gendered division of labor in the household.

Adélia's household is defined by the type of industrialization taking place in northwestern Portugal. Organized around wage work and consumption of wage earnings, the household is dependent upon Adélia's wage because permanent employment is available for women, whereas men, like Adélia's husband, can find only seasonal employment as construction workers and are frequently unemployed. Like other women factory workers, however, Adélia earns a low wage, and the household has difficulty meeting its consumer needs. Also like other young couples, Adélia and her husband would like one day to own a house, but it is impossible for them to accumulate the necessary savings. Worries about money and frustration over their inability to achieve their aspirations are new sources of stress and nervos for young married women.

The structure of Adélia's household is different from the structure of her mother's household, and the two women have differences of opinion about household management. Adélia's mother ran her household based on subsistence and commodity production, but Adélia's household is dependent solely on wage earnings. Adélia does not have time to carry on the subsistence and commodity production activities her mother engaged in. She purchases the food her household consumes, and she has increased her consumer aspirations. Her mother criticizes the way Adélia spends her money. According to Adélia's mother, to spend (gastar) money is to waste money. Spending money, a woman violates the ideal of the trabalhadeira, the ideal of the woman as household manager (governadora), which is to save (poupar) the household's resources.

At marriage, like most young couples, Adélia and her husband had moved in with her parents, but differences between mother and daughter made it impossible for Adélia to continue living there. Differences of opinion between the women were based on their different views of the household. Adélia's mother sees the household as based on a pooling of resources to be managed by her and shared among household members. As a daughter raised in a maritime household, Adélia understands her mother's view, but as a worker, Adélia sees wage earnings as her own to be managed by her for herself, her husband, and her children. She and her husband had carried on the tradition of uxorilocal residence after marriage, but they had lived as a separate household under her parents' roof. They contributed to her parents' expenses by paying the electricity bill for the house, but otherwise they constructed their own household based on their nuclear family. Conflicts between generations of women about household structure and household management intensify a young couple's aspirations for a home of their own.

The separation of productive and reproductive work under capitalism creates two work places and a double workday for women factory workers like Adélia.[8] When economic production was managed by the household, as it was in the maritime economy of Vila Chã, women—like Adélia's mother—were better able to combine their domestic labor, their reproductive work, with their productive work. As a result, women of earlier generations exerted a greater measure of control over the allocation of their time and labor than can factory workers like Adélia for whom productive work (in factories) is separated from reproductive work (in the home). Adélia must do her domestic work—housecleaning, laundry, shopping, child care—in the hours before and after wage work, that is, before 7:00 A.M. and after 7:00 P.M.

Adélia cites numerous instances of conflict between her productive and her reproductive work. She inevitably misses several days of wage work each month in order to look after a sick child at home or to catch up on housework. These responsibilities directly affect her wage work because she will not be paid for the days she misses at the factory. She is caught in a double bind: she wants to do the work of a dona de casa, including keeping an orderly house and caring for her children, but she knows the household will lose much-needed wages if she stays home. Meanwhile, the conditions of her work at the fish plant, combined with worries about her children and the household's finances, affect Adélia's health so that she finds it difficult to do any of her work well. Her life is hard, and she is not optimistic about the future.

The increasing conflict between productive and reproductive work for women is requiring new forms of negotiation between wives and husbands, and women are developing new ideals of conjugal relations. Industrialization in northwestern Portugal has created new inequalities in the gendered division of labor by placing a disproportionate amount of the work of the household (both productive and reproductive) on women. The disparity in the share of work performed by women and men is widening as the construction industry falters and increasing numbers of men become unemployed. Many women are struggling to get their husbands to take on a greater share of the domestic work. Adélia is one of the more fortunate because her husband has assumed some responsibility for meal preparation, shopping, and child care.

WOMEN IN THE HOME

More than two-thirds (67.1 percent) of the eighty-two women with young children in the households of Lugar da Praia and Lugar do Facho worked for wages outside the home in 1985; only 32.9 percent (or twenty-seven) of women with young children worked in the home as full-time housewives (donas de casa). In the household-based fishery prior to 1960, the women of Lugar da Praia and Lugar do Facho had effectively combined work in economic production with the reproductive work of the household. The household was the locus of both production and reproduction. In 1985, the two types of work were being carried out in two separate locations: in the factory and in the home. For women like Adélia, who worked in factories, this separation creates a double workday. For women who work full-time at nonwage domestic work in the home, the separation from economically productive work brings greater dependence on their husbands. At the same time, being in the home also creates the conditions that encourage some women to elaborate the dona de casa role. The elaboration of domesticity and dependence is encouraged further by the images of women on television and in consumer advertising.

Of the twenty-seven women with young children who work in the home as donas de casa, eight are the wives of men with permanent salaries, such as policemen, bank clerks, or factory mechanics; six are the wives of emigrant workers who send home their wages; three are ill and have had to leave their factory jobs; and the others are temporarily home from factory work caring for young infants. The role of dona de casa tends to be a temporary status for the majority of young married women and the permanent status of only a few—those whose husbands earn the highest wages and have secure employment, the new middle class in rural communities. In 1985 the dona de casa ideal is almost as inaccessible to the majority of Vila Chã women as it was in the past, when only the wives of wealthy lavradores worked in the home. Most women will be engaged in wage work for the greater part of their lives.

FÁTIMA: A DONA DE CASA'S STORY

Fátima's story is the story of a woman who has achieved, at least temporarily, the status of dona de casa. Fátima spends her days caring for her small daughter, shopping at the local grocery store, preparing hot meals for her husband at noon and at night, cleaning the house, and washing and ironing clothes. To own and furnish a modern home is the central aspiration in her life.

Like all Vila Chã women, regardless of their work, Fátima insists on showing visitors her house, an old, one-story building owned by her mother. The "house tour" reinforced a woman's identification with the house and her chosen identity as a dona de casa. Fátima's interest in her house and its furnishings is typical.

To the immediate left when one enters the house from the street is the living room she has painted pastel blue. A cupboard in the corner displays a collection of china figurines, every one of which her two-year-old daughter has dropped and chipped. There is an overstuffed chesterfield against one wall below a window and a glass-covered coffee table in front of it. On the opposite wall is a huge wooden cabinet displaying more china ornaments and Fátima's large collection of paperback romances. Across the hall from the living room is the bedroom. The walls are painted Fátima's favorite cream color, and she expressed the hope that one day all her rooms would be painted that color. The space of the small room is filled with a carved mahogany bedroom suite including a bed, vanity table, dresser, and wardrobe. On the bed is an elaborate white bedspread crocheted by Fátima. At the end of the hall is a storage room that she plans to refurbish as a dining room one day when they can afford to buy the furniture. And across the hall is the kitchen. A round table covered with a tablecloth is in the center of the room. A huge color television sits on a diagonal shelf in the corner facing the sink and stove so that Fátima is able to watch television when she is cooking or washing dishes. Like most young women in Vila Chã, Fátima watches the Brazilian *telenovelas* (soap operas) each night after supper. A small room off the kitchen serves as her daughter's bedroom and contains a crib, a changing table, and piles of children's clothing. Outside the kitchen door in a small backyard is Fátima's washtub, and every day she does laundry. She changes her daughter's clothes several times each day, and her husband leaves his T-shirts and work clothes for her to wash. The clothesline is laden with dripping clothes, whites are soaking in bleach in several basins, and the dirtiest clothes soak in detergent in the washtub. Fátima will scrub and rinse these clothes after dinner and hang them on the clothesline before she goes to bed.

Fátima is a friendly and vivacious young woman. She has short, dark curly hair and wears light eye makeup and lipstick. She dresses in tight blue jeans and colorful sweaters. She is happy to have visitors and to have the opportunity to talk about her life.

"My father is a fisherman and my mother is a fisherwoman. I was born in Vila Chã in 1962, the youngest of six children. When I was born my father went to Germany to fish for a company there and to earn more money than he could earn fishing here. When I was five, my mother joined him in Germany and began to work for the same company in the fish plant. For the next six years, I lived with my sister and her husband. I saw my parents only when they came home from Germany on holidays. You would not recognize me if you saw pictures of me then— dirty and barefoot and not smiling. I used to daydream and try to remember my parents' faces, but it was hard. Although my mother sent money home from Germany, my sister put the money into her own savings—she saved it to build her new house. Her husband used to beat her and he used to beat me too. The only happiness in my life at that time was school. I did well in school and I loved to read. The others used to make fun of me. They used to call me "the teacher" (*a professora*) because I was always trying to speak Portuguese correctly. But I had to leave school after grade 6 because there was no money to pay for the bus and the books and the meals at the school in Vila do Conde. Then my parents returned from Germany, and my father took up fishing again in Vila Chã. I hated my mother when she came home because I had been so unhappy.

"In 1977, when I was fifteen, I went to work at a garment factory. Along with the other girls I walked to the train station each morning [three kilometers] and took the train two stops down the line to the village where the factory was located.

"I hated the work. There was too much pressure. The managers were never satisfied with your work. They told us we were lazy, and they often made us stay several hours past quitting time and without pay if they thought we hadn't produced what we should have in that day. It was always the production (*a produção*) that they were concerned with. Many of the women who worked there became sick with nervos from the noise and fatigue and from the pressures to meet the production quotas and from the constant criticism. Two women right here in Facho have had nervous breakdowns because of the stresses of their jobs as factory seamstresses. Both are now seeing psychiatrists. The managers never thought your work was good enough, and they fired women almost daily. They knew they could replace the workers immediately. There were always young women waiting for jobs. I was fired after a year because I didn't work fast enough. Then I got a job in another garment factory closer to Vila Chã and worked there until I became pregnant. Work there was no better, but I wasn't fired so I stayed.

"I married in 1982. I was twenty years old. My husband is five years older than I am. He has a small construction contracting firm of his own and employs four other men. I married him because my parents wanted me to. They really liked him. They liked him because he makes a good living. I married him because they liked him, but it's no great love (*grande amor*). If I had it to do over again, I'd still be single. I'm not happy with my husband. He's ill-bred and lazy (*mal-educado e preguiçoso*). I wish he were better educated and that he spoke proper Portuguese.

"I want my husband to emigrate. I'd be happy to leave Vila Chã. I'd like to go back to work myself one day, but I don't want to return to the factory. I'd like to be a secretary but I need more education. But he wants to stay here. He has no ambition. I'd like to emigrate so that we can build a house of our own. The house we're living in now is not ours. It belongs to my mother, and it is old and *pobrezinha* (very poor). New houses are better than old houses because they're easier to keep clean. Someday I want to have a new house of my own.

"My daughter was born toward the end of our first year of marriage. She's two years old now and I spend my whole day chasing after her. She gets into everything! But children need the attention. They need to be listened to. No one ever listened to me. My mother didn't have time. She didn't know that children need time. Mothers should spend time with their children. So I play with my daughter and I listen to her, and I do the work that needs to be done. I shop and I have my husband's meals ready for him when he comes home. He's very fussy. He doesn't like fish so I have to buy beef. And I try to keep the house tidy, and I do the laundry every day. It's lonely sometimes, but when I have time, I read. I love to read romances."

Fátima's experience as a dona de casa is shared by other young Vila Chã women who work in the home. She, like them, is engaged in a daily and repetitive cycle of domestic work. Fátima is proud to be a dona de casa because of the status she awards the role, and she has elaborated the work she associates with being a dona de casa: she does laundry every day because she changes her daughter's clothes frequently and washes her husband's work clothes several times a week; she cleans the house every day; she shops for groceries every day; she prepares a variety of meals for her husband because he earns a good wage and he expects to live well; and she plays with her small daughter because she believes that children need their mothers, that women should spend time with their children.

Fátima is concerned with the house as a structure: its size, appearance, furnishings, and modernity. She dreams of having a new house one day that she will be able to furnish well and keep clean (something she finds difficult in the old house where she now lives).

Like other young women in Vila Chã, Fátima is an avid consumer of popular romance novels and of the Brazilian telenouvelas shown each night on local television. Through them she has developed a concept of romantic love against which she critically measures her own relationship with her husband. The telenouvelas and the advertising on television have been important in changing local ideas about gender relations because they reinforce the romantic ideal of conjugal love and the dona de casa role for women after marriage.

The conditions of Fátima's work in the home are different in important ways from those of the women of her mother's generation. For Fátima, the house itself and the furnishings it contains are important status symbols. The house is a center of consumption and a place to display manufactured goods. For earlier generations of women, however, the house had been a place for household members to eat and sleep and for storage of foods and other goods produced by the household. Along with other household members, women had spent most of their time outside of the house working on the beach, or selling fish, or in their gardens. The demands of their economically productive work had determined the amount of time they devoted to reproductive work. But the work of young women like Fátima is centered exclusively on housework and child care. Fátima's day is organized around the preparation of her husband's meals and the needs of her child. And unlike Fátima, who works alone in the home, women of previous generations had never been alone in their work. They had worked with their husbands and with other men and women on the beach, and their children had accompanied them as they worked. Finally, women's work as managers of the household's resources has changed. Women of the older generation had decision-making authority over the management of all the household's resources: Alvina's husband never knew the status of the household finances or what Alvina earned from her economic transactions (negócios). Young wives like Fátima, however, are given money by their husbands to meet household expenses, and their husbands' wishes and preferences take precedence over any ideas a wife might have about economizing, saving, or investing the household income: Fátima, for example, buys meat, which is more expensive than fish but which is preferred by her husband.

CONCLUSION: FISHERWOMEN AND FACTORY WORKERS

Today, women of maritime households work in the fishery, but they no longer go to sea. Instead of saying they fish "like men" (as Maria and Alvina say), women say they "help [their husbands] on the beach" (*ajudamos na praia*). The men fish, and the women unload the boats and sell the fish; and women harvest and sell seaweed. As formerly, women manage the economic resources of the household, but these now include income from summer house rentals and wages earned by teen-age children, in addition to the earnings from the fishery. Women's role as managers of household production has receded as their role as managers of household consumption has become more important. Increased sources of cash income encourage increased household consumption of manufactured goods and new foods; increased household consumption increases household dependence on wage earnings. The contemporary household is less an independent unit of production and reproduction (as in the pre-1960 fishery) than a unit of reproduction and consumption in a wage economy where production takes place outside the household. The effect of the transfer of most productive work out of the household is to reduce the control that women can exercise in their role as household managers.

Women who work in factories have less control over their work and their households than do the fishermen's wives of contemporary maritime households. Like Adélia, they cannot control their working conditions in the factories; they cannot increase their earnings by intensifying their labor and increasing their production; and they cannot effectively reduce the cash needs of their households because they have no time to use their labor for subsistence and commodity production for the household—their households are entirely dependent on wage earning and consumption. In addition, they have a double workday: they do wage work in factories and unpaid domestic labor in the home, and the two types of work, productive and reproductive, conflict with one another. Women frequently miss days of wage work in order to catch up on domestic work, and this reinforces employers' tendencies to treat the women as a cheap and expendable labor supply. Other new forces in society, such as television advertising and programming, also reinforce the perception that women are primarily domestic workers in the home and ignore the reality that a majority of young wives and mothers also work for wages outside the home. Women themselves tend to consider that, under ideal circumstances, they would not have to work for wages and they would be donas de casa: most hold the dream that they will one day own a new home, and an unstated part of that dream is that they will work exclusively as donas de casa furnishing and caring for the home. The dona de casa ideal for women restrains them from organizing for better wages and working conditions. Factory workers tend to view their status as wage workers as temporary: in an ideal world they would be donas de casa working at home. And, in an effort to construct themselves as donas de casa, they identify themselves more with their homes and housework than they do with their factory work. This increases the pressures they experience, because they spend their "leisure" (i.e., non-wage-earning) hours trying to meet new standards for housework and child care, standards that assume women are full-time housewives.

Women who actually are full-time housewives have even less control over their work and their households than do women factory workers. They are removed from economic production altogether, and they are economically dependent upon their husbands. They are also effectively removed from household management because their husbands earn the wage, give them money to spend for the household, and make demands about how the money should be spent. The dona de casa experiences other contradictions. On the one hand, she is proud of her social status and her function as a symbol of the household's economic well-being. On the other hand, she has no economic autonomy or decision-making authority in the household and in her marriage. Donas de casa, like Fátima, attempt to increase the importance of domestic work by elaborating the tasks associated with the dona de casa role, including child care, so that these tasks are both more time-consuming and more labor-intensive than they had been in their mothers' maritime households (cf. Bouquet 1984; Cowan 1983; Luxton 1980). They also collaborate with advertising and television imagery in the construction of a romantic ideal of conjugal relations, which may sustain them emotionally, at least temporarily, in their dependent role as dona de casa. For some women, however, these constructions cannot mask the conflicts in the role for long, and they may seek to end their marriages. A little over a year after we recorded her narrative, Fátima had separated from her husband, and she and her three-year-old daughter were living with her mother. She was still living with her mother and suing her husband for a divorce two years later when I visited her in the summer of 1988.

The conditions under which young wives and mothers do productive and reproductive work have changed dramatically from the time when their mothers and grandmothers were able to combine both forms of work in the context of a household economy. In a capitalist economy there is increasing conflict for women who try to combine productive and reproductive work, and some women are removed from productive work altogether and depend on their husbands' incomes. The removal of productive work from the control of the household has been accompanied by the social construction of women as donas de casa, a new source of conflict for the majority of young Vila Chã women, whose households will require them to be wage workers throughout their lives.

"To be a woman is to be a worker," women in Vila Chã say. Contrary to the images of women that have prevailed in the ethnography of South-

ern Europe, it is only recently that the maritime women of Vila Chã
have begun to be defined and to define themselves in terms of their
reproductive work as wives and mothers. Historically, it has been their
work in economic production that has been the primary source of their
identity. A major impact of industrialization in Portugal has been this
change in the social construction of rural women and in the locus of
their gender identity. Despite the fact that women, as factory workers,
continue to be engaged in economically productive work—like their
mothers and grandmothers they are trabalhadeiras—they choose not
to find their identity in their factory work. Instead, they have dissected
the contradiction that gave rise to the fragmented consciousness of
earlier generations of maritime women, women who were socially stigmatized because of their visible role in economic production. Rather
than seeing productive work as a source of their power in the household and of their identity as women, younger women are choosing to
see their work in economic production as an indicator of their low
socioeconomic status. Thus, women like Adélia would like to think that
once they have achieved their goal of a new and fully furnished home,
they will retire from factory work and be donas de casa. Also like
Adélia, however, most know that this aspiration is probably unrealiza-
ble and that they will be factory workers most of their adult lives.

One approach to interpretation would describe the transformation of
women's work and the changes in the social construction of women in
Vila Chã as a classic case study of women and development (Etienne
and Leacock 1980; Fernández-Kelly 1983; Leacock and Safa 1986;
Mies 1986; Nash 1979). Maritime women have become less autonomous in their work in the fishery. Their daughters have become an
unskilled, low paid, wage labor force. Working in factories, the daughters have no decision-making control over their hours and working
conditions and have lost the autonomy earlier generations of women
had found in their work. Establishing households based on the consumption of wage earnings instead of on production for household subsistence, young married women are unable to manage their households with the authority of their mothers and grandmothers and are
unable to make ends meet by intensifying their own labor; they are
entirely dependent on what their wage will buy, on how far they can
stretch their wage. And, as we have seen, they are extremely poorly
remunerated for their work, which makes it difficult, often impossible,
for them to meet their new consumer needs. The gap between their
aspirations and the possibility of achieving those aspirations for themselves and their households is wider than it has ever been, with the
result that young married women live with a constant feeling of fail-
ure—a feeling alien to earlier generations of women, who defined suc-

cess in terms of the local cultural ideal of the trabalhadeira and in the context of the maritime household economy of Vila Chã.

Perhaps most difficult of all is the increasing divisiveness among women. Inveja is intensifying under contemporary socioeconomic conditions: women compete for jobs in factories where they are treated as interchangeable and replaceable; and they compete to have the most modern and best-furnished homes in the parish, striving endlessly in the new consumer society where enough is never enough. Young married women who toil through long double workdays in factories and at home also have little time for building and maintaining the support of other women in similar circumstances. In factories where they are controlled by the vigilance of foremen and the pressure of production quotas, women have little opportunity to share experiences—unlike the maritime women of earlier generations, who came and went freely in their work on the praia, on the street, or in their gardens, always in the company of other women. And, as Adélia describes in recounting her stressful relations with her mother, there is new conflict between generations of women, and it is bringing about the dissolution of the strong bonds and mutual aid system that had existed between consanguineally related women and had been important to the construction of the women-centered maritime household. Different generations hold different ideals for women. Older women, like Alvina, treasure their economic independence and authority in the household and describe young housewives as *mais escravas* (more servile) because they are dependent on a husband's income. They recognize that the younger women have achieved, in relative terms, a higher standard of living, but in their view, the price young women have paid in the loss of their autonomy is too high. The younger women, however, maintain that the older women, the trabalhadeiras, were *escravas* (slaves) because they defined themselves in terms of their economic production and because they lived in material conditions of poverty. Women's different ideals and aspirations under changed socioeconomic conditions have introduced new conflicts between the generations.

A second approach to interpreting the experience of Vila Chã women and economic development would view women as historically constituted subjects and would seek to understand the meaning of these changes from the point of view of the women involved. This approach would enable us to see some of the complexities and contradictions behind the women-and-development case study summarized above. The women's narratives presented in earlier chapters assist us in this task. Through them we see not only that young women today are not merely passive victims in the construction of their circumstances but that older women actively constructed an identity for themselves which assisted them in the reconciliation of the contradictions and conflicts they had internalized. We are able to identify the struggles of factory-working women, like Adélia, to construct a new model of conjugal relations and a new gendered division of labor in the household. We are able to see how, in their low level of commitment to their jobs (signified in part by high rates of absenteeism), they may be using their factory wages to pay them to do their housework—that is, they see themselves as earning factory wages in order to be able to define themselves as donas de casa.

The key to integrating these two interpretive approaches—the objective analysis of women and economic development, and the subjective life stories of individual women experiencing socioeconomic change—lies in a new understanding of the meaning and the processes of the social construction of gender. The social construction of gender is not only a process of constructing ideals about gender roles and relations but also a process of manipulating those ideals—a process of negotiation. Socioeconomic conditions, including circumstances of rapid social and economic change, only define limits within which the construction of gender identity takes place; they do not predetermine gender roles and relations. On the other hand, gender ideals are not constructed independently of material conditions and, once constructed, are not immutable. Rather, through a process of negotiation that originates in the subjective and historical experiences of individuals and groups of individuals, gender ideals are identified and then manipulated in the construction of identities that validate the experiences of those individuals and of those groups. Gender, then, is a historical and social construct, malleable and subject to change. It is actively constructed and negotiated at different, often antagonistic, levels of society—the individual, the household, the community, and the state, for example—resulting in contradiction and in layered systems of social and cultural meaning.

Thus, where state and local elites in rural Portugal defined the subordination of women and the low social status of maritime peoples, the maritime women (and men) defined an alternative gender system that both legitimated the division of labor necessary in their households and enabled the women to find dignity in their lives of hard work. Under contemporary conditions, exploited as cheap and expendable factory labor, women continue to struggle to negotiate gender roles and relations that enable them to withstand the harsh conditions under which they work and to salvage self-esteem. They achieve the latter in part by asserting that they are securing a higher standard of living and are dissolving some of the contradictions that their mothers and grandmothers lived with. The inevitability is that new contradictions and conflicts are created—the double workday for women may be the most difficult—but the hope, for both analyst and social actor, must be that these new contradictions and conflicts can be confronted and resolved in ways that will ensure the continuing dignity of rural women.

NOTES

CHAPTER 1
VILA CHÃ

1. According to the last official census of population in 1981, Vila Chã had a population of 2,781 residents in 665 households (Instituto Nacional de Estatística). Both the secretary and president of the parish council considered these figures to be too low, but they did not have more accurate figures and suggested the estimates of 3,000 population and 700 households used here.

2. The term *lavradores* is used to refer to small landowning peasant farmers and their households. This is the term used locally and follows current ethnographic practice in northern Portugal (Brettell 1986; O'Neill 1987; Pina-Cabral 1986). *Lavradores* also refers to the collective social group comprising landowning households engaged in agriculture. Again, this is a distinction made locally to define group membership and boundaries. The term *pescadores* (fishermen and women) is used to refer to the collective social group comprising households engaged in the seasonal exploitation of marine resources and the production of seaweed fertilizer. In Vila Chã the term is used also to refer to the descendants of pescadores, many of whom in 1985 lived in households based on wage earnings but continued to identify themselves as "of the pescadores" (as opposed to "of the lavradores"). In the Portuguese: *o pescador* (m., s. the fisherman); *a pescadeira* (f., s. the fisherwoman); *os pescadores* (pl. the fishermen *or* the fishermen and fisherwomen); and *as pescadeiras* (f., pl. the fisherwomen).

3. The thirty-two parishes that constitute the concelho of Vila do Conde occupy an area of 146.8 square kilometers in the valley of the Ave River and in the 1981 national census had a total population of 63,788. The term *parish* (*freguesia*) originally referred to a population of parishioners of one church, but, since at least the nineteenth century, the term has referred to a lay community and is the Portuguese administrative division below the municipal level. A rural parish usually comprises several hamlets (lugares) or villages. The term *concelho* (municipality) refers to the administrative division between the levels of the parish and the district. The *câmara municipal* (town council) is the local governmental body at the municipal level, above the level of the parish council

4. Since the fifteenth century, the town of Vila do Conde has been a major fishing port and ship-building center in Portugal. The caravels used during the Portuguese era of colonial expansion in the fifteenth and sixteenth centuries were built here, as were many of the boats used by the Portuguese in the cod fishery on the Newfoundland Grand Banks. Further, over half of the domestic sardine fleet is built in the shipyards of Vila do Conde. In 1985, small-boat fishing (*pesca artesanal*) was important in the economies of six parishes in the

concelho, including Vila Chã. Agriculture is the economic base of the other parishes, and, since the Second World War, local lavradores have developed commercial dairy farming and the production of potatoes as a cash crop. Industry is important in Vila do Conde, as it is on the north coast generally. In the late nineteenth century a British-owned textile factory opened in the town and employed local people. Sardine-processing plants were also established in the nineteenth century. And, since the 1960s, a number of small garment factories and plants that process chocolate and milk products have begun operation in the town. Tourism is also important in the regional economy. The town of Póvoa de Varzim, three kilometers north of Vila do Conde, is a tourist center with luxury hotels, numerous restaurants, a casino, and a large expanse of groomed beach. Vila do Conde has two hotels and a few restaurants; it absorbs some of the overflow of the tourist traffic to Póvoa de Varzim. The tourists are mainly Portuguese, and recently, in search of more economical accommodation, some have come down the coast to Vila Chã. Vila Chã has no hotels or restaurants, but many residents are happy to rent out their homes during the summer months. The beach, however, is small and rocky and offers little potential for tourist development. Furthermore, the beach is the center of the local fishery, and sunbathers must compete with fisherwomen and their seaweed for space on the beach.

5. The fascist-inspired New State came into being after a bloodless military coup toppled the short-lived First Republic on May 28, 1926, and it held power in Portugal until the Revolution of April 25, 1974 and the introduction of democratic government. Dr. António Salazar, who was the first finance minister in 1926, became prime minister in 1932, a position he held until 1968 when he suffered a debilitating stroke and was replaced by Marcel Caetano.

6. Pina-Cabral (1984a:81) explains that, while the word *dote* is correctly translated into English as "dowry," and although in some areas of Portugal the practice of giving dowry to a daughter at marriage has been common, in the Alto Minho of northwestern Portugal the term *dote* has come to be equivalent to "inherited property." A spouse's dote is the amount of property that he or she eventually will contribute toward the common fund of the household. In Vila Chã the term *dote* is also used with this meaning of "inherited property," although it can be received either at marriage or at the death of the parents. If a part of the dote is received at marriage—for example, a small plot of land on which to build a house or a small amount of cash—its value is deducted from the child's eventual total inheritance (and in poorer households often constitutes the entire inheritance).

7. The estimated numbers of households for the years 1877 and 1905 are probably low because they are based on the electoral censuses, and only males who paid more than one thousand réis in taxes per year were enumerated. This excluded the poorer households of the parish, including households headed by women and probably the majority of maritime households. The estimate of households for 1911 is more accurate because it is based on the *X Recenseamento geral da população*, Vol. 2 (Instituto Nacional de Estatística). This census recorded the population and number of households for each hamlet of each parish of the county of Vila do Conde. The earliest census of Vila Chã

is found in the *Memórias paroquiais* (1758), and a second is found in a list entitled *Número dos fogos de cada lugar das freguesias* (Vila do Conde, 1863). These censuses are held in the archives of the concelho at the Biblioteca Municipal de Vila do Conde.

8. The pilado fishery was time- and labor-intensive and hazardous. Two boats each with a crew of two or three worked together. They rowed five to ten kilometers offshore in order to get to the fishing grounds. There, one boat (*o barco da carga*) anchored with one end of the net attached to it. The second boat (*o barco de carreira*), often smaller, rowed out in a circle, dropped the net, and returned to the anchor boat, completing the circle. Then the crew hauled in the full net and emptied the pilado into the barco da carga with the aid of a small hand net (ganha-pão). Two crew members rowed back to shore with the heavily laden boat, raising the sail if the winds were favorable. The others brought in the smaller, empty boat. Tragic accidents occurred when sudden winds overturned the loaded pilado boat, and the men and women accompanying the boat were drowned. Once the boats reached shore, the work continued. The women unloaded the boats and, after rinsing the long nets in fresh water in the river, spread them out on the beach to dry. They also spread the pilado to dry on the beach for two or three days. Once it was dry, they loaded it into baskets that they carried up the beach on their heads, and they deposited it in piles ready for the lavradores to transport inland by cart.

9. According to the anonymous *Inquérito industrial e comercial* (1890), there were at that time sixty-nine boats fishing from the Vila Chã beach. They were of three types. The first was the *mirança*, a notoriously fragile double-prowed boat, 5.6 meters in length and capable of carrying up to four people. The mirança was propelled by two oars or poles and had a carrying capacity of 1,000 kilograms. There were twenty miranças in Vila Chã, and they were used close to shore in the harvest of seaweed. The second type was the *catraia*. The catraia was smaller (4.1 meters in length; 400 kilograms in capacity) and was equipped with a mast and lateen sail (*vela latina*) as well as oars. It was more expensive to build (20$000 réis instead of 12$000 réis), but it was expected to last ten years, twice as long as a mirança. The catraia was used in line and net fishing, and there were twenty-three in Vila Chã. The third type was a reinforced, sturdier mirança built at still greater cost, equipped with mast and sail, and viable for fishing at greater distances from shore. There were twenty-six of these miranças, and they were used in the pilado fishery as well as in sardine and line fishing.

10. In Portugal this kind of inshore fishery is known as *a pesca artesanal*, and, to this day, by far the majority of boats in the Portuguese fleet (15,289 of 16,060 boats in 1984) are engaged in the pesca artesanal (Anonymous 1984:25). These are small boats licensed to fish only on a specified stretch of the coast and only for a certain distance out to sea. In Vila Chã boats are licensed to fish within twelve miles of shore in the coastal zone between Matosinhos and Póvoa de Varzim.

11. For a history and analysis of the participation of rural Portuguese fishermen in the Newfoundland cod fishery, including the life stories of two bacalhoeiros, see Cole (1990).

12. The archives of the concelho of Vila do Conde contain fifty-three petitions to emigrate submitted by Vila Chã residents during the period from 1865
to 1898. Until 1879, all of these emigrants were young unmarried men, and the
majority (86 percent) were under age fourteen; one was only nine years old.
Several petitions were made, on behalf of these boys, by their mothers, who
were either widowed or unmarried, or whose husbands were "absent in Brazil."
For all but six of these young men, their profession was listed as *marítimo*
(seaman) and they were going to Brazil to work on merchant vessels. After
1880 married men began emigrating from Vila Chã, and these were all pescadores. Thus, in the late nineteenth century, the majority of emigrants from Vila
Chã were members of maritime households, and this pattern continues in the
twentieth century.

CHAPTER 2
A FISHERWOMAN'S STORY

1. One tostão had a value of less than 0.01 escudos—so small that they have
not been in circulation for some time.
2. Following Bertaux (1981) I prefer to speak of life *stories* rather than life
histories. The term *life stories* allows for and acknowledges the dimension of
storytelling in the process, the playfulness of memory, and the brevity and se-
lectivity of some subjects' accounts of their lives. Pseudonyms have been used
for the personal names of the subjects whose life stories appear in this book.
3. I worked with twelve Vila Chã women on their life stories. These women
were of different generations, pursued different kinds of work, and constructed
different kinds of households. They included fisherwomen, a fish vendor, a
factory worker, a housewife, a secretary, and a woman of an agricultural household. Among them were women who were married, women who were widowed, and women who had been deserted by emigrant husbands. These were
all women with whom I worked and socialized throughout my year in Vila Chã.
I knew their children, spouses, and siblings, and was welcome in their homes
to share meals and family celebrations. With each of these women, in addition
to the many informal contexts within which we talked, I spent eight to ten
afternoons in their homes tape-recording and/or taking notes on the details of
their lives as they presented them to me. In the initial stages of these sessions,
I remained nondirective in order to enable each woman to emphasize the experiences or parts of her life that she considered most important. At a later stage,
I designed more directed interviews in order to request elaboration or clarifica-
tion, or in order to address subjects we had not discussed at all. I have selected
five of the twelve life stories for presentation in this book because they illumi-
nate various aspects of the relationship between women's work and the social
construction of gender, and because they show different ways in which women
negotiate their gender identity. On the question of the representativeness of
life histories, Langness and Frank, following Margaret Mead, argue that "any
individual, with certain qualifications, can be taken as representative of a culture in some sense" provided that his or her position within the society is specified (1981:53). Sheridan argues that "by its very nature, the life history

method is time-consuming and emotionally demanding, and its contribution can never be judged in terms of quantity" (1984:17). I first wrote the stories of Vila Chã women in colloquial Portuguese; I have translated them into standard English because I believe that this will render the stories accessible to a wider audience and that translation of the colloquial Portuguese into some form of English dialect would be patronizing to the subjects. See Patai (1988) for an important discussion of the ethical problems surrounding the writing down of life stories that have been told orally.

4. Even prior to the publication of Oscar Lewis's now-classic *Children of Sánchez* in 1961, recording life histories had been an important method of data collection in anthropology (Simmons 1942; Smith 1954). But anthropologists have often lamented that the method has been poorly developed and poorly utilized (Langness and Frank 1981). Recent interest in the life history has come, in large part, from European sociologists and feminist scholars who see it as a democratic method of conducting research that lessens the objectification of the subject and "gives a voice" to the nonliterate and the powerless (Bertaux 1981; Geiger 1986; Ginsburg 1989; Knight 1974; Myerhoff 1978; Patai 1988; Personal Narratives Group 1989; Shostak 1983; Thompson, Wailey, and Lummis 1983). In the Portuguese context, the life history method has been used by Brettell (1982), Chinita (1983), Joaquim (1985), and Vicente (1985), all of whom focus on women. Other life histories of European peasants include Buechler and Buechler's recorded autobiography of a Spanish Galician woman (1981) and Hélias's account of his life in a Breton village (1978). At the same time, a long tradition of reflexive writing in anthropology (see, for example, Bowen's *Return to Laughter* [1964]) is incarnated in contemporary ethnography in the work of the self-named postmodernists (Clifford and Marcus 1986; Crapanzano 1980; K. Dwyer 1982; Rabinow 1979). For a history of this tradition, see Cole (forthcoming 1991). For early critiques of postmodernist anthropology, see Geertz (1988); Mascia-Lees, Sharpe, and Cohen (1989); Spencer (1989). On the hazards of endeavoring to connect the "subjective" and "objective" spheres of consciousness, see Bourdieu (1986). Finally, for a recent important review of the ethical issues surrounding writing and *reading* women's life stories—including the feminist concern with appropriation of voice—see Behar (1990b).

CHAPTER 3
THE MARITIME HOUSEHOLD

1. As Sider has pointed out, "The opposition to elite cultural hegemony hardly occurs in the simple act of suggesting alternative values, or spinning oppositional value systems out of bitter critique and thin air. . . . Opposition to hegemonic domination advances values that are, or become, rooted in the ties people have to one another in daily life and in production" (1986:122). In Sider's terms, the positive valuation of the maritime way of life by the pescadores may be understood as the creation of counter-hegemonic cultural forms through the inversion and mockery of symbols borrowed from the existing hegemony in order to express experiences and claims different from the lavra-

dores'. Sider defines counter-hegemony as "an opposition to the prevailing hegemony—by mockery, by distancing and evasion, by denial or by oppositional claims, demands, or values. . . . Counter-hegemonic strategies like other forms of culture do not just emerge out of people's thoughts and individual experiences, but out of their mutual understanding of their social relations" (1980:26).

2. Writing of the hamlet of Fontelas in the interior northern province of Trás-os-Montes, O'Neill has argued that the legal prescription for equal division of property among all heirs, if followed, would have resulted in "collective economic suicide" (1983:53) in the context of scarce resources in that isolated mountainous region. Instead, inheritance practices endeavored to keep the patrimony intact, and this resulted in strategies to limit the formation of new households through marriage. In Fontelas these strategies included late marriage, celibacy, and high ratios of illegitimacy. O'Neill sees reproduction in the parish as constantly motivated by the tension between "matrimony" and "patrimony." Although in coastal Vila Chã, in the mid-nineteenth century, there were similar efforts on the part of agricultural households to keep the patrimony intact, there was less constraint on marriage and on the establishment of new households because, as we have seen, some landless and land-poor households (i.e., nonheirs) were turning to the exploitation of marine resources and were not dependent on land ownership and agricultural production.

3. The prevalence of sibling vicinality parallels Pina-Cabral's observations in interior northwestern Portugal, but it should be clarified that, at least in Vila Chã, it is sisters, not brothers, who live near one another.

4. Actual numbers are unavailable (and, given the size of the community, would be difficult to obtain) as to what proportion of households followed what appears to be a pattern of female ultimogeniture (i.e., younger daughter inheritance). My reading of the data at present suggests that, among households with daughters, it was by far the majority. Where a household had only sons, the son's wife would assume responsibility for practical management of the household property, and, in a succeeding generation, a daughter would inherit the property. For a comparative discussion of household structure, inheritance, and residence patterns in Iberia as a whole, see the special issue of the *Journal of Family History* (Douglass 1988).

5. O'Neill (1983:68) found extraordinarily high illegitimacy ratios in the hamlet of Fontelas, Trás-os-Montes, where, during the first three decades of the twentieth century, illegitimacy ratios were 44.1, 46.0, and 42.3. In Fontelas more than 80 percent of illegitimate children were born to jornaleiras, which indicates a very strong correlation between property and marriage (legitimacy), and between propertylessness and illegitimacy. O'Neill argues that, in the context of Fontelas, illegitimacy was created and perpetuated by the inheritance system, and that jornaleiras and their illegitimate children provided a continual source of necessary labor to the landowning agricultural households without threatening the basis of inheritance of patrimony in those households.

6. Rates of nonmarriage for women were determined from the parish death registers (*óbitos*). All deaths of unmarried women over the age of fifty were recorded. For Vila Chã these rates, expressed as a percentage of all female

deaths by decade, were: (from 1911 to 1919) 11.1 ($N = 36$); (from 1920 to 1929) 8.3 ($N = 36$); (from 1930 to 1939) 12.9 ($N = 31$); (from 1940 to 1949) 21.9 ($N = 32$); (from 1950 to 1959) 11.7 ($N = 60$); (from 1960 to 1969) 29.7 ($N = 64$). These rates are lower than those recorded by Brettell (1985:92) for Lanheses, but they are nonetheless significant, especially during the decades from 1940 to 1949, when more than one-fifth of women were unmarried at death, and from 1960 to 1969, when this figure rose to almost 30 percent. These data suggest that at the turn of the century and again in the 1920s—both periods of high rates of male emigration—it was difficult for all women to marry. The rate of nonmarriage in Vila Chã may have been lower than that recorded by Brettell for Lanheses because women of maritime households married younger than did women of agricultural households.

CHAPTER 4
WOMEN WORK AT SEA AND ON LAND

1. Women may have gone to sea in other Portuguese fisheries, but there has been no research on the subject. Explanation for the local perception that Vila Chã was the only fishery where women regularly went to sea may lie in the intermediate character of its fishery. The fishery in Vila Chã was not a large urban fishery like those of Póvoa de Varzim and Matosinhos where the pescadores were entirely alienated from agricultural work. Nor was the Vila Chã fishery carried out by small landowners as was the case in other small fisheries along the coast north of Póvoa de Varzim. By 1890, for example, the Póvoa fishery employed almost six thousand men and women. The fishery began to industrialize early in the twentieth century, and to use large boats with gas engines and as many as ten men as crew. Women were busy full-time onshore selling and processing the large volume of fish caught, and manufacturing and mending nets. On the other hand, in the smaller northern fisheries, the majority of the pescadores were also small landowners, and women there were busy with agricultural work and seaweed harvesting. The local system of land tenure was different in Vila Chã (and throughout the concelho of Vila do Conde), where land tended to be concentrated in larger plots and held in the hands of a few lavradores. The Vila Chã pescadores were essentially landless in that they did not own sufficient land for farming. At the same time, their population was small in comparison with the landless fishing population in Póvoa de Varzim. An additional factor was the poor quality of the landing beach—there was no natural harbor as in Póvoa—so that the fishery could not develop beyond a small-boat household-based inshore fishery. Remaining essentially a household operation, the Vila Chã fishery depended on all labor, male and female, both at sea and on land.

2. Correspondence on file in the Biblioteca Municipal de Vila do Conde.

3. In Vila Chã the term *illegitimate* is not used. Instead, illegitimate children are said to "have no father" (although in a majority of cases the natural father was known to them).

4. See O'Brien (1977) on female husbands in Africa for a discussion of the possibilities of third genders.

CHAPTER 5
WORK AND SHAME

1. See, for example, Cutileiro (1971); Pitt-Rivers (1971); Peristiany (1965). Cf. O'Brien (1984), who makes a similar point concerning the writing about women in Melanesian ethnography. O'Brien argues that we do not know what Melanesian women do because ethnocentric ethnographers have given priority to men's activities (hunting, for example) and have assumed that women fulfill reproductive roles only.

2. Writing of Spain, Pitt-Rivers (1971:119), however, did note that wealthy *señoritos* demanded "a stricter mode of conduct from their womenfolk" than did poorer men.

3. The question of whether Portugal is "Mediterranean" is not a particularly useful one. Historical geographers certainly have never considered northwestern Portugal to be part of the Mediterranean region—see, for example, Ribeiro (1986), who describes the area as "Atlantic." For over a decade, however, the major ethnography of Portugal published in English (Cutileiro 1971) was a study of a community in southern Portugal that engaged in the then-current Mediterranean discourse among British anthropologists. It is perhaps for this reason that anthropologists working outside Portugal (and lacking evidence to the contrary) have tended to subsume Portugal in a so-called Mediterranean culture area. My purpose in dissecting the honor-and-shame code from the perspective of a community in northwestern Portugal is not to argue that the area is not Mediterranean. Rather, it is to demonstrate just how inaccurate it is to arbitrarily extend the discourse to this region. For a new approach to regional comparison in the "old" Mediterranean, see Pina-Cabral (1989).

4. In order to limit the number of children they have, both husband and wife may exercise restraint in sexual activity. Women are interested in birth control and employ a variety of methods ranging from douching after intercourse to sleeping surrounded by their children so as to be less accessible to their husbands. Ideally, husbands will also assume responsibility for limiting family size, and coitus interruptus was said to be the most common and desirable method of birth control. "My husband is careful" (*O meu homem tem cuidado*), women say. It is probable that, in the past, malnutrition was also a factor in limiting the number of births. Female malnutrition is known to lead to fewer pregnancies' being brought to full term and to shorten the female fertile period (Edholm, Harris, and Young 1977:113). Since the early 1970s the birth control pill has been readily available and fully accepted in the parish. Older women consider that women today are fortunate to have a simple and reliable method of controlling family size.

5. *Ter vergonha* is to have the characteristics of shame, modesty, decency, restraint, propriety. To be *sem vergonha* is to lack these characteristics, to be shameless. *Não ter vergonha* is to have no shame. The expression *Que vergonha!* means "What a shame!" *or* "What an embarrassment!" Interestingly, *perder a vergonha* (to lose one's shame), used in reference to women, has both negative and positive connotations. It can mean, negatively, that a woman

acted shamelessly. Or it can be used approvingly to mean that a woman asserted herself in a situation in which women are generally expected to accept gender inequality and to exhibit submissive behavior.

6. Although it has been argued that the code of honor and shame is probably characteristic of all face-to-face societies (Peristiany 1965), the gender attributions of the code (and of vergonha in the Portuguese context) may be the distinctive characteristic of this system of social control in the so-called Mediterranean societies (Brandes 1987; Gilmore 1987).

7. Pina-Cabral (1986:88) acknowledges the element of contradiction in gender roles in northwestern Portugal, but he does not consider that the existence of contradiction allows for fluidity, change, and negotiation. Herzfeld (1986:217), however, writing of women in Greece, argues that "female" and "male" are symbolic categories which are "manipulable and labile" and are used for "negotiating complex relationships between different levels of identity—kin-group, local, regional, and national."

8. Several women over sixty years of age said that they did not menstruate until as late as age eighteen or nineteen. Today the age at first menstruation has decreased to around twelve or thirteen years.

9. Brettell (1985:94–98) and Pina-Cabral (1986:57) both describe the frequency of premarital sex in northern Portugal.

10. Intergenerational differences among women are further discussed in chapter 7.

11. Cross-cultural studies of fishing societies indicate that this was the case in other nonindustrialized household-based fisheries. Nadel-Klein (1988), writing of Scotland, says that a man could not fish without taking a wife who would perform the shore work. This dependent relationship was reflected in the local expression "A fisher laddie needs a fisher lassie." Faris (1972:75) writes of a Newfoundland fishing settlement, "A man without a wife is like a man without a good boat or a good horse and a woman is, in the division of shares of a voyage, considered an item in her husband's capital, just as a cod trap or an engine." It is unlikely that Faris is presenting the Newfoundland woman's perception of herself (cf. Murray 1979 for a woman's point of view). It is also not clear whether this is Faris's interpretation of a husband's perception of a wife, or if Newfoundland fishermen themselves see the conjugal relationship in this way.

12. Compare Pina-Cabral (1986:88), who says that despite strong feelings of partnership between husband and wife in the agricultural households of northwestern Portugal, men "emphasize the need not to dar confiança (give trust) to one's wife." This contrasts with the Vila Chã maritime woman's ideal of conjugal relations as expressed by Alvina: "I think it's a terrible thing when a husband does not trust his wife."

13. S. Rogers (1975), writing of rural France, argues that women's selective submissive behavior is part of a "myth" of male dominance that serves to maintain nonhierarchical gender relations in peasant societies. According to Rogers, the myth of male dominance occurs in societies with the following characteristics: the domestic sphere is of central importance; women are primarily associated with the domestic sphere; informal relationships and forms of power are

at least as significant a force in everyday life as formalized, authorized relationships of power; and men have greater access to jural and other formal rights. Where men also experience a felt lack of power (for example, in the exclusion of Vila Chã fishermen from the parish administration under the New State), both the relatively powerful position of women and the mythical nature of male dominance are enhanced. Finally, a sixth component ensures that both men and women will "play the game" and maintain a relatively even balance of power. This sixth component is men and women's approximately equal dependence on one other economically, socially, politically, or in other important ways (S. Rogers 1975:732). The long history of male emigration in Vila Chã, however, may have reduced the extent to which women perceived themselves to be dependent upon men.

14. Pina-Cabral (1986:89) says that, in interior northwestern Portugal, sex was so important in a marriage that there was competition between husband and wife to satisfy each other sexually.

15. This statement is similar to one recorded by Brettell (1986:297). A woman who had been pregnant at the time of her marriage explained to Brettell the birth of a child soon afterward: "The first child comes in a short amount of time. After that it takes longer and is more regular."

16. Female sexuality was manipulated in Vila Chã the way Lambek has described the manipulation of virginity by women in Mayotte. In Mayotte "sex is a resource controlled by women and it is their right and responsibility to reserve it for socially productive ends" (1983:266). Virginity signifies respect for social order and adult responsibility, not repression of female sexuality— and it can be faked. Similarly, Boddy, writing of female circumcision, describes how, in the Northern Sudan, virgins are "made, not born" (1982:687). It should also be noted that we are concerned here with the land-poor maritime households of Vila Chã. Among the agricultural households of the parish, where land and property are more important prerequisites for marriage, virginity can assume importance as another resource to be manipulated by households and not only by women themselves. Excessive concern with the anthropological code of honor and shame has, however, glossed over differences in the value that different social classes place on virginity.

17. Following the Revolution of April 25, 1974, the Constitution of the new democracy (A Constituição da República Portuguesa) was passed in 1976, and church and state were officially separated. Divorce was legalized again, and wives achieved the right to equality with their husbands in divorce proceedings. Rights of common-law couples and their children were also recognized.

18. The history and legacy of the New State is the subject of much current writing and debate. For traditional sources, see Delzell (1970) and Oliveira Marques (1972). For recent analyses, see Costa Pinto (1987), Graham and Wheeler (1983), Leeds (1984), Raby (1988), Robinson (1979), and Sousa Ferreira and Opello, Jr. (1985). For ethnographic case studies of the political life of two rural Portuguese communities under the regime, see Cutileiro (1971) and Riegelhaupt (1967; 1979). For an interesting parallel, see Harding's 1984 study of a rural Aragonese village in Spain under Franco.

19. Not until 1978 was the category of *chefe de família* removed from the Civil Code, and a wife defined as her husband's equal and not his dependent. At this time, wives also acquired the same legal rights as their husbands to "acquire, administer, enjoy and dispose of property."

20. Not until the 1976 Constitution did all women and men eighteen years of age and older obtain equal voting rights. The 1976 Constitution declared all citizens, male and female, equal.

21. There is no literal translation for the term *regedor*, a special type of administrative officer created by the New State. The regedor reported to the câmara municipal in Vila do Conde. His (for the regedor was always a man) responsibilities included collecting census materials, policing the parish, collecting agricultural and industrial statistics, posting government decrees, notifying young men of their induction into military service, and informing the câmara of any irregularities in the administration of the parish or the operation of the parish council. The council consisted of three members: president, secretary, and treasurer, and two alternates. It was responsible for ascertaining voting eligibility through a yearly census, certifying the poor, administering the common lands of the parish, undertaking certain public works, and suggesting needed public improvements to the county administration. Common lands (*baldios*), the council's main financial resource, varied in importance from one parish to the next and in Vila Chã were inconsequential. The P.I.D.E. (*Polícia Internacional e de Defesa do Estado*) was a secret police force trained by German and Italian security experts. The P.I.D.E. monitored all aspects of parish life, and, where a P.I.D.E. officer was not resident in a community, the force achieved this surveillance through the use of paid informers. In Vila Chã there was a resident P.I.D.E. officer who was also a wealthy lavrador.

22. Following Riegelhaupt (1973; 1984), I consider the behavior incorporated in the Portuguese tradition of popular anticlericalism to be religious in nature, originating in the people's distinction between "church" and "religion." See Badone (1990a) for a discussion of the dangers of establishing an analytical dichotomy between "elite" and "popular" anticlericalism. For comparative studies of the tradition of anticlericalism in European Catholicism, also see Badone (1990a) (especially the papers by Badone, Behar, and Brettell).

23. In Vila Chã, the dead continue to be considered important members of household and community. During the week preceding Todos os Santos the cemetery is a festive place as groups of women work together scrubbing, polishing, or whitewashing the family graves. On the afternoon of October 31 they place flowers—traditionally homegrown white and yellow chrysanthemums but, increasingly, elaborate and expensive purchased flower arrangements—and light candles or oil lamps on the graves. On the morning of Todos os Santos, men, women, and children dressed in somber colors attend mass and afterward "visit" with dead family members in the cemetery, standing quietly for fifteen or twenty minutes in front of each one's grave. The priest speaks disparagingly of the money the people spend on tombstones and on decorating the cemetery, and he disapproves of the practice of visiting the graves on Todos os Santos. Interestingly, lavradores and pescadores alike give value to this day. See Badone (1989) for a detailed description of the "cult of the dead" in Brit-

tany, which bears some strong resemblances to Vila Chã people's beliefs about the dead.

24. For discussions of women and religion in Europe, see Cutileiro (1971) and Riegelhaupt (1984) on Portugal; Brandes (1980), Christian (1989), and Lisón-Tolosana (1983) on Spain; Badone (1990b) on Britanny; and Dubisch (1990) on Greece. Christian (1989:153–161) offers an especially provocative preliminary analysis of religion in the context of women's life cycle. Although my own data at present do not allow such a comparison, the possibility of an ebb and flow in a woman's religious activity depending on her progression through the stages of the life cycle warrants further comparative discussion.

25. Warner, who has documented the history and form of the cult of Mary throughout Europe, argues that women worship the Virgin not in penitence for sin (such as sex)—the official view promoted by the church—but "to beg for the cure of earthly ills" (1978:310; see also Christian 1989). The cult of the Virgin in Vila Chã, as elsewhere, is an important part of the worship of a whole range of patron saints who are thought to possess powers to cure various illnesses and to heal injuries to specific parts of the body. The Virgin thus plays a major part in local curing practices. The whole subject of women, illness, and curing is an important one in Vila Chã but one on which I have insufficient data at present.

26. Following Stavenhagen (1975), who argues that social classes constitute historical categories whose sociological content is specific to the society under study, I refer to the fundamental division of Vila Chã society into lavradores and pescadores as a class division. In rural Portuguese society the sociological content of social classes is extremely diverse. Cutileiro (1971) describes the highly stratified society of latifundist-landowner (*latifundiário*), sharecropper (seareiro), and laborer (trabalhador) of the Alentejo. Riegelhaupt (1979) considers that the parish of São Miguel in the Estremadura comprises equivalent units—households—that maintain "balanced reciprocal relations," and among whom differences in wealth have not led to local class differentiation. Reluctant to speak of "social classes," Pina-Cabral (1986) has divided his Alto Minho parishes, Paço and Couto, into what he calls "wealth sub-groups" (The Very Rich, The Rich, The Upper Middle, The Lower Middle, the Poor, and the Very Poor), but he is mainly interested in the "cultural differentiation" between bourgeoisie and peasantry, "the two most significant status groups" (30) in local society. O'Neill (1987) writes of the social "hierarchy" of *proprietários* (large landowners), lavradores (middle peasants), and jornaleiras (women day laborers) in Fontelas, Trás-os-Montes—categories the residents themselves employ. In Vila Chã, the operative categories are lavradores, jornaleiros, and pescadores, with the most important cultural division being that between those who work on the land and those who work on the sea.

27. Use of the term "social construction of gender" follows Edholm, Harris, and Young (1977) and assumes that gender is a social and historical construct, malleable and subject to change (see also Bourque and Warren 1981). Ortner and Whitehead speak instead of the "cultural construction of gender," and they view gender as a symbolic construct, a matter of "symbolic analysis and inter-

pretation" (1981:1–2). I combine the two approaches when I speak of the "negotiation" of gender relations. The Althusserian concept of "relative autonomy" refers to "the specification, for a given social and historical context, of the limits to the autonomous operation of ideology . . . [and recognition that a] range of possibilities exist for the ideological processes of a particular social formation, without necessarily being able to predict the specific form they may take" (Barrett 1980:97; see also Rubin 1975). Again, it is through the negotiation of gender relations by individuals and groups that gender systems achieve relative autonomy.

CHAPTER 6

INVEJA

1. Ana is also a distinctive-looking woman. She is lean and blue-eyed. Despite a certain amount of phenotypical diversity on the north coast of Portugal (attributed locally to the historical invasions and visits of seafaring peoples including the Vikings), blue eyes are rare. Ana herself pointed out her blue eyes (*olhos azuis*) to me. Cutileiro, writing of southern Portugal, says that old women with blue eyes are especially associated with the evil eye (1971; see also Herzfeld 1981:570). Pina-Cabral, writing of interior northwestern Portugal, says that "thin, sinewy, wan" people are especially accused of using the evil eye (1986:177). Ana has both blue eyes and a "thin, sinewy, wan" appearance. I am also interested in the possibility that Ana may be the subject of this indictment because she does not fit the local stereotype of what a woman *should* look like: she is not short, round, bosomy, and fecund-looking (although she was married and did have two children).

2. An alternative explanation may be offered. Since the time that I did my fieldwork, Fátima and her husband have separated, and Fátima is suing for a divorce. Her perception of inveja emanating from her sister-in-law might also be seen as her way of trying to explain—to herself and to others—the real experience of unhappiness in her marriage and why marriage (which according to local ideals should last forever) could fail.

3. Lock and Dunk (1985) have similarly described the phenomenon of *nevra* among Greek women living in Canada.

4. See Pina-Cabral (1986:186ff.) for a discussion of the differences between witches and white witches (both of whom are called bruxos), their methods and cures, and how evil forces are perceived among the peasantry of northwestern Portugal. It is Pina-Cabral's view that evil originates in perceptions of inequality in a society that sees itself as fundamentally egalitarian.

5. It is not clear to what extent the New State's ideology of família played a role in defining the importance of familial relations and in undermining the relative importance of communal relations. Certainly the regime endorsed the church's efforts to undermine feelings of allegiance to community by trying to terminate the celebration of local festas and other occasions when a communal identity was expressed. The New State also discouraged (and in some cases defined as illegal) other forms of association based on work, class, sex, neighborhood, or region.

6. The term *Ti'* (Tia, or Aunt) was used among the pescadores as a form of address to all adult women. In 1985, the term was still used for addressing or referring to women over the age of approximately forty. In this highly endogamous community (at least until the 1960s), most residents were, in fact, related to one another, if not by birth, then by marriage. Because of the prevalence of uxorivicinality in Praia and Facho, a group of women (neighbors) who shared the fermento often—but not always—were sisters, their mothers, and their maternal aunts.

7. The visits to the dead take a form similar to that observed by Badone in Brittany (1989:63-64). Upon entering the room where the deceased is laid out, people dip a sprig of laurel (not boxwood as in Brittany) in a dish of holy water that sits on a table by the bed and sprinkle the body while tracing the sign of the cross.

8. Young (1978:151) describes a parallel set of relations among the women of what she calls "self-provisioning" households in rural Mexico that are similar in economic organization to the maritime households of Vila Chã. She writes, "It is these households which are in keen competition for scarce land and other social resources, thus the degree of mutual aid between them is slight, women's solidarity and co-operation with non-kin is equally slight, and interfamilial rivalry and strife is not infrequent." Rosenberg (1988:194), describing competition and *jalousie* (jealousy) in a French alpine community, suggests that the inevitable competition in a small-scale society is intensified under contemporary conditions of increased commoditization and industrialization. She argues that cooperative and communal structures traditionally ameliorated the effects of competition, but that these structures have dissolved under capitalism.

CHAPTER 7
FISHERWOMEN AND FACTORY WORKERS

1. My analysis of the changes in northwestern Portugal from the perspective of the "women and development" literature is, to my knowledge, novel in a European context. Indeed, the subject of women and factory work in contemporary Europe has received surprisingly little attention from anthropologists. Notable exceptions are Giovannini (1985) and Holmes (1989). Important historical studies are Scott and Tilly (1975) on women's proletarianization in nineteenth-century France and Ingerson's work (1982–1983; 1985) on women textile workers in the Ave Valley, northwestern Portugal, under the New State.

2. Since 1960, there has been a decrease in the absolute number of men who fish in Vila Chã. In 1966 there were 115 fishermen; in 1973 there were 105 fishermen; and in 1985 there were only 42 active fishermen.

3. In the parish registers of marriages during the 1930s, five women are identified as *operárias* or *fabricantes* (both terms meaning factory workers). These were daughters of the poorest households. This number is possibly low, as in the parish records the priests tended to identify women as domésticas (housewives) regardless of whether they worked outside the home. It is not clear why the priest chose to identify these five women as factory workers.

4. See table 1.3, chapter 1.

5. Salazar argued that the New State's model of the family was based on the peasant family. As we have seen in earlier chapters, there is no evidence that the pescadores of Vila Chã held the state view of woman as primarily wife and mother, or that their households were organized around the concept of male authority and a male wage. In a study of thirteen textile mills in the Ave Valley inland from Vila Chã, Ingerson (1985) documents how rural women have constituted more than half of all textile workers since the late nineteenth century, and how mill owners, happy to employ women in times of labor shortage, would use the state's ideology of the family to justify laying off women in times of downturn in the industry. In 1939, for example, six hundred married women were laid off from one mill, and the owners, paraphrasing Salazar, published a statement offering the following reason: "In truth, the place of a married woman, with or without children, is in the home. It is there that she can best help her husband and especially look after the children who are so neglected when their mother is not in the home. We are convinced that, in the majority of cases, the decrease in earnings brought about by a married woman's leaving the factory will soon be made up for by a more orderly household" (as quoted in Ingerson 1985:8; translation mine).

6. In a study of factory women in Malaysia, Ong argues that the sexuality of new working women becomes the focus of local anxiety over the social effects of capitalist development. She writes, "A heightened sexuality attributed to Malay female workers by the Malaysian public can be considered the contradictory cultural constructions of a society intensely ambivalent about the social consequences of industrial development" (1987:4). A parallel preoccupation with the sexuality of factory workers in Vila Chã may be similarly and simultaneously understood as both the projection onto women of local anxiety and ambivalence about the social changes taking place, and an expression of resistance to those changes. Resistance in this form may be rooted in what Scott (1976) calls a "moral economy" under siege, rather than in other forms of alliance (such as class interest).

7. For a sensitive description of the working conditions and lives of immigrant women workers in a garment factory in Toronto, see Gannagé (1986).

8. I use the term *reproductive work* to include not only the work of biological reproduction (pregnancy, childbirth, and lactation) but also the work of social reproduction, including the daily and generational reproduction of social forms (like the family and household) through domestic labor and child socialization.

GLOSSARY

This glossary comprises Portuguese words that appear frequently in the text.

adega — tavern
a jornal — paid agricultural work, usually by the day
barraca — hut, shack
barriga — abdomen; also used to refer to a woman's uterus and the reproductive zone of the female body
bruxo, -a — lit., witch; also diviner, sorcerer, faith healer, medium or exorcist
casa — house, household
casa do mar — shack on beach for storage of fishing gear
criado (de servir) — servant
dona de casa — housewife
dono — boat owner
dote — dowry, expectation of eventual inheritance
educado — well brought up
escrava — slave
família — family
homem, -ens — man, men
inveja — envy
jornaleiro, -a, -os — agricultural day laborer(s)
lavrador, -eira, -es — landowning farmer(s)
lota — place where fish are sold by auction
lugar, -es — locality(-ies); hamlet(s)
mulher, -es — woman, women
namorado, -a, -os — sweetheart(s)
namorar — to court
namoro — courtship
nervos — nerves
pescador, -eira, -es — fisherman, fisherwoman, fishermen and women
pilado — a small crab netted and dried for fertilizer
os pobres — the poor
praia — beach
respeito — respect
os ricos — the rich
sargaço — seaweed
trabalhadeira — hardworking woman
trabalhar — to work; also used for "to have sexual intercourse"
vergonha — shame, modesty, propriety

BIBLIOGRAPHY

PRIMARY SOURCES

Parish Archives

Parish Registers: Births. Marriages. Deaths. Vila Chã, 1911–1985 inclusive.

Concelho Archives

Electoral Censuses. Vila Chã. Câmara Municipal do Concelho de Vila do Conde 1862, and 1865–1877, 1905–1928, and 1966–1973 inclusive.
Memórias paroquiais. 1758.
Número dos fogos de cada lugar das freguesias. Vila do Conde, 1863.
Miscellaneous documents and correspondence.

SECONDARY SOURCES

Aceves, J. B., and W. A. Douglass, eds.
1976 *The Changing Faces of Rural Spain*. New York: Wiley.
Acheson, J.
1981 Anthropology of Fishing. *Annual Review of Anthropology* 10:275–316.
Alexander, P.
1982 *Sri Lankan Fishermen: Rural Capitalism and Peasant Society*. Canberra: Australian National University.
Altorki, S.
1986 *Women in Saudi Arabia: Ideology and Behaviour among the Elite*. New York: Columbia University Press.
Amrouche, F.
1988 [orig. 1968] *My Life Story: The Autobiography of a Berber Woman*. London: The Women's Press.
Andersen, R., and C. Wadel, eds.
1972 *North Atlantic Fishermen: Anthropological Essays on Modern Fishing*. St. John's, Newfoundland: Institute of Social and Economic Research.
Anonymous
1890 *Inquérito industrial e comercial: a pesca*. Lisbon: Imprensa Nacional.
1937 "Velharias" Vila Chã I. *Renovação* 153.
1938 "Velharias" Vila Chã II. *Renovação* 155.
1984 *Pesca e navegação* (May): 25.
Ardener, S.
1975 *Perceiving Women*. London: J. M. Dent and Sons.
Arizpe, L., and J. Aranda
1981 The "Comparative Advantages" of Women's Disadvantages: Women

Workers in the Strawberry Export Agribusiness in Mexico. *Signs* 7(2):453–473.

Badone, E.

1989 *The Appointed Hour: Death, Worldview, and Social Change in Brittany.* Berkeley: University of California Press.

1990a *Religious Orthodoxy and Popular Faith in European Society.* Ed. Princeton: Princeton University Press.

1990b Breton Folklore of Anticlericalism. In *Religious Orthodoxy and Popular Faith in European Society*, E. Badone, ed., pp. 140–162. Princeton: Princeton University Press.

Bailey, F. G., ed.

1971 *Gifts and Poison: The Politics of Reputation.* Oxford: Basil Blackwell.

Baldaque da Silva, A. A.

1891 *Estado actual das pescas em Portugal.* Lisbon: Imprensa Nacional.

Barbosa, J.

1985 Algumas achegas sobre a importância das pescarias na Póvoa de Varzim, seu trato com a Galiza no primeiro quartel do século XIX. In *Colóquio "Santos Graça" de etnografia marítima*, 2:143–169. Póvoa de Varzim: Câmara Municipal da Póvoa de Varzim.

Barrett, M.

1980 *Women's Oppression Today: Problems in Marxist-Feminist Analysis.* London: Verso.

1985 Introduction. In *The Origin of the Family, Private Property and the State*, by F. Engels, pp. 7–30. London: Penguin Books.

Behar, R.

1986 *Santa María del Monte: The Presence of the Past in a Spanish Village.* Princeton: Princeton University Press.

1990a The Struggle for the Church: Popular Anticlericalism and Religiosity in Post-Franco Spain. In *Religious Orthodoxy and Popular Faith in European Society*, E. Badone, ed., pp. 76–112. Princeton: Princeton University Press.

1990b Rage and Redemption: Reading the Life Story of a Mexican Marketing Woman. *Feminist Studies* 16(2):223–258.

Behar, R., and D. Frye

1988 Property, Progeny, and Emotion: Family History in a Leonese Village. *Journal of Family History* 13(1):13–32.

Beneria, L.

1979 Reproduction, Production and the Sexual Division of Labour. *Cambridge Journal of Economics* 3:203–225.

1982 *Women and Development: The Sexual Division of Labour in Rural Societies.* New York: Praeger.

Beneria, L., and G. Sen

1981 Accumulation, Reproduction, and Women's Role in Economic Development: Boserup Revisited. *Signs* 7(2):279–298.

Bertaux, D., ed.

1981 *Biography and Society: The Life History Approach in the Social Sciences.* Beverley Hills, Calif.: SAGE.

Boddy, J.

   1982 Womb as Oasis: The Symbolic Context of Pharaonic Circumcision in
   Rural Northern Sudan. *American Ethnologist* 9(4):682–698.

Boserup, E.

   1970 *Women's Role in Economic Development*. London: George Allen and
   Unwin.

Bouquet, M.

   1984 Women's Work in Rural South-West England. In *Family and Work in
   Rural Societies: Perspectives on Non-Wage Labour*, N. Long, ed., pp. 143–
   159. London: Tavistock.

Bourdieu, P.

   1986 L'illusion biographique. *Actes de la recherche en sciences sociales* 62/
   63:69–72.

Bourque, S., and K. Warren

   1981 *Women of the Andes: Patriarchy and Social Change in Two Peruvian
   Towns*. Ann Arbor: University of Michigan Press.

Bowen, E. S. [pseud.]

   1964 [orig. 1954] *Return to Laughter: An Anthropological Novel*. New
   York: Harper and Bros.

Brandão, R.

   1923 *Os pescadores*. Lisbon: Biblioteca Ulisseia de Autores Portugueses.

Brandes, S.

   1980 *Metaphors of Masculinity*. Philadelphia: University of Pennsylvania
   Press.

   1981 Like Wounded Stags: Male Sexual Ideology in an Andalusian Town.
   In *Sexual Meanings: The Cultural Construction of Gender*, S. Ortner
   and H. Whitehead, eds., pp. 216–239. Chicago: University of Chicago
   Press.

   1987 Reflections on Honor and Shame in the Mediterranean. In *Honor and
   Shame and the Unity of the Mediterranean*, D. Gilmore, ed., pp. 121–134.
   Washington: American Anthropological Association.

Brettell, C.

   1979 Emigrar para voltar: A Portuguese Ideology of Return Migration. *Papers in Anthropology* 20:1–20.

   1982 *We Have Already Cried Many Tears: The Stories of Three Portuguese
   Migrant Women*. Cambridge, Mass.: Schenkman Publishing Company.

   1984 Emigration and Underdevelopment; The Causes and Consequences
   of Portuguese Emigration to France in Historical and Cross-Cultural Perspective. In *Portugal in Development: Emigration, Industrialization, and
   the EEC*, T. Bruneau, V. da Rosa, and A. Macleod, eds., pp. 65–81. Ottawa:
   University of Ottawa Press.

   1985 Male Migrants and Unwed Mothers: Illegitimacy in a Northwestern
   Portuguese Town. *Anthropology* 9(1 and 2):87–110.

   1986 *Men Who Migrate, Women Who Wait: Population and History in a
   Portuguese Parish*. Princeton: Princeton University Press.

   1990 The Priest and His People: The Contractual Basis for Religious Practice in Rural Portugal. In *Religious Orthodoxy and Popular Faith in Euro-*

pean Society, E. Badone, ed., pp. 55–73. Princeton: Princeton University Press.

Brochado de Almeida, C.
1983 *Modivas: Uma aldeia Maiata*. Vila do Conde: Câmara Municipal de Vila do Conde.

Brøgger, J.
1987 *Pre-Bureaucratic Europeans: A Study of a Portuguese Fishing Community*. Trondheim: University of Trondheim Occasional Papers in Social Anthropology.

Brox, O.
1964 Natural Conditions, Inheritance, and Marriage in a North Norwegian Fjord. *Folk* 6(1):35–45.

Buechler, H., and J.-M. Buechler
1981 *Carmen: The Autobiography of a Spanish Galician Woman*. Rochester, Vt.: Schenkman Books.

Callier-Boisvert, C.
1966 Soajo—Une communauté féminine rurale de l'Alto Minho. *Bulletin des études portugaises* 27:237–278.

Campbell, J. K.
1964 *Honour, Family and Patronage*. Oxford: Clarendon.

Caro Baroja, J.
1965 Honour and Shame: A Historical Account of Several Conflicts. In *Honour and Shame: The Values of Mediterranean Society*, J. G. Peristiany, ed., pp. 81–137. London: Weidenfeld and Nicolson.

Casselberry, S., and N. Valavanes
1976 "Matrilocal" Greek Peasants and a Reconsideration of Residence Terminology. *American Ethnologist* 3:215–226.

Catedra Tomás, M., and R. Sanmartin Arce
1979 *Vaqueiros y pescadores: dos modos de vida*. Madrid: Akal.

Chinita, I.
1983 *Peste malina (histórias de mulheres)*. Lisbon: Ulmeiro/Fémina.

Christian, W. A., Jr.
1989 [orig. 1972] *Person and God in a Spanish Valley*. Princeton: Princeton University Press.

Clark, C.
1987 The Achievement of Virginity: Sexuality and Social Organization in Sub-Saharan Africa. Unpublished paper.

Clifford, J., and G. Marcus, eds.
1986 *Writing Culture: The Poetics and Politics of Ethnography*. Berkeley: University of California Press.

Cole, S.
1990 Cod, God, Country, and Family: The Portuguese Newfoundland Cod Fishery. *Maritime Anthropological Studies* 3(1):1–29.
Forthcoming 1991 Anthropological Lives: The Reflexive Tradition in a Social Science. In *Essays in Life Writing*, M. Kadar, ed. Toronto: University of Toronto Press.

Collier, J.
1986 From Mary to Modern Woman: The Material Basis of Marianismo and

Its Transformation in a Spanish Village. *American Ethnologist* 13(1):100–107.

Colson, E.

1953 *The Makah Indians.* Manchester: Manchester University Press.

Corbin, M. P.

1987 Review of Sex and Gender in Southern Europe: Problems and Prospects, D. Gilmore and G. Gwynne, eds. *Man* 22(4):756.

Costa, L.

1980 *A-Ver-O-Mar crónicas.* Figueirinhas.

Costa Pinto, A., et al., eds.

1987 *O Estado Novo: das origens ao fim da autarcia (1926–1959).* Vols. 1 and 2. Lisbon: Fragmentos.

Coull, J. R.

1972 *The Fisheries of Europe.* London.

Cowan, R. S.

1983 *More Work for Mother: The Ironies of Household Technology from the Open Hearth to the Microwave.* New York: Basic Books.

Crapanzano, V.

1977 Introduction. In *Case Studies in Spirit Possession*, V. Crapanzano and V. Garrison, eds., pp. 1–40. New York: John Wiley and Sons.

1980 *Tuhami: Portrait of a Moroccan.* Chicago: University of Chicago Press.

Cutileiro, J.

1971 *A Portuguese Rural Society.* Oxford: Clarendon.

Davis, D. L.

1983 *Blood and Nerves: An Ethnographic Focus on Menopause.* St. John's, Newfoundland: Institute of Social and Economic Research.

Davis, J. L.

1977 *People of the Mediterranean: An Essay in Comparative Social Anthropology.* London: Routledge and Kegan Paul.

Deere, C., and M. León de Leal

1982 Peasant Production, Proletarianization, and the Sexual Division of Labour in the Andes. In *Women and Development: The Sexual Division of Labour in Rural Societies*, L. Beneria, ed., pp. 65–93. New York: Praeger.

Delzell, C.

1970 *Mediterranean Fascism, 1919–1945.* New York: Harper and Row.

Descamps, P.

1935 *Le Portugal: La vie sociale actuelle.* Paris: Firmin-Didot.

Dionisopoulos-Mass, R.

1976 The Evil Eye and Bewitchment in a Peasant Village. In *The Evil Eye*, Clarence Maloney, ed., pp. 42–62. New York: Columbia University Press.

Douglass, W. A., ed.

1988 Iberian Family History. Special Issue. *Journal of Family History* 13(1).

Dubisch, J.

1986 *Gender and Power in Rural Greece.* Ed. Princeton: Princeton University Press.

1990 Pilgrimage and Popular Religion at a Greek Holy Shrine. In *Religious*

Orthodoxy and Popular Faith in European Society, E. Badone, ed., pp. 113–139. Princeton: Princeton University Press.

du Boulay, J.

1974 *Portrait of a Greek Mountain Village.* Oxford: Clarendon Press.

1976 Lies, Mockery and Family Integrity. In *Mediterranean Family Structures*, J. G. Peristiany, ed., pp. 389–406. Cambridge: Cambridge University Press.

1986 Women—Images of Their Nature and Destiny in Rural Greece. In *Gender and Power in Rural Greece*, J. Dubisch, ed., pp. 139–168. Princeton: Princeton University Press.

Dundes, A.

1981 Wet and Dry, the Evil Eye: An Essay in Indo-European and Semitic Worldview. In *The Evil Eye: A Folklore Casebook*, A. Dundes, ed., pp. 257–312. New York: Garland.

Dwyer, D.

1978 Ideologies of Sexual Inequality and Strategies for Change in Male-Female Relations. *American Ethnologist* 5(2):227–240.

Dwyer, K.

1982 *Moroccan Dialogues.* Baltimore: John Hopkins University Press.

Edholm, F., O. Harris, and K. Young

1977 Conceptualizing Women. *Critique of Anthropology* 3(9):101–130.

Elson, D., and R. Pearson

1981 The Subordination of Women and the Internationalisation of Factory Production. In *Of Marriage and the Market: Women's Subordination in International Perspective*, K. Young, C. Wolkowitz, and R. McCullagh, eds., pp. 144–166. London: CSE Books.

Elworthy, F.

1895 *The Evil Eye: The Origins and Practices of Superstition.* London: John Murray.

Etienne, M., and E. Leacock, eds.

1980 *Women and Colonization: Anthropological Perspectives.* New York: Praeger.

Faris, J.

1972 *Cat Harbour: A Newfoundland Fishing Settlement.* St. John's, Newfoundland: Institute of Social and Economic Research.

Fernandez, J.

1983 Consciousness and Class in Southern Spain. *American Ethnologist* 10:165–173.

Fernandez, J., and R. Lellep Fernandez

1988 Under One Roof: Household Formation and Cultural Ideals in an Asturian Mountain Village. *Journal of Family History* 13(1):123–142.

Fernández-Kelly, M. P.

1983 *For We Are Sold, I and My People: Women and Industry on Mexico's Frontier.* Albany: State University of New York Press.

Fiadeiro, M. A.

1984 Untitled. *Diário de Notícias.* May 16.

Filgueiras, O. L.
  1984 Fishing Crafts in Portugal. In *The Fishing Cultures of the World*, B. Gunda, ed., pp. 143–180. Budapest: Akadémiai Kiadó.
Firestone, M.
  1967 *Brothers and Rivals: Patrilocality in Savage Cove*. St. John's, Newfoundland: Institute of Social and Economic Research.
Firth, R.
  1946 *Malay Fishermen: Their Peasant Economy*. London: Routledge and Kegan Paul.
  1984 Roles of Women and Men in a Sea Fishing Economy: Tikopia Compared with Kelantan. In *The Fishing Cultures of the World*, B. Gunda, ed., pp. 1145–1170. Budapest: Akadémiai Kiadó.
Foster, G.
  1965 Peasant Society and the Image of Limited Good. *American Anthropologist* 67(2):293-315.
  1967 *Tzintzuntzan: Mexican Peasants in a Changing World*. Boston: Little, Brown.
  1972 The Anatomy of Envy: A Study in Symbolic Behaviour. *Current Anthropology* 13:165–201.
Freeman, S. T.
  1987 Egalitarian Structures in Iberian Social Systems: The Contexts of Turn-Taking in Town and Country. *American Ethnologist* 14(3):470–490.
Friedl, E.
  1967 Appearance and Reality: Status and Roles of Women in Mediterranean Societies. *Anthropological Quarterly* 40(3):97–108.
Galt, A.
  1982 The Evil Eye as Synthetic Image and Its Meanings on the Island of Pantelleria, Italy. *American Ethnologist* 9:664–681.
Gannagé, C.
  1986 *Double Day, Double Bind: Women Garment Workers*. Toronto: The Women's Press.
Geertz, C.
  1988 *Works and Lives: The Anthropologist as Author*. Stanford: Stanford University Press.
Geiger, S.
  1986 Women's Life Histories: Method and Content. *Signs* 11(2):334–351.
Gilmore, D.
  1985 Introduction. Special Issue No. 3, Sex and Gender in Southern Europe: Problems and Prospects. *Anthropology* 9(1 and 2):1–10.
  1987 Introduction: The Shame of Dishonour. In *Honor and Shame and the Unity of the Mediterranean*, D. Gilmore, ed., pp. 2–21. Washington: American Anthropological Association (Special Publication No. 22).
Ginsburg, F.
  1989 *Contested Lives: The Abortion Debate in an American Community*. Berkeley: University of California Press.

176 BIBLIOGRAPHY

Giovannini, M.
  1981 Woman: A Dominant Symbol within the Cultural System of a Sicilian Town. *Man* 16:408–426.
  1985 The Dialectics of Women's Factory Work in a Sicilian Town. *Anthropology* 9(1 and 2):45–64.
Gluckman, M.
  1963 Gossip and Scandal. *Current Anthropology* 4(3):307–316.
Graham, L., and D. Wheeler, eds.
  1983 *In Search of Modern Portugal: The Revolution and Its Consequences.* Madison: University of Wisconsin Press.
Harding, S.
  1975 Women and Words in a Spanish Village. In *Toward an Anthropology of Women*, R. Reiter, ed., pp. 282–308. New York: Monthly Review Press.
  1984 *Remaking Ibieca: Rural Life in Aragon under Franco.* Chapel Hill: University of North Carolina Press.
Harris, O.
  1981 Households as Natural Units. In *Of Marriage and the Market: Women's Subordination in International Perspective*, K. Young, C. Wolkowitz, and R. McCullagh, eds., pp. 49–68. London: CSE Books.
  1982 Households and Their Boundaries. *History Workshop Journal* 13:143–152.
Hartmann, H.
  1981 The Family as the Locus of Gender, Class and Political Struggle: The Example of Housework. *Signs* 6(3):366–394.
Hélias, P.-J.
  1978 *The Horse of Pride: Life in a Breton Village.* Trans. by J. Guicharnaud. New Haven: Yale University Press.
Herzfeld, M.
  1980 Honour and Shame: Problems in the Comparative Analysis of Moral Systems. *Man* 15:339–351.
  1981 Meaning and Morality: A Semiotic Approach to Evil Eye Accusations in a Greek Village. *American Ethnologist* 8(3):560–574.
  1984 The Horns of the Mediterraneanist Dilemma. *American Ethnologist* 11(3):429–454.
  1986 Within and Without: The Category of "Female" in the Ethnography of Modern Greece. In *Gender and Power in Rural Greece*, J. Dubisch, ed., pp. 215–233. Princeton: Princeton University Press.
Holmes, D.
  1989 *Cultural Disenchantments: Worker Peasantries in Northern Italy.* Princeton: Princeton University Press.
Ingerson, A.
  1982–1983 Uma história cultural e comparada da indústria têxtil no vale do Ave. *Análise social* 18(72, 73, 74):1465–1500.
  1985 Women and the Family in the Textile Industry of Northwestern Portugal under Salazar, 1930–1970. Unpublished paper.
Instituto Nacional de Estatística
  Recenseamentos gerais da população (General population censuses) 1864,

1878, 1890, 1900, 1911, 1920, 1930, 1940, 1950, 1960, 1970, 1981. Lisbon.

Iszevich, A.
1975 Emigrants, Spinsters and Priests: The Dynamics of Demography in Spanish Peasant Societies. *Journal of Peasant Studies* 2:292–312.

Iturra, R.
1985 Casamento, ritual e lucro: a produção dos produtores numa aldeia portuguesa (1862–1983). *Ler história* 5:59–81.

Joaquim, T.
1983 *Dar à luz: ensaio sobre as práticas e crenças da gravidez, parto e pós-parto em Portugal*. Lisbon: Publicações Dom Quixote.
1985 *Mulheres de uma aldeia*. Lisbon: Ulmeiro/Fémina.

Johnson, M.
1984 Domestic Work in Rural Iceland: An Historical Overview. In *Family and Work in Rural Societies: Perspectives on Non-Wage Labour*, N. Long, ed., pp. 160–174. London: Tavistock.

Kertzer, D.
1987 Review of Honor and Shame and the Unity of the Mediterranean, D. Gilmore, ed. *American Anthropologist* 89(4):991.

Knight, R.
1974 *A Very Ordinary Life*. Vancouver: New Star Books.

Lamas, M.
1948 *As mulheres do meu país*. Lisbon: Actuális Lda.

Lambek, M.
1983 Virgin Marriage and the Autonomy of Women in Mayotte. *Signs* 9(2):264–281.

Langness, L., and G. Frank
1981 *Lives: An Anthropological Approach to Biography*. Novato, Calif.: Chandler and Sharp Publishers.

Leacock, E.
1978 Women's Status in Egalitarian Societies: Implications for Social Evolution. *Current Anthropology* 19(2):247–275.
1981 History, Development, and the Division of Labour by Sex: Implications for Organization. *Signs* 7(2):474–491.

Leacock, E., and H. Safa, eds.
1986 *Women's Work: Development and the Division of Labour by Gender*. South Hadley, Mass.: Bergin and Garvie.

Leeds, E.
1984 Salazar's "Modelo Económico": The Consequences of Planned Constraint. In *Portugal in Development: Emigration, Industrialization, the European Community*, T. C. Bruneau, V. da Rosa, and A. Macleod, eds., pp. 13–51. Ottawa: University of Ottawa Press.

Lever, A.
1987 Honour as a Red Herring. *Critique of Anthropology* 6(3):83–106.

Lewis, O.
1961 *Children of Sánchez: Autobiography of a Mexican Family*. New York: Random House.

Lima, M.
1963 Matozinhos: contribuição para o estudo da linguagem, etnografia e folclore do concelho. *Revista Portuguesa de filologia* 11(2):323–462.

Lino Netto, M. de M.
1949 *A linguagem dos pescadores e lavradores do concelho de Vila do Conde.* Coimbra: Caso do Castelo, Editora.

Lisón-Tolosana, C.
1971 *Antropología cultural de Galicia.* Madrid: Siglo XXI.
1973 Some Aspects of Moral Structure in Galician Hamlets. *American Anthropologist* 75:823–834.
1976 The Ethics of Inheritance. In *Mediterranean Family Structures*, J. G. Peristiany, ed., pp. 305–315. Cambridge: Cambridge University Press.
1983 [orig. 1966] *Belmonte de los Caballeros: Anthropology and History in an Aragonese Community.* Princeton: Princeton University Press.

Lock, M., and P. Dunk
1985 "My Nerves are Broken": The Communication of Suffering in a Greek Canadian Community. Unpublished paper.

Löfgren, O.
1979 Marine Ecotypes in Preindustrial Sweden: A Comparative Discussion of Swedish Peasant Fishermen. In *North Atlantic Maritime Cultures*, R. Andersen, ed., pp. 83–109. The Hague: Mouton.

Long, N., ed.
1984 *Family and Work in Rural Societies: Perspectives on Non-Wage Labour.* London: Tavistock.

Lopes de Oliveira, A.
1973 *Caxineiros: gentes de Vila do Conde.* Vila do Conde: Edição-Centro Paroquial das Caxinas.

Luxton, M.
1980 *More Than a Labour of Love: Three Generations of Women's Work in the Home.* Toronto: The Women's Press.
1986 Two Hands for the Clock: Changing Patterns in the Gendered Division of Labour in the Home. In *Through the Kitchen Window: The Politics of Home and Family*, M. Luxton and H. Rosenberg, eds., pp. 17–36. Toronto: Garamond Press.

MacCormack, C., and M. Strathern
1980 *Nature, Culture and Gender.* Cambridge: Cambridge University Press.

Mackintosh, M.
1979 Domestic Labour and the Household. In *Fit Work for Women*, S. Burman, ed., pp. 173–191. London: Croom Helm.
1981 Gender and Economics: The Sexual Division of Labour and the Subordination of Women. In *Of Marriage and the Market*, K. Young, C. Wolkowitz, and R. McCullagh, eds., pp. 1–15. London: CSE Books.

Maloney, C., ed.
1976 *The Evil Eye.* New York: Columbia University Press.

Mascia-Lees, F., P. Sharpe, and C. Cohen
1989 The Postmodernist Turn in Anthropology: Cautions from a Feminist Perspective. *Signs* 15(1):7–33.

Matos, M. da Conceição Faria
1969 A vida rural na Apúlia. *Finisterra* 8(15):66–103.
Mendonsa, E. L.
1982 Turismo e estratificação na Nazaré. *Análise social* 28(2):311–329.
Mies, M.
1986 *Patriarchy and Accumulation on a World Scale: Women and the International Division of Labour.* London: Zed Books.
Mohanty, C. T.
1984 Under Western Eyes: Feminist Scholarship and Colonial Discourses. *Boundary* 2 and 3:333–358.
Moreira da Silva, R. F.
1983 Contraste e mutações na paisagem agrária das planiches e colinas minhotas. *Estudos contemporâneos* 5:9–115.
Munson, H., Jr.
1984 *The House of Si Abd Allah: The Oral History of a Moroccan Family.* New Haven: Yale University Press.
Murray, H. C.
1979 *More Than Fifty Percent: Women's Life in a Newfoundland Outport 1900–1950.* St. John's, Newfoundland: Breakwater Books.
Myerhoff, B.
1978 *Number Our Days.* New York: Simon and Schuster.
Nadel, J.
1984 Stigma and Separation: Pariah Status and Community Persistence in a Scottish Fishing Village. *Ethnology* 23(2):101–115.
Nadel-Klein, J.
1988 A Fisher Laddie Needs a Fisher Lassie: Endogamy and Work in a Scottish Fishing Village. In *To Work and to Weep: Women in Fishing Economies*, J. Nadel-Klein and D. L. Davis, eds., pp. 190–210. St. John's, Newfoundland: Institute of Social and Economic Research.
Nadel-Klein, J. and D. L. Davis, eds.
1988 *To Work and to Weep: Women in Fishing Economies.* St. John's, Newfoundland: Institute of Social and Economic Research.
Nash, J.
1979 *We Eat the Mines and the Mines Eat Us: Dependency and Exploitation in Bolivian Tin Mines.* New York: Columbia University Press.
Nunes, J. Arriscado
1986 On Household Composition in Northwestern Portugal: Some Critical Remarks and a Case Study. *Sociologia Ruralis* 26:48–69.
Oakley, A.
1972 *Sex, Gender and Society.* New York: Harper and Row.
O'Brien, D.
1977 Female Husbands in Southern Bantu Societies. In *Sexual Stratification: A Cross-Cultural View*, A. Schlegel, ed., pp. 109–126. New York: Columbia University Press.
1984 "Women Never Hunt": The Portrayal of Women in Melanesian Ethnography. In *Rethinking Women's Roles: Perspectives from the Pacific*, D. O'Brien and S. Tiffany, eds., pp. 53–70. Berkeley: University of California Press.

O'Laughlin, B.
1974 Mediation of Contradiction: Why Mbum Women Do Not Eat Chicken. In *Woman, Culture and Society*, M. Rosaldo and L. Lamphere, eds., pp. 301–318. Stanford: Stanford University Press.

Oliveira Marques, A.
1972 *History of Portugal*. 2 vols. New York: Columbia University Press.

O'Neill, B. J.
1983 Dying and Inheriting in Rural Trás-os-Montes. In *Death in Portugal: Studies in Portuguese Anthropology and Modern History*, R. Feijó, H. Martins, and J. Pina-Cabral, eds., pp. 44–74. Oxford: Journal of the Anthropological Society of Oxford.
1987 *Social Inequality in a Portuguese Hamlet: Land, Late Marriage, and Bastardy 1870–1978*. Cambridge: Cambridge University Press.

Ong, A.
1987 *Spirits of Resistance and Capitalist Discipline: Factory Women in Malaysia*. Albany: State University of New York Press.

Ortner, S., and H. Whitehead
1981 Introduction: Accounting for Sexual Meanings. In *Sexual Meanings: The Cultural Construction of Gender*, S. Ortner and H. Whitehead, eds., pp. 1–27. New York: Cambridge University Press.

Ott, S.
1981 *The Circle of Mountains: A Basque Shepherding Community*. Oxford: Clarendon.

Paine, R.
1967 What Is Gossip About? An Alternative Hypothesis. *Man* (n.s.) 2:278–285.

Patai, D.
1988 Constructing a Self: A Brazilian Life Story. *Feminist Studies* 14(1):143–166.

Peristiany, J. G., ed. 1965 *Honor and Shame: The Values of Mediterranean Society*. London: Weidenfeld and Nicolson.

Personal Narratives Group, ed.
1989 *Interpreting Women's Lives: Feminist Theory and Personal Narratives*. Bloomington: Indiana University Press.

Phillips, L.
1990 Rural Women in Latin America: Directions for Future Research. *Latin American Research Review* 25(3):89–107.

Pi-Sunyer, O.
1977 Two Stages of Technological Change in a Catalan Fishing Community. In *Those Who Live from the Sea*, M. E. Smith, ed., pp. 41–55. New York: West.

Pina-Cabral, J. de
1984a Female Power and the Inequality of Wealth and Motherhood in Northwestern Portugal. In *Women and Property, Women as Property*, R. Hirschon, ed., pp. 75–91. London: Croom Helm.
1984b Comentários críticos sobre a casa e a família no Alto Minho rural. *Análise social* 20(2 and 3):263–284.
1986 *Sons of Adam, Daughters of Eve: The Peasant Worldview of the Alto Minho*. Oxford: Clarendon.

1989 The Mediterranean as a Category of Regional Comparison: A Critical View. *Current Anthropology* 30(3):399–406.

n.d. Household and Family in Mediterranean and Atlantic Europe. Unpublished paper.

Pitt-Rivers, J. A.

1965 Honour and Social Status. In *Honour and Shame: The Values of Mediterranean Society*, J. G. Peristiany, ed., pp. 19–78. London: Weidenfeld and Nicolson.

1971 [orig. 1954] *The People of the Sierra*. Chicago: University of Chicago Press.

Porter, M.

1982 Women and Old Boats: The Sexual Division of Labour in a Newfoundland Outport. Unpublished paper.

Rabinow, P.

1979 *Reflections on Fieldwork in Morocco*. Chicago: Chicago University Press.

Raby, D.

1988 *Fascism and Resistance in Portugal: Communists, Liberals and Military Dissidents in the Opposition to Salazar, 1941–1974*. Manchester: Manchester University Press.

Radin, P.

1927 *Primitive Man as Philosopher*. New York: Dover.

Rapp, R.

1978 Family and Class in Contemporary America: Notes toward an Understanding of Ideology. *Science and Society* 42:278–301.

Ravis-Giordani, G., ed.

1987 *Femmes et patrimoine dans les sociétés rurales de l'Europe Méditerranéenne*. Paris: C.N.R.S.

Redclift, N.

1985 The Contested Domain: Gender, Accumulation and the Labour Process. In *Beyond Employment: Household, Gender and Subsistence*, N. Redclift and E. Mingione, eds., pp. 92–125. New York: Basil Blackwell.

Reis, J.

1984 O atraso económico português em perspectiva histórica (1860–1913). *Análise social* 20(80):7–28.

Reiter, R.

1975 Men and Women in the South of France: Public and Private Domains. In *Toward an Anthropology of Women*, R. Reiter, ed., pp. 252–282. New York: Monthly Review Press.

Ribeiro, O.

1986 [orig. 1945] *Portugal, O Mediterrâneo e o Atlântico*. Lisbon: Livraria Sá da Costa Editora.

Riegelhaupt, J.

1967 Saloio Women: An Analysis of Informal and Formal Political and Economic Roles of Portuguese Peasant Women. *Anthropological Quarterly* 40:109–126.

1973 Festas and Padres: The Organization of Religious Action in a Portuguese Parish. *American Anthropologist* 75(3):835–851.

1979 Peasants and Politics in Salazar's Portugal: The Corporate State and Village "Nonpolitics." In *Contemporary Portugal: The Revolution and Its Antecedents*, L. S. Graham and H. M. Makler, eds., pp. 167–190. Austin: University of Texas Press.

1984 Popular Anti-Clericalism and Religiosity in Pre-1974 Portugal. In *Religion, Power and Protest in Local Communities: The Northern Shore of the Mediterranean*, E. Wolf, ed., pp. 93–115. Berlin: Mouton.

Roberts, J. M.

1976 Belief in the Evil Eye in World Perspective. In *The Evil Eye*, C. Maloney, ed., pp. 223–278. New York: Columbia University Press.

Robinson, R.A.H.

1979 *Contemporary Portugal: A History*. London: George Allen and Unwin.

Rocha, E.

1984 Crescimento económico em Portugal nos anos de 1960–73: alteração estrutural e ajustamento da oferta à procura de trabalho. *Análise social* 20(84):621–644.

Rogers, B.

1980 *The Domestication of Women: Discrimination in Developing Societies*. London: Tavistock.

Rogers, S.

1975 Female Forms of Power and the Myth of Male Dominance: A Model of Female/Male Interaction in Peasant Societies. *American Ethnologist* 2(4):727–756.

Rosenberg, H.

1988 *A Negotiated World: Three Centuries of Change in a French Alpine Community*. Toronto: University of Toronto Press.

Rowland, R.

1984 Sistemas familiares e padrões demográficos em Portugal: questões para uma investigação comparada. *Ler história* 3:13–32.

Rubin, G.

1975 The Traffic in Women: Notes on the Political Economy of Sex. In *Toward an Anthropology of Women*, R. Reiter, ed., pp. 157–210. New York: Monthly Review Press.

Safa, H.

1981 Runaway Shops and Female Employment: The Search for Cheap Labour. *Signs* 7(2):418–433.

Sampaio, A.

1979a [orig. 1923] As vilas do norte de Portugal. *Estudos históricos e económicos*. Vol. 1. Lisbon: Vega.

1979b [orig. 1923] As póvoas marítimas. *Estudos históricos e económicos*. Vol. 2. Lisbon: Vega.

Santos Graça, A.

1982 [orig. 1932] *O poveiro*. Póvoa de Varzim: Câmara Municipal da Póvoa de Varzim.

Santos Júnior, J. R.

1985 Os lavradores de Mindelo lavravam a terra e o mar. In *Colóquio "Santos*

Graça" de etnografia marítima, 2:171–183. Póvoa de Varzim: Câmara Municipal da Póvoa de Varzim.

Schneider, J.

1971 Of Vigilance and Virgins: Honour, Shame and Access to Resources in Mediterranean Society. *Ethnology* 10:1–24.

1981 Trousseau as Treasure: Some Contradictions of Late Nineteenth Century Change in Sicily. In *Beyond the Myths of Culture*, E. Ross, ed., pp. 323–356. New York: Academic Press.

Scott, J.

1976 *The Moral Economy of the Peasant: Subsistence and Rebellion in Southeast Asia*. New Haven: Yale University Press.

Scott, J., and L. Tilly

1975 Women's Work and the Family in Nineteenth Century Europe. *Comparative Studies in Society and History* 17(1):36–64.

Segalen, M.

1983 *Love and Power in the Peasant Family*. Trans. by S. Matthews. Chicago: University of Chicago Press.

Sen, G., and C. Grown

1987 *Development, Crises, and Alternative Visions: Third World Women's Perspectives*. New York: Monthly Review Press.

Serrão, J.

1982 *A emigração portuguesa*. 4th ed. Lisbon: Livros Horizonte.

Sheridan, M.

1984 The Life History Method. In *Lives: Chinese Working Women*, M. Sheridan and J. Salaff, eds., pp. 11–22. Bloomington: Indiana University Press.

Shostak, M.

1983 *Nisa: The Life and Words of a !Kung Woman*. New York: Vintage Books.

Sider, G.

1980 The Ties That Bind: Culture and Agriculture, Property and Propriety in the Newfoundland Village Fishery. *Social History* 5(1):1–39.

1986 *Culture and Class in Anthropology and History: A Newfoundland Illustration*. Cambridge: Cambridge University Press.

Silva Lopes, A. M. Simões da

1975 O vocabulário marítimo português e o problema dos mediterraneísmos. *Revista Portuguesa de filologia* 16 and 17.

Simmons, L.

1942 *Sun Chief: The Autobiography of a Hopi Indian*. New Haven: Yale University Press.

Smith, M. E., ed.

1977 *Those Who Live from the Sea: A Study in Maritime Anthropology*. American Ethnological Society Monograph 62. St. Paul: West.

Smith, M. F.

1954 *Baba of Karo: A Woman of the Muslim Hausa*. London: Faber and Faber.

Sousa Ferreira, E. de, and W. Opello, Jr., eds.

1985 *Conflict and Change in Portugal 1974–1984 / Conflitos e mudanças em Portugal 1974–1984*. Lisbon: Teorema.

Spacks, P.
1985 *Gossip.* Chicago: University of Chicago Press.
Spencer, J.
1989 Anthropology as a Kind of Writing. *Man* 24:145–164.
Stavenhagen, R.
1975 *Social Classes in Agrarian Societies.* Trans. by J. A. Hellman. New York: Anchor Books.
Stivens, M.
1981 Women, Kinship and Capitalist Development. In *Of Marriage and the Market*, K. Young, C. Wolkowitz, and R. McCullagh, eds., pp. 112–126. London: CSE Books.
Strathern, M.
1984 Domesticity and the Denigration of Women. In *Rethinking Women's Roles*, D. O'Brien and S. Tiffany, eds., pp. 13–31. Berkeley: University of California Press.
Thompson, P.
1981 Life Histories and the Analysis of Social Change. In *Biography and Society*, D. Bertaux, ed., pp. 289–306. Beverley Hills, Calif.: Sage.
1985 Women in the Fishing: The Roots of Power between the Sexes. *Comparative Studies in Society and History* 27(1):3–32.
Thompson, P., T. Wailey, and T. Lummis
1983 *Living the Fishing.* London: Routledge and Kegan Paul.
Veiga de Oliveira, E.
1984 *Festividades cíclicas em Portugal.* Lisbon: Dom Quixote.
Veiga de Oliveira, E., F. Galhano, and B. Pereira
1975 *Actividades agro-marítimas em Portugal.* Lisbon: Instituto de Alta Cultura, Centro de Estudos de Etnologia.
Vicente, A., ed.
1985 *Mulheres em discurso.* Lisbon: Imprensa Nacional.
Wall, K.
1982 A outra faça da emigração: estudo sobre a situação das mulheres que ficam no país de origem. *Cadernos condição feminina* 14.
Warner, M.
1978 *Alone of All Her Sex: The Myth and the Cult of the Virgin Mary.* London: Quartet Books.
Willems, E.
1962 On Portuguese Family Structure. *International Journal of Comparative Sociology* 3:65–79.
Yanagisako, S.
1977 Women-Centred Kin Networks in Urban Bilateral Kinship. *American Ethnologist* 4(2):207–226.
Young, K.
1978 Modes of Appropriation and the Sexual Division of Labour: A Case Study from Oaxaca, Mexico. In *Feminism and Materialism: Women and Modes of Production*, A. Kuhn and A. Wolpe, eds., pp. 124–154. London: Routledge and Kegan Paul.

Young, K., C. Wolkowitz, and R. McCullagh, eds.
   1981 *Of Marriage and the Market: Women's Subordination in International Perspective.* London: CSE Books.
Zavella, P.
   1987 *Women's Work and Chicano Families: Cannery Workers of the Santa Clara Valley.* Ithaca: Cornell University Press.